ACROSS
SIXTEEN COUNTRIES

*An account of what was seen and heard
on the author's journey to historic and interesting places
in sixteen countries in the years of 1920–21.*

C. J. Larson

———◆———

*Michael Timshel, Translator
Rhonda Erlandson, Editor
Swedish Roots in Oregon Press
Portland, Oregon*

Originally published in Swedish as a travel serial in the *Oregon Posten* newspaper, Portland, Oregon, 1920–21; published as *Genom Sexton Länder*, Oregon Posten Press, 1927.

Second-edition English translation © 2016 by Michael Timshel, Portland, Oregon.
Book compilation © 2016 Swedish Roots in Oregon, Portland, Oregon
Original narrative and photographs © 2016 C. J. Larson Family
Additional photographs © 2016 as credited to contributors

Cover designed by Tricia Brown

All photos courtesy of Larson and Hammerback families, except as noted: Front cover, top, from left: Anna Larson, C.J. Larson, and Signe Ekström [courtesy of Bethany Evangelical Lutheran Church, Warren, Oregon]; Bottom, clockwise from top, left: Anna with Syrian children; on the road in the U.S.; visiting the Sphinx; in the Holy Land. Back cover, left: the home place in Warren, Oregon; right, C.J.'s ancestral home in Sweden, 2015 [courtesy of Lars Nordström].

Translator: Michael Timshel
Editor: Rhonda Erlandson
Acquiring Editor: Lars Nordström
Associate Editor: Tricia Brown
Design: Sophie Aschwanden
Mapmaker: Penny Panlener
SRIO Consultant: Ingeborg Dean

ISBN-13: 978–0692702468
ISBN-10: 0692702466

Published by:

SRIO

Swedish Roots in Oregon
8740 S.W. Oleson Road
Portland, OR 97223
swedishrootsinoregon.org
Book orders, questions, and comments may be directed to
president@swedishrootsinoregon.org

Printed in the United States of America

For Ingeborg

Gud var med oss tills vi mötas igen.

[God be with us until we meet again.]

CONTENTS

FOREWORD
To the English Edition

A Rare Bookstore Discovery

The book *Genom Sexton Länder* [*Across Sixteen Countries*], by C. J. Larson, was originally written as letters to the editor and serialized in the newspaper *Oregon Posten* of Portland, Oregon. The letters recounted Mr. Larson's travels through the U.S., Europe, and the Near East in 1920 and 1921. *Oregon Posten* published them in a single volume in 1927. [1]

Mr. Larson was a successful farmer and entrepreneur, who settled in Warren, Oregon, in 1906. He was active in the Evangelical Lutheran Church, and was a great promoter of Swedish settlement in western Oregon. After his wife, Betty, died in 1918, the fifty-eight-year-old began planning an epic trip. It would be more than a year long, and he would be accompanied by his twenty-year-old daughter, Anna, and her friend, Signe Ekström. After their return, Miss Ekström and Mr. Larson were married.

The trio began their travels in western Oregon, traveling by train mostly, spending a few weeks visiting Tillamook, Corvallis, Cottage Grove, etc. Then they headed south through Oregon and California, traveling as far south as Tijuana. Turning east, they saw places such as the Mesa Verde cliff dwellings at a time when they were accessible only by foot or mule-back. At one point they bought an automobile and traveled by road when few, if any, roads were paved (the car did not survive). Along the way they visited numerous Lutheran congregations, including those at Bethany College in Lindsborg, Kansas, and Bethphage, in Axtell, Nebraska. After reaching New York, they embarked for Europe. Mr. Larson's descriptions of street-level life in France and Italy are immediate and personal. True, it is all filtered through Mr. Larson's eyes, but his vision is sharp, and his commentary is sometimes piquant.

A major part of the journey is in the Near East, the "Holy Land." Nearly every place that Mr. Larson and company visit is referenced in the Bible. Often Mr. Larson calls places by their old names, or Swedish names, that no longer appear on the map under those names. I derived a lot of pleasure looking up all of the obscure places, and learning their history, both from Mr. Larson's vivid and factual descriptions, and from reference material. Everywhere Mr. Larson went, from Oregon to England, he had a keen eye for the terrain and how the land was used. Especially in the Near East, he seemed to know the history of every foot of ground that they walked, and they walked a lot.

Their travels in Sweden are just as much fun. They traveled most of the length of the country, as far north as Kiruna and the Midnight Sun. They spent months visiting all sorts of interesting places and people. With them we visit the Sami in their *kåta*, a Laestadian prayer meeting, and a museum dedicated to Gustav Vasa.

As the son of an immigrant, I always had an interest in learning Swedish. However, my father was more focused on being American, and I didn't get much help. So, after a few sporadic, unsuccessful attempts to learn on my own, I enrolled at the University of Oregon and learned the language there. Since then, I have tried to keep it fresh and alive by reading and writing every day. I found a copy of *Genom Sexton Länder* in a used-book store and thought it would make a fun translation project. I was right. Some of it was challenging, and some of it was really challenging. Mr. Larson was so quirky and such an odd combination of provincial and cosmopolitan. He was a farmer who knew his way around. From this distance, his biases are amusing. For me, the very best part is getting firsthand reporting on what the world really looked like in 1920, just a couple of years after the end of World War I.

I did this translation entirely for myself, and never thought about it being published. However, now that it is done, I think it could be of interest to a number of audiences. First of all, Mr. Larson, although an immigrant, was also a hometown boy, and a promoter of settlement and development of western Oregon. His detailed, first-hand accounts of everyday life in the U.S., Europe, and The Levant would interest historians and anthropologists, armchair as well as professional. Those with a religious bent, especially Lutherans, can derive a lot from Mr. Larson's commentaries, especially those of the Holy Land. In the end, it's an absorbing road story, and I hope you like it.

— Michael Timshel, Translator
Monmouth, Oregon
March 2016

ACKNOWLEDGMENTS

From the translator: I wish to thank Amy Timshel, Joanne Timshel, Marianna Timshel, and Mary Dulebohn, with a special acknowledgement to Michael Hanneson.

— Michael Timshel

From the editor: This project has been such a labor of love by so many people whose interest and assistance have brought it to fruition. Three years before I was aware of C. J. Larson's travel memoir, Pastor Rory Scott of Bethany Lutheran Church in Warren, Oregon, loaned me the church's founding records: dozens of binders filled with notes written in old Swedish chronicling the church's development as a fledgling congregation in that bastion of preserving Swedish heritage, the Augustana Lutheran Synod. C. J. Larson's signature is everywhere in those records, reflecting his careful stewardship of the little church. It was in these documents that I discovered the sense of close-knit community and commitment of the Swedish Oregonians to their homes, families, and friends. My hearty thanks go out to Pastor Scott and to the congregation of Bethany Lutheran for welcoming me and sharing these precious primary documents with me.

A huge debt of gratitude goes to the staff and volunteers of the Columbia County Museum Association. Thank you to Joanne Pellham and Les Watters for your support and enthusiasm around this project. Les, you're a photo wizard—thank you so much for all the hours you spent enhancing our photos and for going the extra mile to attend a Bethany Lutheran Council meeting to learn more of the history behind C. J.'s story. Your assistance was absolutely vital to this project.

Tusen tack to Abbey Gaterud of Ooligan Press and her Portland State University students, and special thanks to designer Sophie Aschwanden. Abbey, you were so gracious to embrace this project, and I thank you for encouraging me when I balked at the enormity of what lay ahead. C. J. would be delighted to know that his humble memoir helped advance the skills of your students learning the art and science of modern book design. Discovering that you, too, claim a Swedish emigrant ancestor was one of many coincidences that have made this project so magical.

A shout-out to the Cedar Mill Community Library: to Sarah, Rob, and Laura in the Interlibrary Loan Department for so deftly helping me get my hands on research materials in record time; and to Director Peter Leonard, my boss, for granting me all that time off. I owe many thanks to my friends and family for their patience and understanding while I was incommunicado for the better part of this year doing this good work.

Ingeborg Dean, you're an angel. Thank you so very much for your generous financial support and for lending your native speaker's eye to fine-tune the translation. Thanks to my fellow Swedish Roots in Oregon board members. Our monthly meetings always buoy my spirits, and I value all the support and advice you've shared along the way. A tip-'o-the-hat goes to Lars Nordström for taking the time to visit C. J.'s ancestral home in Sweden and providing that idyllic photo for our use. Mike Timshel, you're a Renaissance man if ever there was one.

And finally, my deepest gratitude goes to the Larson family. *Tack så mycket* to Rolf, Donna, and Rhonda Larson for welcoming me into your home and spending an afternoon sharing your family history with me. Rolf, I've so enjoyed getting to know your father. I still smile when I imagine C. J. finding you swimming in Scappoose Bay with your buddies after he had assigned you chores at home on the farm. Della Larson, thank you for responding so warmly to my tentative inquiries when I first contacted you two years ago. Thank you for introducing me to your family's ancestor Albert Larson and sharing insights into his relationship with his brother, C. J., and for all your help in arranging family meetings and gathering family photos. I have especially loved learning about the bond you felt with my Aunt Ruth and that your mother-in-law, Katherine Larson, was her best friend. We've only recently become acquainted, yet we've always been close by virtue of belonging to the old Warren Swedish immigrant extended family.

And Tricia Brown . . . those lipstick smudges on your shoes? Mea culpa! You have been the energy behind this endeavor. Your expertise and knowledge of writing and publishing have made the dream that Mike and I had for this little project come true in so many wonderful ways. Thank you for connecting us with essential assistance at every juncture, for bringing Les and Abbey and Penny into the project, for translating the language of the book-making industry for me, and for the many, many hours you spent assisting with editing and formatting the manuscript for the designers—all this while working simultaneously on your own book deadlines. You are a true heroine!

— Rhonda Erlandson
May 31, 2016

Father and daughter, C. J. and Anna Larson

Signe Ekström

INTRODUCTION
The Journey Begins

After all, not to create only, or found only,
But to bring perhaps from afar what is already founded,
To give it our own identity, average, limitless, free.
—Walt Whitman

Across Sixteen Countries offers a unique opportunity for armchair traveling in the early twentieth century. Moreover, it illuminates the unique perspective of travelers who were new Americans, immigrants already experienced in enough travel to fill numerous lifetimes. Ultimately, it brings to life the story of C. J. Larson, a remarkable man whose legacy lives on today.

When C. J. Larson and his traveling companions, twenty-year-old daughter Anna, and her friend, twenty-three-year-old Signe Ekström, embarked on their journey in early 1920, C. J. was fifty-nine years old, a widower, and at the pinnacle of his life's accomplishments. Behind him lay more than a half-century of overcoming unlikely odds. Ahead in the final third of his life, he would not only continue as a successful farmer and community leader, but would also fall in love, remarry, and raise a second family. Although C. J.'s first daughter, Anna, was born in the United States, her childhood traced her parents' moves from Colorado to Kansas and finally to the Pacific Northwest, where the failed prospects of the Midwest yielded to prosperity in the rich farmland along the Columbia River in northwest Oregon. Signe Ekström emigrated in 1912 from the north of Sweden when she was fourteen years old. Arriving in Oregon, Signe joined her father, Gustaf, and stepmother, Hannah, who had arrived before her in 1903.

In many respects, the story of C. J. Larson (aka Carl Johan and the Americanized versions of his name: Charles, Charlie, or Charley) is the story of tens of thousands of Swedes who left their home country in the late nineteenth century to make new lives in America. In the years between 1820 and 1930, more than 1.2 million Swedes came to America, leaving areas of Sweden completely depopulated, farms abandoned, and communities decimated. During the great wave of European migration of the mid-nineteenth and twentieth centuries, Sweden followed Norway and Ireland in contributing the third-largest ethnic group of emigrants to the movement. In his 1887 lyric poem, *The Great Migration*, Swedish Count Carl Snoilsky (1841–1903) wrote of the "/. . . *long long lists of passengers / Like death reports from a battle.*"

> *Every route that crosses the ocean*
> *I would mark on the map in red,*
> *For there our hearts' blood flows*
> *From open wounds towards the west. . . .*[2]

Reasons for emigration were varied. The social and economic push-pull factors that led to Sweden losing more of its citizens to emigration than any other European nation in proportion to its population have been widely covered in historical sources. By the middle of the nineteenth century, Sweden's population had doubled in the prior hundred years and showed no indication of leveling off. Arable land was scarce while famine was plentiful, killing twenty-two out of every thousand Swedes. Between 1861 and 1881, one hundred fifty thousand Swedes emigrated to America with two-thirds of that number coming in the five-year period of 1868–73, the same window of opportunity in which C. J.'s parents struck out for the United States.[3]

For such land-starved people, the Homestead Act, signed into law by President Abraham Lincoln in 1862, proved to be an irresistible pull factor. This act offered settlers 160 acres of public land in exchange for a small filing fee and an agreement to complete five years of continuous residence on the land. Such a commitment culminated in the homesteader receiving ownership of the land at the end of the five-year period. Alternately, after only six months of residency, homesteaders had the option of buying the land from the government for $1.25 per acre. The Homestead Act resulted in the distribution of 80 million acres of public land by 1900.[4]

Other factors that induced Swedes to leave their homeland were a rigid class system, lack of suffrage, and religious oppression. Reflecting on his reasons for emigration, one Swedish man in 1880 mused that, ". . . the bread question was much of it, class differences, too, and then there was the question of personal worth, for I felt myself valueless for both the community and myself. . . . Still I have nothing to condemn Mother Svea for, because I have a least inherited from her good principles."[5]

C. J.'s story begins in 1861 in the southeastern Swedish province of Södermanland, situated just southwest of Stockholm. Here, in Strångsjö, near the town of Katrineholm, he was born in a little log house that his father and grandfather had built. C. J.'s parents were

Anna Charlotta Andersson Larson. After immigrating at age thirty-seven, she would live out her life in Kansas. She was buried in the Zion Lutheran Church cemetery in Brantford in 1912. (Courtesy Jim and Linda Maroud)

Lars Johan and Anna Charlotta (née Carlson) Andersson. In personal biographical notes written many years later, C. J. describes his parents as common laborers who worked long days and late into the night by candlelight. The Andersson family did not hold title to the land upon which their house was built. Instead, Lars did general farm work for the land owner in exchange for the privilege of residing on the land in his own house. In addition to farm work, he did carpentry and blacksmithing, and he was engaged in the making of utilitarian crafts such as spinning rope and making buckets and tubs out of wood. Anna Charlotta (family tree records show her as Anna Lotta Carlsdotter) kept house and was adept at spinning yarn, weaving it into cloth, and sewing by hand for the family's needs. She wove cloth from flax for summer fabrics and household linens and from wool for warm winter clothing and blankets.

On Sundays one or more of the family members would walk one Swedish mile (roughly equivalent to seven American miles) to the Stora Malm Parish church, one of many Lutheran churches throughout the nation that were organized under the State Church of Sweden. The State Church was charged with administrative tasks that supported the government, such as keeping civic records. The Church Parish handled municipal tasks and was largely responsible for school curricula and supervising teachers. Parish priests wielded significant influence on the citizens, the culture of the parish, and ultimately on the country as a whole.

By the time C. J. was seven years old, his family had grown to include five children ranging from an older sister, Anna Augusta, age nine, to an infant brother, Otto Elias. Between them were brothers Albert Lars, two years old, and Gustaf Emil (known as Emil), four. About this time, it happened that Anna went to a nearby fair to shop for a range of manufactured goods, household items like spoons, dippers, and containers made of bone or wood. Such fairs were occasions for socializing with people from all over the parish as well as taking advantage of business opportunities that only came around once or twice a year. It was here that what seemed to be a chance meeting changed the course of the Andersson family's life. Anna Charlotta encountered a man distributing religious tracts that promoted unorthodox views running counter to the established State Church doctrine. These writings encouraged Christians to trust in personal revelation, embrace independent thinking, and to welcome fellowship with other Christians holding various views and scriptural interpretations. Historically, individuals who followed this unorthodox path were known as Pietists. Devotions and services were typically held in private homes and led by laymen and pastors who were disillusioned with the authoritative State Church. This movement would have sweeping effects on established Lutheranism in Sweden and would go on to form the foundation for scores of Swedish-American immigrant communities in the United States, particularly under the auspices of the Swedish Evangelical Lutheran Augustana Synod in North America.

Anna was struck by what she read in the tract and took it home to share with her husband. Lars, too, found it compelling, and soon the couple were inviting itinerant preachers and missionaries into their home to expand on these revolutionary views. From a modern perspective, Pietism would be viewed as very conservative, eschewing such worldly distractions as dancing and the evils of drinking alcohol while devoting as much time as possible to reading and discussing the Bible. But to Anna and Lars, Pietism opened up a world of (relatively) free thinking that bordered on radicalism. In Sweden, followers of this movement were known as *läsare*—"readers"—because they read outside the body of literature prescribed by the State Church: the official catechism, Psalm-book, liturgy, and designated Bible version.

In time, Anna and Lars formed a Sunday school for children in their home and held regular services of prayer, singing, and Bible study. The State Church deemed it illegal for citizens to host such worship services without the presence of a Lutheran clergyman. Soon the word came down from Stora Malm Parish that the Andersson family must cease and desist these religious activities in their home. When they refused to do so, the landowner on whose property they resided issued an eviction order.

We can only imagine what a blow this must have been to the family. Their home was their whole world, and although far from affluent, they were comfortable and happy in the life they had carved out among friends and family that could be traced back in church records for hundreds of years. Nevertheless, Lars and Anna realized they were fundamentally changed by months devoted to free thinking. They couldn't go back—only forward—and that meant emigration: leaving Sweden and starting their lives over in America, where they would be free to practice their faith, free from the authority of a state-sanctioned church. On September 27, 1869, as required by law, the Anderssons registered with the police regarding their intent to leave Sweden.[6] Lars built a wooden trunk into which they placed their most valuable belongings. They traveled by train from Katrineholm to Göteborg (Gothenburg) and from there, they crossed by ship over the North Sea to England and on to New York. C. J. was eight years old when he stepped onto American soil for the first time.

Within a year, C. J.'s baby brother, Otto, would be dead, and his father would also die of pneumonia only two months later. Anna

Charlotta and the remaining four children would be left devastated by grief and destitute in a land where they seemed to have neither viable prospects nor the ability to communicate in English.

———•———

The family's journey had started out well enough. C. J.'s biographical notes describe how they traveled from New York to Chicago in search of employment. Finding none, they got a tip that work was available in Kansas City and sure enough, Lars was hired to make railroad ties at Pomeroy, a small rail station fifteen miles from Kansas City. Anna and the children stayed behind in a rooming house in Kansas City, and the older children even attended school for a few weeks. Within a short time, however, the family was reunited, overjoyed to move into a small log cabin that Lars had quickly built near his work site. While the family settled in, Lars worked in the woods hewing railroad ties out of oak and black walnut timber with a broad ax.

In his notes, C. J. wrote, "One day Father caught a hard cold that settled on his lungs and ran into consumption, which laid him up so he could not work and, after some time, he passed away. . . . A neighbor made a box for a coffin out of common boards that Father was laid in, and he was buried in a new burial place on a hill near Pomeroy."

In the weeks and months that followed, while coping with the loss of her husband and youngest child, Anna managed to scrape by, keeping house for a few men who had worked alongside Lars in the woods. In exchange for room and board, she was able to keep little Albert, now three years old, and Emil, five, with her. The two older children were separated from each other and the rest of their family, taken in by others who provided room and board in exchange for chores. Fostering children was a common practice at this time when families were struggling to survive and another reason why it was vital for immigrants to bond with others from the home country. Little Anna Augusta helped with housekeeping and caring for the children of a nearby family, while C. J. moved in with another family where he helped make railroad ties using a small ax his foster father gave him. Now only eight years old, C. J. described how he accompanied this man to the woods, where "he would put me on one side and he on the other to chop away until the tree would fall. . . . After getting a tree down [the man] would mark off eight-foot lengths on the tree and then put me to trim off the leaves while he started to make the first butt cut."

No doubt Anna Charlotta and the children were buoyed and ultimately saved by their strong faith and a network of fellow evangelical Lutheran immigrants. Through these connections Anna managed to secure better living arrangements with a Swedish missionary in Keokuk, Iowa. Still, a happy ending was a long way off for the family. Lacking enough money to purchase train tickets for all of the children, C. J. was left behind where he continued to work and live near Pomeroy. In a hand-written memoir, C. J. recalls that this parting was "a hard experience, but what could I do? I cried and worried but finally consoled myself with the thought that when Sunday came, I could go to a little Sunday school not so far away that good Christian people were leading [who] would be a comfort to me and cheer me up some."

In the months it took C. J. to gather the amount needed to pay his fare to Keokuk, he lived with at least three different families, some of whom inflicted severe physical and emotional abuse upon him. C. J. tells the harrowing story of how one man mistreated him with such cruelty that the man's wife took pity on the little boy and placed him with her brother, Alfrid, who lived a few miles away.

C. J. and Alfrid went on to be lifelong friends; however, a serious illness forced C. J. to move yet again. Desperately ill for several weeks, he stayed in the home of a couple who, having no children of their own, were willing to care for him. Once recovered, C. J. was determined to reunite with his mother, brothers, and sister. Because he could not yet speak English, "a good neighbor boy" accompanied him to Kansas City and helped him purchase the needed tickets. About nine years old by this time, C. J. traveled by himself on the train to Quincy, Illinois. From there, he sailed on the Mississippi River to his destination in Iowa, where he was overjoyed to see his mother waiting for him on the dock.

Although elated to be reunited with his mother, C. J. was met with the sobering news that his brother Emil had been adopted by another family.[7] Anna believed adoption was the only path to a better life for the little boy, and considering the same option for C. J., she arranged for him to live for a time with a prospective adoptive family. Happily, about a year after the death of Lars, Anna remarried, and C. J. found himself back with his own family. His new stepfather, a stone mason named Andrew M. Larson (known as A. M.) welcomed the children; they assumed his last name and called him "Father."

The newly formed Larson family left Illinois and took up homesteading in Washington County, Kansas, near the township of Brantford. While Anna worked in Brantford as a cook and housekeeper, earning $2.00 a week, C. J. joined his stepfather in herding cattle and building a sod house on the homestead. C. J. writes, "Father and I dug a basement on the homestead during the winter, which was hard work being it froze every night. We had to dig in frozen ground every day. But we got it dug anyway. Then I hauled stone from a nearby hill with one blind horse that Father had gotten in pay for building a stone house for a new settler in the neighborhood." C. J. and his new father walled in their new home and then covered it with hay, brush, and grass from a nearby creek. When the family moved into their new home in February, it was still so cold that a coat of ice sheathed the dirt floor.[8]

The family now settled into the rhythms of pioneer life on the prairie. A baby sister, Amanda, was born on September 26, 1873. C. J.'s notes recall boyhood memories of making sorghum molasses with a cane mill, fashioned with two iron rollers that pressed the cane as a horse plodded in circles, driving the pole around the mill. The end product, thick sweet syrup, would be put into twenty gallon barrels that retailed at twenty-five cents per gallon. The family gradually took on livestock and depended on a team of oxen and horses to leverage the heavy lifting that such farming required. They grew crops of corn and wheat. C. J. writes, "Father sowed some wheat on the ground, broadcasting it by hand, and I harrowing it down with the one blind horse [and] a small harrow that we borrowed from a neighbor. The wheat made a nice growth and Father cut it when ripe with a scythe, and I gathered it in bundles with a rake. Mother bound [the] bundles to be thrashed and sacked and then hauled thirty miles with our blind horse on a little wagon to Waterville to a grist mill, where it was ground to flour and part of it taken back home to be used to make bread.... Grain was thrashed with a small thrashing machine which was worked by five horse teams traveling around and around. The corn was shelled with a sheller turned by hand and then hauled to [Waterville] and sold at twenty to twenty-five cents per bushel at the railroad station, scooping it with shovels from our wagon into box cars to be shipped to bigger markets. And so time went on year after year while I was growing up."

By the time C. J. was eleven, his community was able to support a school and a "grown girl as teacher." The young woman was paid

$25 per month to teach three months out of the year during the winter. C. J. began his education in this little school house at a level we would now identify as the third grade. Going to school for a few months each winter allowed him to complete the fifth grade by age twenty-one. He was particularly good at math and able to help with bookkeeping on the farm. At twenty-two, he and his seventeen-year-old brother Albert took full responsibility for the farm while their stepfather made a year-long trip to Sweden in 1883.

Zion Lutheran Church, Brantford, Kansas. The church was organized in 1874; the building was erected in 1880. (Courtesy Howard and Della Larson)

A group of Swedish Evangelical Lutherans lived in Brantford and for a number of years had made the weekly six-mile round-trip to the nearest church by wagon or simply walking. Before A. M. Larson made his year-long sojourn to his home country, he decided it was time to build a church in Brantford. As a young man in Sweden, A. M. had studied architecture and stone masonry. Now, many years later, he put that expertise to work drawing up plans, raising funds and galvanizing the community to work together in constructing the church. The new church was named Zion Lutheran and was built from natural lime rock the settlers hauled from a hillside two miles away. C. J. participated alongside his stepfather and fellow community members in building the church. The experience left an indelible impression on the young man, instilling a lifelong love of architecture and providing a model that he would replicate in Stockholm, Kansas, and a quarter-century later in Warren, Oregon. Those churches would be named Bethany

C. J.'s stepfather, A. M. Larson, posed with two unnamed granddaughters in Brantford, Kansas, date unknown. The photo hangs in the Brantford church today. It is labeled, "He was the builder of our church." (Courtesy Zion Lutheran Church)

Lutheran in honor of the home where Jesus loved to gather with his friends Mary, Martha, and Lazarus.

———•———

At age twenty-six, C. J. Larson moved a distance of thirty miles from Brantford to Scandia, Kansas, where he married eighteen-year-old Betty Helgren in 1887. Although born in the United States, Betty's parents were among those immigrants who struggled to gain a foothold in the new country. Just as C. J.'s brother Emil had been adopted by another family, Betty had been raised as the adopted daughter of a Swedish family with the means to support a child. As a young married couple, C. J. and Betty farmed and were active in Scandia's Augustana Synod Lutheran church, where C. J. formed a choir. A great lover of music and singing, C. J. recalled how, as a young child in Sweden, his father accompanied the family's singing with an instrument he made called a psalmodicon that was box-like with violin strings stretched over it.[9] With his own first earnings as a twenty-one-year-old, C. J. invested a substantial amount of money to purchase an organ for $140.00, an amount that would be valued at more than $3,000.00 in today's currency. No doubt C. J.'s little Lutheran choir in Scandia appreciated the benefit of his organ and understood very well what a luxury it was. Later, that same organ would travel three hundred miles by covered wagon with C. J. and Betty when they secured homestead land of their own in Wallace

FARM RESIDENCE OF A.M.LARSON. SEC.32.GRANT TP., WASHINGTON CO., KAN.

From a dugout to an admirable farm. An illustration of the A. M. Larson farm accompanied a biography of the man in the 1890 book published by Chapman Brothers, Chicago, titled *Portrait and Biographical Album, Washington, Clay, and Riley Counties, Kansas.*

County. Once again, C. J. was instrumental in forming a Sunday school, and soon he and his fellow homesteaders were building another Lutheran church located near Sharon Springs in Stockholm, Kansas, in the western part of the state.

According to C. J.'s notes, the next several years were challenging as he and Betty struggled with drought in Wallace County. Water was scarce and it took three attempts at drilling wells before they hit water at 205 feet below the surface. The well was a half-mile from the house, and carrying water that distance only intensified their hard work. Eventually the dry conditions got so bad, they were forced to abandon the homestead. The couple moved to Pueblo, Colorado, where C. J.'s brother Albert had found some measure of success renting irrigated farmland. In 1897, C. J. borrowed $1,000.00 at 10 percent interest and rented 320 acres of land not far from Albert's location. His notes describe how he loaded the household goods and farm machinery on two wagons and drove his cattle and horses nearly two hundred miles to Pueblo.

In the second year of farming in Colorado, C. J. recounts an illness (he called it "inflammatory rhumitis") that incapacitated him for more than a month and necessitated hiring farmhands to

Betty (Hellgren), Anna, and C. J. Larson, ca. 1900, photographed in Clyde, Kansas, just south of Brantford. (Courtesy Howard and Della Larson)

The Albert Larson Family. Albert Larson, right, paused for a photo with his children and the sister of his late wife, Selma. Front, from left: Nora, Leroy, Hulda Sandstedt, and Albert. Back: Alvin and Myrtle Larson. (Courtesy Jim and Linda Maroud)

keep the operation going. It is at this juncture that C. J.'s personal notes end on a poignant note, "It looked pretty hard now to get me through living in a new community when we were strangers. [We had] no one to neighbor with and felt forsaken and lonesome and no one to tell our troubles to." Brighter days were ahead, however. Within two years of moving to Colorado and after twelve years of marriage, C. J. and Betty welcomed the birth of their daughter Anna on November 5, 1899.

As C. J. explains in his preface to *Across Sixteen Countries*, the next several years were transitional periods for him and his family. Four years of farming in Colorado were followed by three years back in Kansas assisting his parents, who were having financial difficulty on the Brantford homestead. A year in Texas preceded C. J.'s visit to the Pacific Northwest where he would discover his heart's home. In an interview conducted in January 2016, C. J.'s youngest son Rolf recalled family history that placed C. J. on the West Coast, visiting relatives in Gresham, Oregon, sometime in 1904. During his stay, he got a job with the *Oregonian* [newspaper] that involved traveling by train between Portland and Astoria, promoting and selling subscriptions to the paper. According to an article written by Katherine R. Larson and published by the Columbia County Historical Society in 1969, C. J. got his first glimpse of Warren one day when the train stopped at the little station to load produce, milk, and cream. He got out to stretch his legs and was immediately struck by the beauty of the area, just twenty-five miles northwest of Portland, with its views of the snowcapped Cascade Mountains forming

Bethany Lutheran Church, Stockholm, Kansas, was established in 1888. (Courtesy Howard and Della Larson)

a backdrop for Scappoose Bay. And there was rolling, verdant farm land as far as the eye could see. When he learned that a few Scandinavians had already settled in the area, he returned as soon as possible, and in 1906, he purchased a Donation Land Claim in Warren with a farmhouse and barns already established on the property. In this home, C. J. would spend the rest of his days, until his death in 1951. Katherine Larson writes, "This house was a landmark for many years and a haven for newcomers in the old days. . . ."[10] The classic two-story white farmhouse stood squarely above fields, orchards, and pasture land that stretched in every direction. In the middle distance, Scappoose Bay lay before them and, on clear days, magnificent views of five stratovolcanoes. A simple country road and railroad tracks linking Portland and Astoria divided the property on its lower end. C. J. had found his heaven on earth.

The Warren, Oregon, home place. In 1906, C. J. bought a working farm, a Donation Land Claim that overlooked Scappoose Bay. He operated a dairy, and grew crops and fruit. Larson increased his acreage with more land purchases. C. J. and Betty would donate a portion of the land for a new Lutheran Church and an adjoining cemetery. (Larson Family photo)

With his family successfully relocated to their new home in Warren, C. J. focused on establishing Lutheran fellowship for the rural community. He organized services in private homes, leading some of these services himself. In January 1907, a Swedish Evangelical Augustana Lutheran congregation was officially organized, a pastor was called, and a year later the congregation set out to build a church. C. J. donated land for this purpose as well as acreage to be used as a cemetery. Modeled after its sister churches founded by C. J. and his stepfather in Kansas, the little Warren pioneer church was named Bethany Lutheran, and for the next three and a half decades, its services were conducted in Swedish.

In forming the church, C. J.'s vision for Warren extended to the creation of a vibrant and sizable community of Swedish immigrants. With contacts all over the Midwest, he advertised for settlers to join him in Warren.[11] Swedes in Iowa, Kansas, and other Midwestern states enthusiastically responded. In time, immigrants also came directly from Sweden as they learned from friends and relatives how good life was in Warren. Membership rolls of Bethany Lutheran Church record that Albert, now a widower, came with his children from Pueblo, Colorado, to reunite with his brother in 1909. The brothers had adjoining farms on the same road and helped each other out.

Over the course of the next decade, as the Swedish community in Warren flourished, C. J.'s farm and dairy also prospered. C. J. also gave generously of his time and resources to the broader community as evidenced by the fact that he was among the first to serve on the Board of Directors for the Emanuel Charity Board, a Swedish Lutheran organization that established Emanuel Hospital in Portland, Oregon, in 1912.[12] Bethany Lutheran Church records reflect that he remained very active in the church while the congregation took a lively interest in current events and engaged in outreach efforts around the world. Members supported the temperance movement in the United States and sent money to foreign missions abroad. In addition to song and prayer, meetings often included squaring off in formal debate sessions with designated individuals on teams to represent opposing viewpoints in the civil discourse of the day. The

Church roll. A page from Bethany's records is written in Secretary C. J. Larson's hand. (Courtesy Bethany Evangelical Lutheran Church)

Bethany Lutheran Church, Warren, Oregon. (Courtesy Francis Anderson Collection; Columbia County Museum Association)

ladies' Dorcas Society sewed items of clothing for the needy, and young people socialized together in Luther League. As the years passed, new members were welcomed into the church, babies were born and baptized, and loved ones were laid to rest in the serene cemetery behind the church. The members of the Swedish Warren community shared a unique history with one another that each could relate to and in this way offered support and encouragement for one another. This must have been a great source of comfort for C. J. and Anna when, in 1918, at age forty-nine, Betty Larson passed away.

In the years immediately following Betty's death, Anna's health declined. Concerned for his daughter, C. J. considered options to hasten her recovery and settled on the idea of an extended trip abroad. Traveling is always more enjoyable with a friend along, so Anna invited Signe Ekström to join her and her father. Census records for 1920 show that Signe was working as a domestic servant at the time. No doubt she welcomed the prospect of joining Anna and C. J. in this great adventure that would span the length of nearly nineteen months' time. But how could C. J. leave the Warren farm for so long?

Back in Brantford, Kansas, C. J.'s older sister, Anna Augusta, had married Charles Hammerback, and at her death in 1898, she

Good hard work. C. J. stands in the foreground of a work party at haying time. The image once graced the menu of a popular local restaurant, the Warren Country Inn. (Courtesy Rolf Larson)

Bethany Lutheran Church Class of 1915. Seated, from left: Anna Larson, Ellen Johnson, Pastor B. S. Nystrom, Signe Kallberg, Agnes Anderson. Standing, from left: Laurie Lind, Theodore Norbeck, Alvin Larson, Albert Johnson, Charles Erickson, John Nystrom. (Courtesy Bethany Evangelical Lutheran Church)

Bethany Lutheran Church Young People's Society, March 1913. Front, left to right: Esther Lindahl, Signe Newman, Ellen Nystrom, Anna Peterson, Elsie Kallberg, Mary Dahlgren, Anna Larson, C. J. Larson, Mrs. C. J. (Betty) Larson, Hannah Sandstrom, Emmy Dahlgren, Sigrid Anderson, Ella Muhr. Back row: Clara Muhr, Matilda Carlson, Signe Ekström, Nora Larson, Emil Muhr, Sam Dahlgren, Elmer Dahlgren, Charlie Johnson, Arvid Anderson, Leroy Larson, Pastor B. S. Nystrom, Carl Muhr, Dave Anderson, Emil Hammerbeck, Ernest Anderson, Eddie Benson, Harold Carlson, Arthur Lindahl, and Louis Muhr. (Courtesy Bethany Evangelical Lutheran Church)

left four young children. By 1919, two grown sons decided to come to Oregon and manage their uncle's farm in his absence. The 1920 federal census of Warren shows Anna Augusta's eldest son, William Oscar Hammerback, as head of household, newly married and renting the Larson farm, along with his single brother, Emil. (C. J. is included as "uncle" and Anna as "cousin" in the household, even though they were touring at the time of the census.) After the travelers returned, the Kansas-born Hammerbacks settled in the area. Many of their descendants, with a slight name change to *Hammerbeck*, live in Columbia County. While their elders, Charles and Anna Augusta, were buried in the Zion Lutheran Church cemetery in Brantford, Kansas, generations of their offspring now rest among the founding families in Bethany Memorial Cemetery in Warren.

To fully understand early twentieth-century Swedish Lutheran communities in general, and C. J. Larson in particular, the influence of the Lutheran Augustana Synod cannot be overstated. A good

A gathering at the Swedish Lutheran Church, not long before Betty's death. C. J. and Betty are visible seated in the middle row, center, of this group photo taken outside Bethany Lutheran Church in Warren. (Courtesy Columbia County Museum Association)

many Swedish immigrants were not interested in religion, but even they benefited greatly from the Swedish-speaking communities that clustered around the little pioneer churches. In an era when writing letters and bearing messages for friends and loved ones while traveling were foremost methods of staying in touch, the Augustana Synod provided a solid framework for communication across long distances. Its ministers and professors from Augustana College and Theological Seminary in Rock Island, Illinois, traveled back and forth across the country, forming relationships with members of affiliated churches. Through this channel, the depth of C. J.'s commitment to the Swedish Evangelical movement afforded him access to nationwide contacts and acquaintances. He was a gregarious individual who loved talking to others and was not shy about introducing himself and striking up a conversation, particularly when it came to meeting ministers, missionaries, and fellow Christians. Although his writings reveal a deeply devout individual, he does not seem rigid or judgmental. And while C. J. certainly held biases typical of his milieu, his eyes sparkled with intelligent good humor, and his observations while traveling revealed insight and curiosity for other cultures and religions. This should not surprise us when we remember how his forebears, the *läsare*, "readers" who broke away from the State Church in Sweden, valued intellectual freedom above all else.

A vehicle of communication even more vital to the immigrants was the native-language newspaper. The *Oregon Posten*, printed in Swedish and started in 1908 by Fredrik Wilhelm Lönegren, was a lifeline for Oregon Swedes. For twenty-eight years, the *Oregon Posten* provided weekly news stories about Swedish communities and businesses in Oregon and throughout the United States, as well as news from the Swedish-American News Bureau in Stockholm. An entire page was devoted to brief articles from each of Sweden's twenty-five provinces. The paper contributed to preserving, not only the language, but also the heritage, culture, and identity of the Swedish immigrants. Author Lars Nordström describes how the *Posten*

Hammerbacks and Larsons. C. J. Larson, seated with his mother, Anna Charlotte, posed for a portrait with three of the Hammerback children in Kansas. From left are William, Emil, and Emma. In Oregon, the name was changed to Hammerbeck. (Courtesy Jim and Linda Maroud)

"emphasized Oregon's rich natural resources and moderate climate, while simultaneously building a strong, cohesive community feeling," thereby opening a portal for Swedish Oregonians to connect in a statewide network.[13] C. J. carried several copies of the *Oregon Posten* with him during his journey through sixteen countries and proudly shared these with friends and relatives in Sweden who were "completely delighted and could not praise its editor enough . . ." The *Oregon Posten* serialized C. J.'s reports of their experiences as he and "the girls" traveled across the United States, around Europe, and through the Middle East. In each locale

The Oregon Posten. News in their native language was welcomed by Swedish-Americans.

where C. J. encountered and named individuals or families, the paper was essentially relaying personal greetings from friends and loved ones all over the country and throughout the world to the Swedes in Oregon.

For C. J., Anna, and Signe, the journey was deeply meaningful, even pivotal, in the trajectory of their lives. For C. J., visiting the Holy Land was a dream come true. Anna and Signe were intelligent and capable traveling companions for this seasoned man in his late fifties, who seemed to have no problem keeping up with them, even if they hiked thirty miles one day only to strike out for another twenty the next. Perhaps most importantly for C. J., the trip gave him an opportunity to experience closure around some of the most intensely emotional events in his life, such as spending a night alone to reflect and dream in the little house in Katrineholm, where he was born. His biographical notes describe a personal pilgrimage he made to his father's grave while the travelers were in Kansas. Searching for whatever was left to memorialize Lars Johan

Andersson, C. J. wrote, ". . . I walked up on the hill to the little old cemetery to see my father's grave, but how could I find it after thirty-five years of absence? I remembered that there was a black walnut tree growing at the head of Father's tomb, forming a known marker where my father was buried . . . if I could find that tree, I would know that I was on the right spot. And since here was the walnut tree, how could it be that it was not any bigger than when Father was buried there? . . . I began to rake the leaves off the ground around the tree and sure, here was a stump. The tree growing there now was a sprout from the stump. . . . I was now sure that here was my father's grave. I remembered him from my boyhood as a good Christian father who tried to teach me the will of God and lead me in the right way."

As he traveled across the United States, C. J. marveled at its grandeur and beauty, its history, and its promise for the future. He was energized by the antiquity and romance of Europe even as he paused to acknowledge the wounds—so recent and still raw—of post-war battlefields and bullet-riddled villages. Throughout the Middle East, he reveled in his passion for biblical events and peoples. In Sweden, he relaxed and enjoyed the company of friends and relatives, understanding that he would most likely never see them again. Returning to America, he embraced the final westward leg of his journey and welcomed the prospect of resuming life in Warren. After all, there was much to look forward to. In January of 1922, sixty-year-old C. J. and Signe, soon to turn twenty-five, were married, creating somewhat of a local scandal that was overshadowed by the well-known reputations of the bride and groom. Three children—Carl, Naomi, and Rolf—would be born and raised on the farm. After C. J.'s death in 1951, grandchildren came along. Anna, too, had married, and although plenty of family land was there for her to cultivate, she and her husband chose to sell her share and leave farming behind. The couple relocated to California, where they raised their own family and lived out the rest of their lives. Anna would name her firstborn daughter Betty Jean, after her mother.

The journey *Across Sixteen Countries* provided both passage and threshold to the future in the lives of three individuals for whom such an adventure might have seemed highly improbable given the obstacles they had overcome up to that point. How fortunate that C. J. loved to write, and how lucky that the *Oregon Posten* captured his experiences for the enjoyment of countless others. With this new edition of C. J.'s travel memoir, masterfully translated to English for the first time by Mike Timshel, a path opens for a new generation of twenty-first century readers to appreciate this man's story and his unique contribution to the history of Swedish immigrants in Oregon.

—Rhonda Erlandson, President
Swedish Roots in Oregon
Portland, Oregon

FIRST-EDITION PREFACE

The author of this travelogue was born in Nästorpstugan near Strångsjö station in Stora Malm's parish, Södermanland, Sweden, on November 18, 1861. At the age of eight, he accompanied his parents to America. His father died just after their arrival to America, leaving in poverty the family, consisting of the wife and five children, the oldest ten years of age and the youngest just one. The eight-year-old Carl [Charles] had to leave the family and earn his bread working in the woods near Kansas City. After one year, the mother remarried and the family settled as homesteaders in Washington County, Kansas. There Carl's childhood and youth were spent in hard labor and toil with a meager education in the English language. He had learned Swedish from his parents. At twenty-six he married and moved to Scandia, Kansas, and lived there for a year before moving on to Wallace County, Kansas, where he homesteaded on the wild prairie. After six and a half

View of Portland, Oregon, with Mount Hood in the background

Swedish Lutheran Church and parsonage in Warren

years, he was forced to move away as a result of two consecutive years of drought. He then farmed on irrigated land near Pueblo, Colorado, for four years after which he returned to his parents' home in Kansas to help them out of financial trouble that threatened them with the loss of their rural home. He stayed there for three years and then headed for Texas where a sister lived. He stayed for a year and then undertook a journey to Portland, Oregon, to visit relatives there.

As a result of that trip, his family came to live there, in Oregon. In 1906 they moved to a piece of property in Warren, twenty-five miles from Portland, where he founded a successful Swedish community and a Swedish Lutheran congregation.[14] In 1918 his faithful wife [Betty] passed away, and thereafter he undertook the travels described here, accompanied by his daughter [Anna], just twenty years old, and her friend [Signe Ekström]. His daughter's eyesight and health had been weakened by rigorous study, and the father believed the trip would restore her health and vision, which it did.

The trip was very interesting and educational for all three, and the undersigned has, during the journey, recorded the following travelogue according to the knowledge and understanding of the places and circumstances he experienced, and should any errors or unfactual information be presented, the reader is kindly asked to overlook them. Last, he expresses the hope that these simple missives may be of interest and information to the reader.

—C. J. Larson
Warren, Oregon
1927

LIST OF ILLUSTRATIONS

List of Illustrations

TRAVELS ACROSS THE UNITED STATES

• Southern Pacific RR • Denver & Rio Grande Western RR • Missouri-Pacific RR
• Burlington RR • Milwaukee RR • Michigan Central RR • New York Central RR

----- By RAIL —— By CAR ~~~ By STEAMSHIP

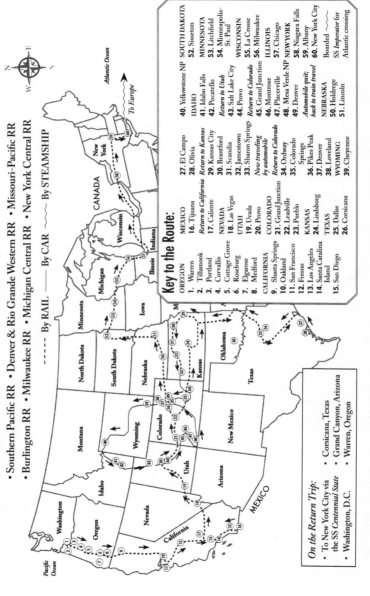

Key to the Route:

OREGON	MEXICO		40. Yellowstone NP	SOUTH DAKOTA
1. Warren	16. Tijuana		IDAHO	52. Sisseton
2. Tillamook	17. Caliente	*Return to California*	41. Idaho Falls	MINNESOTA
3. Portland	NEVADA		42. Pocatello	53. Litchfield
4. Corvallis	18. Las Vegas		*Return to Utah*	54. Minneapolis-St. Paul
5. Cottage Grove	UTAH		43. Salt Lake City	WISCONSIN
6. Roseburg	19. Uvada		44. Provo	55. La Crosse
7. Elgarose	20. Provo		*Return to Colorado*	56. Milwaukee
8. Medford	COLORADO		45. Grand Junction	ILLINOIS
CALIFORNIA	21. Grand Junction		46. Montrose	57. Chicago
9. Shasta Springs	22. Leadville		47. Placerville	NEW YORK
10. Oakland	23. Pueblo		48. Mesa Verde NP	58. Niagara Falls
11. San Francisco	KANSAS		49. Denver	59. Albany
12. Fresno	24. Lindsborg		*Automobile quit;*	60. New York City
13. Los Angeles	TEXAS		*back to train travel*	
14. Santa Catalina Island	25. Dallas		NEBRASKA	
15. San Diego	26. Corsicana		50. Holdrege	
	27. El Campo		51. Lincoln	
	28. Olivia	*Return to Kansas*		
	29. Kansas City			
	30. Branford			
	31. Scandia			
	32. Jamestown			
	33. Sharon Springs			
	Now traveling by automobile			
	34. Ordway			
	35. Colorado Springs			
	36. Pikes Peak			
	37. Denver			
	38. Loveland			
	WYOMING	*Return to Colorado*		
	39. Cheyenne			

On the Return Trip:

• To New York City via the SS *Centennial State*
• Washington, D.C.

• Corsicana, Texas
• Grand Canyon, Arizona
• Warren, Oregon

THE UNITED STATES

From Warren, Oregon, to California

Time flies, and it is now more than two weeks since we left home, family, and friends in dear Warren, Oregon, but we have not made it out of Oregon yet.

From Portland we undertook a trip to Tillamook, as we had long had a desire to visit that part of our good state, but never before had the chance. Now we had the last opportunity for a long time, if ever. The way there, which begins from Hillsboro, winds between high hills and along rivers and creeks until it attains an altitude of 1,811 feet above sea level at Cochran in the Coast Range. Then it descends the western slope through a number of tunnels and over bridges to

The travelers—Signe Ekström, Anna Larson, C. J. Larson

1

A part of the Warren community

salt air on the coast down to Tillamook. Here the even, fertile valley spreads out at the upper end of Tillamook Bay. This tract is famous for its lucrative dairying and cheese manufacturing.

The return to Portland was by way of Barlow, twenty-five miles south of Portland, where we visited some old friends. Then it was off to Corvallis where our old friends the Olof Johnsons had lived for many years. Mr. Johnson had been employed for many years as the most distinguished of carpenters at the state college situated there.[15] Here we spent a couple of half days touring the school buildings. There was much of interest for visitors as well as for students. We also met some young people here from Warren, Colton, and Portland with whom we were acquainted. Also we had the pleasure of chatting with Professor Bextell for a time.[16]

After a couple of days' stay at Corvallis, we continued our journey to Saginaw and Cottage Grove, where we visited a couple of old schoolmates who I hadn't seen since we were in school in Kansas thirty-eight years ago. They now had good homes in our beautiful, multifaceted state of Oregon. We had to travel on and our next stop was in Roseburg and from there another eight miles to Melrose and Elgarose. By getting a ride with the postman, the trip was both cheaper and more comfortable. The weather was beautiful and the roads are good and, although it appears that one is surrounded by high hills, there were indeed always openings for the roads to follow the larger and smaller valleys. Our people in the Swedish community were, in general, healthy and optimistic and were engaged in logging, driving, and cultivating the land. In particular they grew prunes for which they could expect a return of good profits for the effort when they began to bear fruit. We had the pleasure of attending Sunday school and services at the lovely church at Elgarose, where people assemble for edification and strength to fight life's battles. What invaluable benefit to have the Lord's temple to assemble in and hear and contemplate God's word!

We had the pleasure of staying at the home of our friends, Mr. and Mrs. J. W. Hawkins, which is situated on a height where they have a magnificent view of the valleys below. We also had a chance to visit the lovely homes of several of our countrymen, all of which exhibited diligence and order. We had first met some of these friends seven years ago when we saw this area for the first time, others we had never met before but they were all happy and hospitable and we were soon acquainted.

Of those we were with the most were: P. A. Anderson and his wife—Mr. Anderson is Elgarose's postmaster and shoemaker and has continued to expand his fine farm; Mr. Pehrson, who is postman between Melrose and Elgarose; Mr. and Mrs. Lindgren, who have lived there for many years and were the first Swedes to settle in the Melrose area, and who now own a large parcel of land and gardens; Mr. and Mrs. Stenberg, who live at Pastor Stures's former place; and Mr. Johnson, who is owner of Pastor Carlson's modern home, among others.

Big changes have been made by our countrymen since I last visited here. Forests have been cut down, the land cultivated, gardens planted, homes built, and so on. It demonstrates that wherever our Swedes settle, lovely homes are built and the future looks brighter.

The trip continued on the Southern Pacific line which winds along the Umpqua River valley twenty-eight miles to Riddle and then up Cow Creek Canyon thirty-five miles to Glendale, 1,441 feet above sea level. These deep valleys, often with vertical walls and winding rivers create an entrancing sight where nature in its spectacular wildness is an ever-changing panorama. We then follow Wolf Creek's winding path, and at last we arrive at Grants Pass, which got its name as a tribute to General U. S. Grant and Oregon's troops who battled the Indians here in the 1850s. We continued up the magnificent Rogue River, and then we were in the fertile Rogue River Valley with its many fruit orchards where Medford lies and in whose vicinity many Swedes have their fruit production.

Our route then led up the valley to Ashland, where two locomotives were added to haul our train of twelve cars up the steep slope to the top of Mount Siskiyou, 4,125 feet high, and in seventeen miles we ascended 2,235 feet. Here was the so-called "Horseshoe curve" where, at the same time, one can see the tracks in three places below, with the one tunnel below the other.[17] We then descended the south slope, which is nearly as steep. Soon we reached the Oregon–California line. When we look back toward Oregon, what diverse and magnificent nature it has with its year-round snow-covered mountaintops, its many clear, fresh creeks and rivers, its forested and evergreen heights and valleys, the greater and lesser fertile valleys with their multitude of products of so many different types and, not the least, its wonderful climate. Yes, they may count themselves as lucky who live in that state.

In California

Now we are in California. In the beginning it is a continuation of Oregon's landscape but as one comes south, it gradually changes. The heights become less forested and the valleys drier. But now we catch sight of 14,380-foot-high Mount Shasta, and for several hours we may admire its snow-covered crown as we are carried through grassy valleys which provide grazing and fodder for many cattle.

The train stops for a while at Shasta Springs to allow all to drink as much of the naturally effervescent water as they like.[18] Then we are off again down the watercourse of the Sacramento River, which begins at Mount Shasta and runs down to San Francisco Bay after a journey of three hundred fifty miles. The valley widens at Redding and now we travel through the beautiful, flat Sacramento Valley with its twelve million acres of fertile land where wide stretches are sown with wheat, alfalfa, and other crops. There are even fruit trees of various kinds. Part of the valley is irrigated and part of it is farmed without. At Benicia we come to the Carquinez Straits which connect the Suisun Bay with San Francisco Bay. Here the train is transported on a ferry, the largest in the world. It can carry twenty Pullman cars and four locomotives at once.[19] Porta Costa lies on the other side of the sound, which is a mile broad. The track then follows the bay shore through Richmond and Berkeley, and so we arrive at the quiet residential city of Oakland, where we took quarters for a couple of days.

In the City of the Golden Gate

To cross from Oakland to San Francisco, one takes the trolley to Oakland Pier and then a big steam ferry which carries thousands of people every day over the miles-wide San Francisco Bay. We took a tour to Golden Gate Park. The park encompasses 1,013 acres of hilly land which, in the 1870s, consisted only of sand dunes. Now they are covered with many different kinds of trees and flowers and a seventeen-mile-long motorway winding alongside artificial lakes. The park is also home to the "Golden Gate Memorial Museum," which contains much of interest for visitors. In front of the building is displayed, among other things, a German airship that had been shot down and damaged during the war.

We couldn't linger there, but had to make our way to Seal Rock, where the waves of the Pacific beat against the cliffs and where sea lions quarrel and fight and drive each other from the rocks down to the frothing billows.

We then embarked on a tour of Chinatown, where the Chinese are engaged in commerce. That part of the city, as well as a number of other parts of the city, serves as a reminder of the earthquake and its devastation. A number of partly tumbled-down brick walls are still to be seen in many places. Indeed, many have been rebuilt. But the awful subterranean opium dens are no more. They have been destroyed. And so another day has come to an end in San Francisco.

The next day it rained, just as it does in Oregon, and we had to stay in for the morning. In the afternoon we traveled by cable car up the hills, upon which part of the city is built, and many of the rich have their expensive homes. From there one is afforded a magnificent view of the city. Then it was off to the Presidio, where hundreds of cannons are emplaced. It is thought that all of the world's fleets could not force their way in past their vigilance. Also one has a splendid view of San Francisco Bay from here, and as we stood and watched, the sun sank into the western sea and splashed glittering gold upon the waves beyond the Golden Gate as far as the eye could see.

Southward to Los Angeles

To travel southward from Oakland one has two rail lines to choose from, namely the coastal route, which mainly follows the coast with some stretches that lead several miles inland—that way is the one that has the prettiest and most varied scenery to offer—and the line that follows San Francisco Bay to the north and east and then swings to the south up through the San Joaquin Valley. That valley is almost three hundred miles long and about thirty miles wide. It is divided by the San Joaquin River and several minor tributaries.

The water from these rivers has transformed a part of this naturally dry, sandy desert to fertile stretches where grain, hay and fruit of many kinds are cultivated by irrigation.

Here too are several successful Swedish communities such as Turlock, Kingsburg, Vinland, Fresno, and others.[20] Since Mr. O. J. Israelson and family live in Vinland, we directed our travel there. The Israelsons were our neighbors in Warren, Oregon, from 1906 to 1908. They were among the first Swedes who settled there and were part of the founding of the congregation. They now have their home in this warm, sunny valley and seem to be quite happy.[21]

It was nice to stay at their home for a few days. We got to go to the lovely church and hear the Lord's Word presented by Pastor M. A. Nordström, who was the minister. We also had the privilege to have dinner at Pastor Nordström's lovely home. It was a really beautiful respite for a traveler to stay at one of our Swedish communities, particularly on a Sunday, and see the people gathered around God's Word in the temple. And in every corner of this great land, where our people have driven down stakes and established congregations, so are they after all to be judged blessed in every regard.

We couldn't stay any longer, but had to continue our travels up the valley and over the Tehachapi Mountains where the tracks reach a height of over four thousand feet and where it was necessary to make many bends and crooks in order to cross the pass. Then we headed back down again and soon we are in the beautiful valley, where oranges and lemons blossom even while the fruit is harvested. It is in that fragrant valley that the beautiful city of Los Angeles lies.

Los Angeles and Environs

In and around Los Angeles, there are many things of interest to a traveler. A tour up Elysian Hill, from which one can see nearly the whole city all around, is a splendid panorama. We paid a visit to the zoological park and the many wild animals and to the alligator and ostrich farms. We even made a trip by trolley car to San Gabriel Mission, with its old buildings and their old furniture, books, cooking utensils, etc. They date from 1769, when the Spanish Catholics founded their mission among the Indians in California.

A twenty-eight-mile voyage on the Pacific Ocean to Santa Catalina Island gives a little foretaste of a real ocean voyage. A tour along the island in a glass-bottomed boat, over the "underwater garden" with its many types of seaweed and its multitude of fish gave a little insight into the life on the sea bottom.[22]

We also undertook a nineteen-mile rail trip through the beautiful orange and lemon orchards, where the ripe fruit gleam like gold amid the leaves, and the white flowers that attest to a new harvest exude the most pleasant fragrance that one could imagine. So our travels took us up through Pasadena to Ruby Canyon, prized for its rich beauty. Then we ascended three thousand feet up the slopes in wagons holding thirty people each, hauled up the sixty-two-degree rail line by electrically driven steel cables, to the top of Echo Mountain. From there we rode five miles in an electric trolley, which winds constantly up the steep mountainside to "Ye Alpine Tavern." Then it's two and a half miles by foot, horse, or donkey back up a steeply winding mountain trail to the top of Mount Lowe, where one finds himself one mile above the ocean, which one can see in the distance.

The San Gabriel Valley lying below, with its fields, orchards, and towns, spreads itself out now for the moment with all its splendid beauty. That trolley line, which was laid down in 1891–93 and cost over $700,000, was built by T. S. C. Lowe. But when the panic began at that time and tourism ceased, he lost everything and the trolley fell into other hands. Although he was impoverished in that enterprise, he felt himself well-rewarded to see so many get to enjoy the trip up the mountain on that, the most wonderful rail line in the world. The mountain that bears his name will be a lasting memorial to him.[23]

We got to stay over a Sunday in Los Angeles and go to church where Dr. Lincoln "carried the shepherd's crook."[24] Since it rained and blew worse than it does in Oregon, there weren't so many there for the service. We enjoyed the service just the same. It was those who let the weather scare them away who were the losers.

We met up here with our old friend J. P. Eklund and spent an uplifting afternoon at his hospitable home.

We had thought we could keep our overcoats, galoshes, and umbrellas in the steamer trunks when we came to California, but there we were wrong. We needed all of them. Californians, and the farmers in particular, were not unhappy over the rain, for they had had hardly any over the winter, and they would welcome us Oregonians back if we brought rain with us.

The distance to San Diego was one hundred nineteen miles, and even that trip was interesting. The journey leads through orange and lemon groves. Further south, where there is no water, they cultivate corn and lima beans on the slopes above the sea shore instead. San Diego is a fine, clean city and has, indeed, many points of interest. There remain many interesting sights to see in the large, well-planned park where the Mid-Winter Exposition was held in 1915.[25] The Old Missions were interesting too. We took a tour to Tijuana, in Mexico. There the Americans have built big gaming halls with strong drink and race tracks and other things that are not permitted in the United States.[26]

From Los Angeles to Lindsborg, Kansas

Since we had visited beautiful California for a while, but wished to celebrate Easter in Lindsborg, now we must undertake a journey of over eighteen hundred miles. There were three different rail lines that we could take, and when the Los Angeles–Salt Lake City line offered the best scenery, we chose that one.

On one stretch of seventy miles, the tracks pass through tracts where orange and lemon orchards stand in bloom. Then one travels through barren areas until, at Summit, an altitude of thirty-eight hundred feet is attained. It was March 26, and a blanket of snow covered the hills. It eventually disappeared as we descended to a lower plateau and traversed the one hundred seventy miles through the broad sandy desert in eastern California. There one sees nothing but round hills, like sugar cones, large cactus species, and "Spanish daggers."[27] At Las Vegas, at the lower end of Rainbow Canyon, there are springs and natural pasturage. Here people and animals could find water and food after the arduous journey over the burning hot sandy desert during the California gold fever in the 1850s and 1860s before any roads were built in these tracts.

The seventy-seven mile long Rainbow Canyon with its multicolored walls creates an interesting change of scenery in the middle of the desert. Arriving at Caliente, situated at the upper end of Rainbow Canyon, we set our watches ahead one hour just as we had during war time. It is now "Mountain Time." We crossed the hundred-mile broad Mojave Desert, and at Uvada, one crosses over the border into Utah. In Utah the mountains were again covered with snow. Here and there we could see some small shacks and cattle trying to assuage their hunger by eating sage brush and it reminded me of pioneer life in western Kansas twenty-five years before. Gradually we began to see more vegetation and better houses and after thirty-three hours of train travel we arrive in Salt Lake City, famous for its natural beauty, productivity and history. It looked winter-like with a twelve-inch snow cover which had fallen the day before and coats and galoshes felt pretty nice when we stepped off the train.

It was a Sunday morning, and since we had to stay over until evening, we had the pleasure of getting to visit our friends, the Hultquist family, and together with them attend Sunday school and church services. Here we could hear Dr. Kowl, with whom we were acquainted in Oregon when he was "Camp Pastor."[28] He served the congregation, who were waiting until the new pastor arrived. In our countryman Lund's home we had a good dinner and a pleasant visit together. Mr. Lund is a florist and has a thriving business.

So we were away on the Denver & Rio Grande railroad through a fertile, irrigated valley to Provo. The landscape gradually rose and became more uneven and at Soldier Summit attains a height of 7,440 feet. Then it goes back down again along the Green River. At Mack we cross the border into Colorado, and in a while we arrive in Grand Junction, famous for its peaches. Along winding rivers and around hills and mountains, the journey continued ever upward with three puffing locomotives until we reach Tennessee Pass at the backbone of North America, "The Continental Divide," at approximately the same altitude as Mount Hood. Soon we pass Leadville, the highest city in the United States, 10,200 feet above sea level. Then we descend along the winding Arkansas River until we reach Royal Gorge, famous for its grandeur, where the tracks press forward through the narrow pass with its vertical and overhanging rock walls, thousands of feet high, and where bridges over the roaring river are hung from the cliffs in order to make forward progress. Soon we arrive in Canyon City, whose area is famous for its apple orchards. Another forty miles and we are in Pueblo, which has been called The Pittsburg of the West, for the many smelters, steelworks, and foundries there, which make the town pretty smoky, like Pittsburg, Pennsylvania. We stayed over in Pueblo because our train was two hours delayed and the Missouri Pacific train, on which we were to continue, had already left. We thereby had a chance the next day to look up old friends and go out to the graveyard where my brother's wife lies buried,[29] and thirteen miles out of the town to the old place by Oman & Crook Reservoir where we lived from 1887–88. The way there goes through "Mexico-town," with its adobe shacks and through the Italians' vegetable gardens and orchards, where everything looks just as it did twenty-three years before.

A night journey by train over the wide prairie and we arrive at the lovely Swedish community of Lindsborg, Kansas,[30] which has won respect and fame through the Kansas Conference's school, Bethany College, which is a center for song and music in this and several other states. It is here that the beautiful oratorio Händel's *Messiah* is presented annually to great crowds.[31] During Palm Sunday, Good Friday, and Easter evening, the oratorio is performed by a choir of five-hundred-and-twenty voices and an orchestra of forty instruments, which sang and played in a most praise-worthy way. In that choir sang and played youths and gray-haired men and women, some of whom had sung in that choir for over thirty years.

When one listens to that song and music one gets a taste of what the Apostle John heard, "Where the thunder was like a great water, but still as airy as harpists playing on their harps."

But on Easter Sunday we got a reminder that we still live in a stormy world, for a great blizzard raged and closed the roads and rail traffic so that very few could assemble for services in the great temple, and so there were only a few for the Messiah song that evening. However, the members of the choir and orchestra were all there and sang and played with all their hearts of "God's Lamb, who took away all the world's sins."

Through Oklahoma and Texas

When one travels over the wide plains of Kansas, which to a great extent are sown with wheat, it looks so rich, as it does in Oklahoma and northern Texas. But by the time one is in Oklahoma, the wheat fields give way to cotton and further south into Texas, we no longer saw any wheat fields at all. It was mainly cotton and a little corn.

There is even a lot of rice grown in southern Texas, particularly in the El Campo area. Also they cultivate sugar cane in some tracts in the south.

In El Campo we had the pleasure of meeting August Nordin's sons and daughters, and they did everything to make our little visit as nice as possible. Also, we met with M. Noyd and other old friends who live there. We made a trip to Olivia, Texas, near Wolf Point on Matagorda Bay by the Gulf of Mexico. Here we stayed at the home of our old friend, Pastor C. J. Danstrom. Pastor D., who confirmed me in my youth, is eighty-two, but still preaches as he did in the old days and is still spry and healthy. Also, we met the father and brother of Carl Wilson, who lives in the Warren community in Oregon. They have Oregon in their thoughts. After we stayed a while at my sister's home in Corsicana, Texas, we headed north and traveled back through the great wheat fields of northern Texas, Oklahoma, and Kansas.

Back in Kansas

In Osage City, where the Kansas Conference[32] meetings are held, we met many old friends. We made a tour to Kansas City where we had a loving visit with Pastor H. E. Sandstedt and his family, and with N. P. Carlson and M. Julius. Then we went to Keats, Kansas, where my niece and a number of friends from my youth live. Then it was off to Swedesburg, Kansas, where my cousin, Pastor Charles Pehrson, who led the English-speaking congregation in Astoria a number of years ago, is now pastor. The Brantford congregation in Kansas, where I spent eighteen years of my youth, was a beloved place to

Signe Ekström's passport application. She completed the paperwork while in Sharon Springs, Kansas, one of C. J. Larson's former hometowns.

visit. Also we visited relatives and friends in Belleville, Scandia, Courtland, Kackley, and Jamestown, Kansas. Then we were off to Sharon Springs and Stockholm in the western part of the state on whose broad plains buffalo, wild horses, and deer ran free thirty-five years ago. Now the tract is sparsely populated with farmers and cattlemen who make a good living off the land. There are also Swedish communities and congregations which, however small, are brave and strong in their faith. They were founded in 1888 and remain despite drought and poverty at the beginning.

In Colorado and Wyoming

From Kansas we undertook a journey of nearly three thousand miles by automobile through Colorado, partly through the state's wide eastern plains to Rocky Ford, Olney, and Ordway, where we lived from 1894–98. From there we drove through Pueblo, "the Smoky City," to Colorado Springs and Manitou. Then we took a twelve-hour hike up Pikes Peak to its top at 14,109 feet above sea level, where it snowed for several hours on August 12. The next day we saw the "Cave of the Winds," "Cliff Dwellings" (a reproduction of the old cliff dwellings in Mesa Verde national park in southwest Colorado), "Garden of the Gods," South Cheyenne Canyon, and Seven Falls. The

Cog Railway, Pikes Peak, Colorado

next day we continued on to Denver, where we had a two-day rest and visited some old friends. Then we continued our travels to Berthod, Colorado, where our friends the Olof Johnsons and their children live. Here we stayed over Sunday, but as there was no opportunity to go to a Swedish Lutheran church, we went to the United Brethren,[33] of which

O. Johnson's daughter is a member and teacher in the Sunday school. We travelled on to Loveland, Colorado, and from there to Cheyenne, Wyoming. Through Colorado from Rocky Ford to Pueblo, the road follows the Arkansas River and most of the land is in irrigation. Here there is cultivated an abundance of alfalfa, wheat, oats, sugar beets, corn, melons, cucumbers, tomatoes, and apples.

Equipped for our 3,000-mile journey in 1919 Ford Model T Touring automobile.

From Pueblo to Colorado Springs one follows the Fountain River and little land is cultivated even along the river. From Colorado Springs to Denver, there is hardly any land cultivated; just here and there where water can be had from little creeks and streams. The land is beautiful and bears good crops of alfalfa, wheat, oats, beets, corn, etc. Around Cheyenne, Wyoming, it is dry desert land, and from there to Cody, Wyoming, there is alternating partly cultivated and irrigated land, and long stretches of wild, dry desert land. Also the road was very bad in some stretches.

In Wonderful Yellowstone Park

From Cody to the eastern entrance to Yellowstone Park, the road goes up along the Shoshone River's narrow mountain pass, which is very scenic. After some hours of travel we are at Yellowstone Falls, which is over three hundred feet tall and the water casts itself vertically in the narrow, multicolored mountain pass. We climbed down the steep cliff wall to the falls, where we had the most beautiful view of it. There we could drink hot water that spurts up from the rocks and cold, fresh water from a spring right next to it. Near the road, a black bear came out of the woods, and when we stopped the

Lone Star Geyser, Yellowstone Park

car he came right up to it. My daughter Anna reached out her hand and petted him on the nose, but he did not like that, as he snapped at her like an angry dog and bit her hand. Then he wanted to get into the car, but since we had hardly any room I threw him a cracker, which he immediately swallowed. He was indeed not satisfied and came right back, so I threw several more to him and we hurried away.

Among the most beautiful sights in the park are Mammoth Hot Springs with its many high, multicolored terraces and the many geysers that periodically eject boiling hot water hundreds of feet into the air. One never tires of admiring these natural wonders and many tourists come from far away and stay for a long time to enjoy the wonderful and beautiful spectacle and for the high, clean, cool air. One Sunday we had to stay in the park. We had no opportunity to go to any church, but in a forest grove by a clear stream we held services in God's great temple with prayer, song, and God's word. The singing was accompanied with guitar and violin, which we had with us.

Through Idaho to Salt Lake City, Utah

We left the park through the western entrance of Yellowstone and then drove through the southwestern part of Idaho through Idaho Falls and Pocatello. The road was winding and sometimes difficult and passed through forests, mountains, and valleys until we came to the Snake River. Around Idaho Falls was a broad irrigated valley, rich with crops and that gave a pleasant change after spending days in forest and mountains. We traveled again through Salt Lake

City and Provo, Utah. The cities lie in a
broad valley at the foot of the mountain
chain to the east, and that valley is, for
the most part, irrigated, so that there
are good harvests there. From Provo to
Utah's eastern boundary it is desert, inhabited by very few.

In the Utah desert

At Grand Junction, Colorado,
which is famous for its fruit production,
we steered southward to Mount Rose (Montrose). Around that city,
agriculture and fruit-growing is practiced by means of irrigation.
Then, from there we went to Placerville, Rico, Delores, and Mancoes.
That area is thinly populated and a bad road winds forth over hills
and mountain chains and through deep passes. However, there was
much natural beauty to be seen. From Mancoes, the road, which the
government built some years ago, leads to Mesa Verde National Park,
fifteen miles east of the southwest corner of Colorado. The way there
is very romantic, as it winds itself up and down over thirteen heights
and ridges covered with beautiful foliage and conifers. It's slow-going
to climb these slopes, for the automobile gets hot and has to rest from
time to time. But, it's easy going downhill. Indeed, one must drive
carefully to make it around the curves in the road.

Ruins from the Cliff-Dwellers' Time

Cliff Palace has over one hundred rooms with different shapes
and dimensions, all under an over-hanging cliff which constitutes
a roof over the whole thing. Spruce-Tree House, Balcony House,
Sun Temple, and other smaller buildings under and above the cliff
are interesting to see. Many are occupied with researchers studying
the time and circumstances when these prehistoric people built and
lived here. Still, not much is known.

Cliff Palace, ruins of cliff dwellings in Mesa Verde National Park

These buildings, which, for the most part, are walled with cut stone, carved with flint tools and mortared with a tough clay, show these people's diligence and skill at masonry. Finds of corn, beans, etc. in these buildings show that they practiced agriculture, possibly on the highlands. These buildings were first discovered in 1888 by cowboys.[34]

Some mummies, vessels, and stone, bone, and wooden tools from the site were displayed at the 1893 exhibition in Chicago.[35] In 1898 this author visited that area, but as there were no roads at that time, the distance of twenty-five miles had to be traversed on horseback along a very steep and stony mountain trail. There were some Ute Indians there in the narrow canyons who were helpful in finding our destination through simple instructions they could give in very bad English. One of them lifted the shoe of my horse and said, pointing at the shoe, "White man's horse. White man all time go see Cliff House." Then, pointing up a steep ridge back: "White man's trail." Now it is different since our government made it into a national park and built good roads so that people from every direction can come here in comfort.

From Mancoes our journey took us past the mining towns of Durango and Pagosa Springs (where there are hot springs), over the ten-thousand-foot high mountain pass to Del Norte in the San Luis Valley, and to Salida, Canyon City, Colorado Springs, and Denver, where our automobile finally quit, and we now have only memories remaining. But it was an interesting and educational tour.

From Denver Eastward

When one leaves Denver on the Burlington railroad eastward over the wild plains of, by turns, wilderness and cultivated, irrigated land, and one looks back at the Rocky Mountains whose backs are covered with new-fallen snow already at the beginning of September, one feels wonder and reverence. They stand so high and visibly hard, but still there flow from them the blessing of many streams and creeks that flow down from the mountain passes and valleys that are then used to irrigate the otherwise dry prairies and make them productive.

Indeed, the further one travels east and into Nebraska, the more cultivated land one finds. Wide stubble fields, grain, and hay stacks that testify to a real harvest, cornfields with their heavy yellow ears, all witness to the success of the hardy farmers who live independently in their fancy or simple homes on the wide plains.

Toward evening, we arrived at Holdredge, Nebraska, where we visited Pastor C. G. Olson, who we had not seen since 1892 during the pioneer times in western Kansas. The next morning we reached Axtell, Nebraska, where we met Pastor J. A. Edlund who soon after moved to Oregon. Because they had lived there before, they longed to return and that they are welcome to the Columbia Conference hardly needs to be said, for there is plenty of room for hard workers.[36]

The Bethphage Mission in Axtell, Nebraska

We were able to visit the Bethphage Mission as we had long wished.[37] We made the acquaintance of Dr. C. A. Lönnquist, who showed us around the operation, and on Sunday morning sent his son by car to bring us from town to his home and to the church. The Bethania congregation's church lies four miles from Axtell, and there we celebrated a beautiful service and then had dinner at the hospitable parsonage. Then we rode in the company of Pastor Lönnquist to the chapel at Bethphage where services for the home's residents were held at three o'clock, followed by the evening meal at the home. Dr. Lönnquist seems to be the right man in the right place, where he, in his friendly way, goes around among the weak, suffering, and cripples, who have found a good refuge in the home, where goodness and loving care under Christian influence is given to many of the suffering. That Dr. Lönnquist is admired by all is demonstrated by the radiantly smiling faces that meet him. Yes, it is a labor of love that deserves all our support. The only thing that seems to be lacking is room for more, for all of the space was occupied and many had to be turned away. In the evening we got to listen to a good sermon by G. A. Edlund in his church. So, we have celebrated Sunday in Axtell, Bethphage, and Bethania and came away with the best of impressions.

In South Dakota, Minnesota, and Wisconsin

On Monday our trip continued to Sisseton, South Dakota, through Lincoln, Nebraska, Sioux City, Iowa, and Sioux Falls, South Dakota. Sisseton is located in the Sioux Indian reservation, and many Indians were in town to shop.[38] Our friends, the John Ölunds, who live twelve miles from town, met us with a car and we could more closely observe the farming in the area which twenty years before had been wilderness with Indians roaming around. When the government gave them other land to choose, they withdrew to the west where the land was hillier and more wooded, and let the white man take over the flat lands. There grain, corn, and hay are cultivated on broad fields with little ponds here and there. Thousands of wild ducks make it their home, and it is a hunter's paradise.

After a pleasant couple of days visiting our friends' hospitable homes, they gave us a ride back to Sisseton and our journey continued through Millbank and Granite Falls (which lies along the beautiful Minnesota River), to Willmar and Litchfield, Minnesota. Here we were met at the station by Mr. Edwin Enberg. Mr. Enberg lived, several years ago, with his parents in Colton, Melrose, and Warren,

Oregon. They moved then to Rock Island, where Edwin studied for a time at our school and thereafter in St. Peter, Minnesota. As his parents had passed away some time ago, he had to take care of his younger siblings. Therefore, he had to end his studies to be able to take care of them. They live together in

On South Dakota's plains

a little rented house, and Edwin does his best for them although he is only twenty-one years old. We spent a Sunday with these friends and visited the Sunday school and services in our Lutheran church there. Mr. Enberg said that he longed for Oregon, where he hoped to live in the future.

On Monday we continued our travels to Minneapolis, where we had the joy of meeting friends and acquaintances and stayed at their good homes for a few days. We also visited our friend Einar Anderson who had stayed for a time in Warren, but after mustering out of the Army, he stayed in Minneapolis. The Twin Cities, Minneapolis and St. Paul, are very large, progressive cities. St. Paul is nearly as large as Portland, and Minneapolis is one-fourth larger. They are pleasant cities, and the landscape in this area is beautiful. It's a little hilly with groves of trees and lakes here and there. From here we traveled on to Chicago on the Milwaukee rail line, which follows the Mississippi River to La Crosse, Wisconsin, through the natural beauty on the way to Milwaukee, Wisconsin, and then along the shore of Lake Michigan to Chicago.

Chicago

In Chicago, one of America's greatest cities, everything is about being in a hurry. The streets swirl with vehicles and foot traffic, and trolley cars wedge themselves along through it all. But, as there is no room for all the trolleys on the streets, they also run on tracks up above it all. In Chicago we visited Pastor C. A. Tolin, who had been our pastor at the Augustana congregation in Portland and who founded the Bethany congregation in Warren.[39] We loved staying at their home and once again hearing Pastor Tolin's good and instructive preaching. On Sunday afternoon we visited the old folks' home. It is a good thing for the old people who did not have any earthly support to have such a place and get the care they need. Also we visited Dr. Edwin Sandstedt,[40] and he made our visit very pleasant. We made a tour of Hyde Park, where the exposition of 1893 was held and now only the administration building and the German building remain. Now there is a big park, with nice streets, little lakes, and shady trees where Chicagoans can enjoy some fresh air and a little greenery if they find time to go there, something they might well need, as most of the time they breathe smoke and dust. Also we visited Lincoln Park. There they also have several statues of famous men, among which is one of Carl von Linné, Sweden's "Flower King."[41]

At Niagara Falls

Our journey on the Michigan Central Railroad passed through the naturally beautiful areas of Michigan and Canada to Niagara. We had to stop over there to see the mighty waterfall or, rightly said, waterfalls, for Goat Island divides the river a little above the falls so that Canada has Horseshoe Falls on its side and the United States has American Falls. The roar is loud when the great mass of water crashes down from one hundred sixty feet high. The scenery, as we passed through in New York State, was beautiful and reminded us of some parts of Oregon, and apples hung from the trees, just as they do there. We got to ride along the beautiful Mohawk River on the oldest railroad in New York, where the first train began in 1831 with a speed of seven miles an hour and pulling three cars carrying about ten people each. We got to see that train in Grand Central Station where it is on exhibit.

In New York City

At Albany the train crosses the Hudson River and follows it for several miles and after a few hours, we are in the biggest city in America, where millions of people of all nationalities swirl around each other and where the trolley cars must be built under the streets, on the streets, and above the streets in order to get the population to and from work. Still, it is very crowded in all of the cars. Most of the streets are narrow and crooked, and the tall buildings hide the sun, so that electric lights must be used in many buildings all day. "The Cathedral of Commerce," or the Woolworth Building, is the tallest and most beautiful office building in the world. It is 792 feet high, and from its top there is a wonderful view of the city and over the Hudson west of the city and the East River, which separates Brooklyn from New York and over which there are now three bridges hanging from steel cables. The first was built 1869–83 and is 6,538 feet long. Three hundred and fifty thousand people are carried daily over it by trolley, automobile, horse carts, and on foot. "The Subway," the underground trolley, travels under the river to Brooklyn.

We sought out the Lutheran Swedish immigrant home[42] at number 5 Water Street and stayed there a few days until the ship *Imperator*, on which we were to travel to France, was to depart. Here, many Scandinavians and Finns traveling back and forth have found a temporary home at modest cost compared to what others charge for lodging. Of all the cities we have visited on this trip,

New York is the most expensive regarding lodging, as is everything here, and there are many dishonest businessmen who charge three prices for everything.

On Sunday we went to the great Gustaf Adolf's church for services.[43] For several days we had been occupied with getting all the paperwork in order for the trip. There is so much trouble these days. Of course everyone wanted money, but now everything is ready and in the morning we shall embark the ship and bounce on the billows for several days.

The Trip across the Atlantic

We stepped aboard the steamship *Imperator* on October 7.[44] At 2:00 P.M., they cast off the mooring lines and we glided slowly out of the harbor on what is said to be the largest steamer on the Atlantic. The Germans built it to compete with other countries' steamers. It is 940 feet long with a displacement of 52,000 tons. It was taken from the Germans after the war and is now used by the British line, Cunard. After several days of battling the passport office, internal revenue agents, ticket office, etc., we took our places in the well-appointed liner with a sense of relief. But at the same time we felt melancholy at the thought that we, for a time, would be separated from the land of the free, that has so many cherished memories for us, where I have spent almost my entire life and experienced both failure and success, joy and sorrow. Indeed, all that time the Lord has led us wonderfully and reminds us that that land is so dear to us. The "Statue of Liberty" stands so tall, as if welcoming the arriving immigrants who come from every country to this great, free, and—for the time being—prosperous land, where everyone who can work, and will work, gets the chance to improve himself and where many got their own home and won independence for themselves and their children, which they could not have in their homelands. As it receded into the distance, we can well say this is a good land. May righteous freedom live on here.

After two hours travel down the Hudson River, we came out into the Atlantic. We heard a cannon shot, the ship stopped, and everyone rushed to the railing to see what was happening. A little steamer came out and stopped. A rowboat with three men aboard pushed off from our ship, and they boarded the little steamer. It was our pilot leaving after he, with his steady hand, had steered our vessel past rocks and shoals out into the wide ocean. We could still see the outskirts of New Jersey and Long Island's coast in the distance, but soon they disappeared from view and there was only the expanse of the sea to be seen on all sides.

The weather was the most beautiful one could wish for: clear, calm, and mild and a good beginning for the 2,845-mile-long voyage. Soon the sun sank into the sea and left a golden glitter on the waves that then disappeared and gave way to twilight. The bell rang and everyone hurried down to the dining hall, where a simple but good meal was served. We then passed the time strolling on the deck, making conversation, reading and writing in the ladies' salon, where men, in the company of a lady, too can visit if they don't smoke. In the men's salon, smoking and card-playing was permitted, and I was glad to have ladies in my company, so that I could go to the ladies' salon. At nine o'clock everyone had to leave the salons. A bugle sounded and that meant that all ladies had to leave the deck. Men could stay so long as they wished. Some collected in the mess hall, where there was a piano and there was song and music. The lights were turned off at ten o'clock as a signal for all to leave. It was now time to get some sleep. We slept well to the rumbling of the engines, which also caused a little vibration. The next morning we arose early to see the sunrise on the sea, and it was beautiful.

The weather was still lovely and the sea was nearly mirror smooth. One or another steamer passed us during the day.

At dawn on Saturday the 9th, a high, black wall of clouds stood before us, looking like mountain cliffs. But the sun made its appearance like an opening in them, and we passed through. The wind gradually increased, and the ship rocked a little. On Sunday there was a bit more rocking, and some of the passengers became seasick and others just felt bad. My girls had a little bit of that, but soon felt well again. At ten o'clock, Catholic Mass was held in the men's salon. There was a good number of Catholics present. Prayers were led in Latin, so that no one understood a word. Communion was held, but we could not understand what use that was for anyone, as the priest drank the wine himself. There were no songs. A little talk was held in English in which the priest told the Catholics to pray to the Holy Mother for the Pope, "the Holy Father," who was now in some badly embarrassing situation.[45]

Even we Protestants were not without services. I had become acquainted with a Norwegian Lutheran missionary who was on his way to the mission fields in Africa, where he had previously worked for several years to prepare a field and was back in America to enliven interest in the work. He promised to preach for us and the people assembled on deck in the afternoon when missionary Gundersson held a good service on the Apostle Paul's words, "I am not ashamed of Christ's evangelism, for it is God's power of salvation for each and everyone who believes." We sang a song and missionary Savaas, from Hillsboro, North Dakota, who was on his way to Madagascar, spoke for a while on the importance of serving the Lord. Also, others declared that they were not ashamed to confess devotion to Christ. So, we got to celebrate a beautiful service although we were on the wide ocean.

In the evening, some collected around the piano and one song was sung after the other until the lights were turned out at ten o'clock and we went to bed. On Monday the sun came up clear and promising a beautiful day, but the wind picked up in the course of the day. Tuesday morning was cloudy and blustery, rain showers drove over the water, and the ship rocked significantly. Wednesday was more changeable with sunshine and rain showers. Today, Thursday, we expect to arrive in Cherbourg, France.

TRAVELS ACROSS EUROPE

Key to the Route:

FRANCE
1. Cherbourg
2. Evereaux
3. Paris
4. Verdun
5. Meaux and
   Chateau Thierry
6. Chalons-sur-Marne
   and St. Michel
7. Belfort

SWITZERLAND
8. Basel
9. Lucerne
10. Lugano
11. Marcato

ITALY
12. Chiasso
13. Milan
14. Venice
15. Florence
16. Rome
17. Naples
18. Pompeii
19. Pozzuoli (Puteoli)
20. Bacola
21. Brindisi

CORFU
22. Corfu

CRETE
23. Khania
24. Kandia

Return to Italy
25. Brindisi
26. Bari
27. Trieste

AUSTRIA
28. Viloch (Villach)

GERMANY
29. Munich
30. Wittenberg
31. Berlin
32. Warnemunde

See Travels across Scandinavia map

From Norway to Britain
33. Newcastle, England
34. Aberdeen, Scotland
35. Glasgow, Scotland
36. Ayr, Scotland
37. London, England

Leaving Europe
38. Tilbury, England
39. Boulogne, France
40. Queenstown
    (Cobh), Ireland

FRANCE

In the evening of October 14, we sighted the lighthouse on Scilly Island, which belongs to England, and the next morning at seven the ship stopped. The anchor was dropped, and soon we were ready to board a little steamer which would carry us to the dock, as the harbor at Cherbourg was not deep enough for a big ocean liner to enter.

We could tell right away that we were in another country on the steep, narrow gangplank that made it difficult to make way with the luggage. But we managed and in a while the lines were drawn in. We had left our temporary home and as we regarded it from the outside it looked big and heavy and it seemed nearly impossible that it could have carried us over the Atlantic's billows over three thousand miles in seven and a half days.

From Cherbourg to Paris

Coming ashore at Cherbourg we opened our luggage, and the customs agent wanted first and foremost to know if we had cigars or

An old street in Paris

tobacco with us. Since we didn't, we passed easily through after they saw that we spoke the truth. The railroad cars stood waiting for us to board but they were very different from American ones. We entered at the end of the car and the passage along one side gave us access to a little room with two benches across from each other and room for eight passengers. There were glass doors that could be closed, if desired, and curtains that could be drawn so that one was separated from the others. One could talk as much he wanted without disturbing the other passengers and if one became sleepy one could lie down and sleep on the long cushioned benches undisturbed.

We had to wait until twelve-thirty before the train departed, but it rolled away up a valley with rock walls and a winding creek followed for several miles. The valley widened out and small stone houses with little fields and orchards with red and yellow apples hanging on the branches could be seen on the slopes. Gradually we came up out of the valley onto more even ground with bigger fields, planted for grazing and hay. Herds of cattle grazed on the pastures between groves of trees and creeks, and it looked really pleasant. Buildings are of stone with tile or straw roofs, and barns and stables are built attached to the houses.

Eventually there was more cultivation of grain and potatoes, and a little fall grain sprouting here and there. Some plowed with one horse; others had one horse in front of the other. Some worked with two horses abreast but walked and led the horses. Here and there a woman could be seen sitting and milking a cow out in the field at three o'clock in the afternoon.

We passed several small towns without stopping, so long as there was no need to change locomotives and take on water. In Evereaux we had to stop for an hour while the tracks were cleared of the wreckage of a freight train that a passenger train had run into and whereby thirty people had been killed and many injured. That delay meant that we didn't get to Paris before nine o'clock. We should have been there at seven-thirty.

In Paris

We felt a little lost in such a big city, where we did not know the language, but luckily we had in our company a man from New York who knew a little French. He booked us a room at a hotel for eight francs each, corresponding to fifty-eight cents. We wanted to eat at a restaurant. We got *Soupe, Beurre, Pain*, and *Pommes de Terre* [soup, butter, bread, and potatoes]. We were asked if we wanted to have wine, beer, or cognac. They seemed amazed when we shook our heads and instead asked for milk [*de lait*], which we also got. But it was condensed. There seems to be a dearth of fresh milk in Paris. In France it is quite common to pour a little cognac in the coffee instead of milk. Wine is drunk by most people with and between meals. The party cost seven and a half francs (fifty cents) per person.

The next day, Saturday, October 16, began clear and mild, like the previous day. Led by an interpreter, we ventured off to see something of Paris. We descended down to an underground trolley. The air down there was stuffy, dank, and oppressive. After riding for a while, we stepped out of the trolley and into an elevator, which carried us

Wash day in Paris

Coal delivery in Paris

seventy-five feet up to the street. It felt good to inhale fresh air again. We were near the "Church of the Sacred Heart" [Sacre Coeur],[46] which is situated on the highest point in Paris. A stone stairway led up the height to the church. One can also get there by cable car. The church, which is Catholic, is almost exclusively built of stone. It is large and expensive and decorated with many grand paintings and so forth, as is common in Catholic churches. A stone staircase of three hundred fifty steps took us up in the tower where one had a spectacular view over the city and surroundings. The bell, which weighs nineteen tons, is the largest in France. We wandered then through the oldest districts of Paris, where the streets are no more than sixteen to twenty feet broad and the sidewalks, three to four feet. Streets and sidewalks are paved with stone and are fairly uneven. In this part of the city there stands a very old windmill, and inside it is now a dance pavilion.[47]

There was much that was unusual to be seen on the streets. There comes a cart loaded several feet high with household goods and drawn by a man walking between the bows who hauls it with a strap over his shoulders and knuckles like a horse up the uneven street. And here comes a big, heavy cart with five-foot wheels, loaded with coal sacks and drawn by a horse. And on the harness a big, broad yoke on a shapeless collar, heavy iron links to haul with fastened to the bows with no swivel. The driver has a sack hung over his head and shoulders, but when we take a snapshot of it all he throws off the sack. And here comes an ice-cart, just as heavy and shapeless as the others, with a big covering, drawn by two horses, one in front of the other. There one can see a driver with a tall black

hat sitting high on the driver's seat on a little coach with a gentleman inside and drawn by a little horse with jingle bells trudging
up the hill as fast as he can. There comes a boy on a three-wheeled
velocipede with a big box on it containing all kinds of wares. And
rattling, shapeless automobiles, big omnibuses among others, make
up a motley but interesting sight for us Americans. So people walk,
run, carry all sorts of things in baskets, sacks, or in their arms. Bread
is of rye flour and baked in narrow, three- to four-foot-long rolls,
which are carried from the bakery in the arms like firewood without wrappings, for it is said that there is a lack of paper in France.

The shop stalls are narrow, and the wares are set out on the
sidewalk for sale. At cafes and restaurants stand little tables and
chairs out on the sidewalks, and people sit there while they drink
their coffee, wine, beer, cognac, etc.

In the afternoon we boarded a trolley without knowing where it
was going. We handed a bill to the conductor, who handed it back as
it was too much—all money here, down to a half-franc, is paper. We
rode for a long time and passed over the little River Seine, which
flows through the city. At last the conductor came back and gave us
the sign that we should get off. I pointed back and he nodded. The
wagon made a swing around the block and went back the same way
we had come. We paid another thirty-five centimes (two and a third
cents) each. When we rode for a while we caught sight of the Eiffel
Tower, which was built before the exhibition of 1889 and is 984
feet high. It is the highest tower in the world and is built of steel
and iron. As always, we admired height. We got off of the trolley
and walked to the tower. For five francs one can ride to the top in
an elevator, and as it is a quick way to rise up in Paris, we went.

The sun sank in the west, and below us famous Paris spread
itself out with its crooked, winding, and sometimes narrow
streets. But there are also a number of broad boulevards with

thirty-two-foot-wide sidewalks. The streets run at every imagin-able angle and it is not so easy for a stranger to find the way he wants to go. That was our experience when we went to the American Church[48] at 21 Rue de Berry.

Sunday morning, October 17, was raw and rainy, but we wished to go to the American Church and were told by someone who knew a little English that we should take a trolley on which stood the number twenty-three. We stood a long time and waited. All the other numbers came, but no twenty-three. So, we asked a policeman and showed him the address and he pointed that we should walk down the street. We asked if we should take the "tramway," but he pointed that we could walk, and we could get there quickly. We set off, but soon became unsure of where we should turn. We showed the address to another policeman and he pointed in another direction. We followed his advice and at another corner asked a woman. She talked for a long time and pointed in several different directions, but it was incomprehensible to us.

We walked on, and at the next corner asked two women for advice. Once again it was a long and incomprehensible flood of words. Anna said that she did not want to ask any more women, for they were even more unintelligible than the men. At last we met a man who showed us the street, and soon we were in sight of the American Church. We entered a little late, but were glad to be there for we understood what was being said. We got to listen to a good sermon, and after the services the pastor asked that all foreign-ers come forward so he could meet them. The pastor greeted us very cordially and gave us good advice and information and the address to the "American Women's Club,"[49] which is a home for American women. We sought it out in the afternoon and were well-received and got much valuable information, especially from a young woman from Illinois, who had arrived in Paris in September. It is of great value to travelers that there are churches that understand the language and such homes as the Women's Club. At these places they do not accept tips, otherwise tips are expected for the least service. When one eats at a restaurant, the waiter always expects a tip after one pays for the meal.

At the Battlefields of France[50]

On Sunday night, it rained hard. Monday was rainy, too, so we used the time mostly to get our things ready to continue the journey. On Tuesday morning, which was clear, we undertook a trip to Verdun and the surrounding area to see the battlefields. The train departed at 7:35 A.M. and passed through changing scenery, sometimes along the Marne River valley, then through hilly land, with tunnels every so often. Hay and grain fields testified of a good harvest to come. Small towns lay close to each other, and it seemed that the farmers lived there. We passed Meaux and Chateau Thierry, where the war's destruction showed itself with holes in stone walls and roofs, and tumbled-down walls and pits in the ground showed where bombs had exploded. Here and there were piles of barbed wire that had been rolled up so that the land could be tilled where they had been stretched, shot-to-pieces trees everywhere and so forth.

We passed Chalons-sur-Marne and St. Michel, and just before twelve we arrived at Verdun, where we stepped off the train and spent a little time viewing the destruction the German bullets wrought on this old, well-defended city. The streets are very narrow and crooked. The buildings that had not been destroyed were ugly with

The fortress Fort de Vaux, France

low doors and dark passages. We also saw a large, old church and nunnery that had been badly shot up, although the Germans had not approached nearer than four miles from the city.

We also saw fortifications and cannons that had been much used. Then we boarded one of Thomas Cook's big automobiles[51] that took us out to the battlefield, and the farther we got from the city, the greater was the devastation. Former villages and towns were now only heaps of stone and where a dense forest had stood, there were now only one and another stump to be seen. Deep holes right next to each other showed that the bombs had fallen densely. The land is hilly with great heights and deep valleys. The soil is mixed with white stone shards which tell of poor ground. Trenches and snarls of barbed wire everywhere showed how difficult it must have been for the soldiers to advance through these obstacles.

In a while we came to Fort Souville, which the Germans took with a loss of a half-million men. It was the point where the Germans penetrated the farthest. The fortress is in bad shape. Fort de Vaux, which had been thought to be impenetrable, was also destroyed. Germans and Frenchmen battled for five days and nights in the fortress's underground passages with bayonets, but for lack of water, the French were overrun, and the Germans held the fortress for five months.

We wandered through some of the underground passages that the soldiers must have occupied for several months. The floors were mostly paved with cement, but water stood in puddles and even ran down the walls and made the place cold and damp. We toured Fort Douaumont, which is situated on the highest point in the area. The Germans took that fort, too. We went down into the trenches, which led from one fortress to another, and where soldiers marched single-file to stay out of sight of the enemy and even electric wires were strung for light and telephone communications. At Theaumont, where one hundred seventy men were buried alive in the trenches, the bayonets were left in place and are sticking up out of the ground. We passed many cemeteries where one white cross after another show the resting places for thousands of soldiers. Thousands were never found and never will be. Their shattered bodies are mixed with the earth. We returned to Verdun where our train awaited. We had seen what a war had done, and we hope that such will never happen again.

Back in Paris

One day we saw some of the most notable sights in Paris, in one of the big "Cook's Tours" automobiles. An English-speaking guide followed along and gave information on what we saw. To tell everything we saw would take up all too much space. I will only name a few. We visited seven Catholic cathedrals and they were all expensively built and richly furnished. The same was true for the Louvre Museum, built beginning in 1841, which contains the largest collection of artwork in the world. We saw Napoleon's grave and monument and several other graves and monuments to other great men. We even got to go into the Supreme Court, which was very expensively appointed.

One can see much in Paris that one is not accustomed to. So we saw, for example, a load of unthreshed wheat with four horses in a span and another with five horses across. The driver walked next to them. There were even trolley cars with two levels.

We had to stay in Paris one more Sunday. We visited, once again, the American Church and stayed for Sunday school. The sermon was good and bore the stamp of a serious fear of

The American cemetery at Argonne, France

God. The pastor and people were very friendly and outgoing. A fairly good number of people were assembled, mostly Americans. In the afternoon we boarded a trolley outside the city walls to a little suburb. A band of musicians walked up the street. We followed them until they came to a place where there was a carousel and where a whole lot of comedy was performed. It was right next to an old, gray church. We pressed forward to the church steps and entered a dark Greek Orthodox Church. The mass, or service, was going on the best they could and a good many were assembled. The priests, dressed in red skirts, performed the ceremonies. The people seemed very serious in their prayers, and the sign of the cross and rosaries and holy water were in general use. It seemed strange enough that such noise and uproar were permitted right outside the church. On the way home we came to a Roman Catholic church into which a long line of women in big white hoods were entering, and we supposed that mass or some such was being held. We went in, too, and there was a man in a fine uniform, carrying a staff with a big gold knob. The priest was dressed in an elaborate robe, boys dressed in red jingled their bells, and monks went around with their shaven pates. Then long prayers were said and the prayer beads came in handy. Songs were sung alternately by the monks and the congregation, and music was performed on a big pipe organ and other instruments. But, since it was all in Latin, we did not understand a single word.

SWITZERLAND

After a ten-day stay in France, we started off to Italy. We traveled first through southeastern France, which is beautiful and mostly fertile land, where hay, grain, and fruit are cultivated. In some areas where the land is hilly, they grow a lot of grapes. At Belfort we came into an area that had been German before the war, but now belongs to France and stretches almost to Basel, in Switzerland. At the border our passports were inspected and our bags were searched by both the French and Swiss authorities. We stayed in Basel overnight until eleven o'clock the next day. We saw here a museum containing many old things of interest. Basel is a clean and well-situated city, but the streets run in all directions like they do in Paris, and a number of them are very narrow. Between Basel and Lucerne, the

The city of Lucerne and Mount Pilatus

landscape was very beautiful. The train runs through valleys with sloping green hills, alternating with fields and orchards, and high up on the hills were yellow copses that witnessed it was autumn.

In Lucerne

Lucerne is situated in among the Alps and is nearly surrounded by them. The city lies 1,489 feet above sea level on the beautiful "Lake of the Four Cantons." Many steamboats make regular tours between cities on the shores. The city has a very pretty location on the southwestern end of the lake, and stretches up the beautiful green hills on whose slopes hotels, summer homes, sanatoria, etc., make up a captivating panorama when one views them from the train station. We crossed the stately bridge over the river Reuss where it exits the lake, and we arrived in the western part of the city. We followed the river to the left and come to the marketplace, which sits before and under some of the buildings. Here everything possible is for sale, from beautiful flowers to Swiss cheese. From there we come to an old wooden bridge, which is called the Chapel Bridge and was built in the 1300s. It is about ten feet wide and is used only for foot traffic. It is built in many crooks and angles, which make it three times as long as the distance over the river. It is covered, and under the roof there are one hundred twelve oil paintings showing different events from the land's history during war and peace.[52]

Near the bridge in the middle of the river stands an old fortress tower from the 1300s. On the other side of the bridge, to the right along the river we see odd old buildings with narrow passages and vaults here and there where people live completely hidden away. In a while we come to another old wooden bridge, built like the first one but not so crooked. Under its roof are oil paintings depicting the *Dance of Death*, painted by Casper Meglinger.[53] Having crossed the bridge, we see before us several fortress towers and a twenty-foot high old wall over the heights. The wall and towers, which were also built in the 1300s, surrounded the town at the time and were a protection against enemy armies who all too often tried to take the city. Inside the walls is the oldest part of the city with its very narrow streets and passages between the houses, which were built in the 700s. Now the city has been built up even outside the walls and on the other side of the river.

We viewed several places of interest, Glacier Garden,[54] among others. A little further along is a great panorama depicting General Bourbaki's retreat to Switzerland in February, 1871, a masterpiece by M. Castres.[55] We also saw the famous *Lion of Lucerne*. It is carved into an overhanging cliff. It constitutes a memorial for the Swiss Guards who heroically fought and died when they were attacked by the Austrian army on August 10, 1792. The image is sixty feet high and carved into the cliff after a model by Thorvaldsen.[56]

One day we made a trip to the top of Mount Pilatus, which is 6,962 feet high and situated some miles from Lucerne. The weather was cloudy and foggy. After an hour's ride on the train to Alpnach, we rode a cog railway up a forty-three-degree slope through seven tunnels. When we were half-way up we saw the fog lying like a lake in the valleys below us and at the top, the Alp's snow-covered pates were spread almost all the way around us to view. After a couple of hours wandering on the rocks we headed back down. It was cloudy, cold and grey the whole time we were in Lucerne until the last morning, when it cleared up and became quite lovely.

Southward to Italy

Saturday, October 30, we traveled southward to Italy. The scenery in the Alps as we traveled through it was spectacular and in places looked like the Columbia River Gorge, where it cuts through the Cascade Mountains, and in other places like the valleys in southern

Oregon. We passed through about fifty tunnels in four hours. The longest took nineteen minutes to pass through. A little after sundown we came to the city of Lugano in the southern part of Switzerland and stayed there until Monday. That city lies on Lake Lugano on steep slopes. It is an unusually romantic place and is much visited by tourists.

On Sunday morning we sought out the English Episcopalian church (the only English there) and participated in the services. It was much better than Catholic services, for God's word was read and sung, so we understood what the cape-clad priest was saying. The content was not what one could want: fairly little of the Law or Gospel. Mostly it was about England and its leaders, and as it was the Sunday before All Saints Day, the congregation was exhorted to remember the departed holy men in their prayers.

We noted a great difference between that one and the American Church in Paris. The pastor did not approach us and no one else did either before I spoke to someone and introduced myself. Even then they were quite taciturn. I was informed that there was a German church in the city; otherwise all the others were Catholic. The city has about fourteen thousand residents. We visited another little town nearby called Marcato. The Catholic church there was built in the 1300s. At the church, which is built on a mountain slope, there is a cemetery with graves built into the rock. The houses in that town were very old and the streets and alleys very narrow, some only four feet wide and looked dirty and disgusting. When we, on the morning of the November 1, looked out the window, there lay a white blanket on the ground, and the tree branches whose leaves are still green, bowed down under the weight of the wet snow. At nine o'clock we continued our journey and in a few hours we were in Chiasso, on the border of Italy.

ITALY

In Chiasso our baggage, once again, had to be searched and our passports scrutinized and stamped. Everything went unexpectedly well and in a little while we climbed aboard another train that carried us to Milano. The snow continued to fall through the whole day, and it was fairly cold as there was no heat in the cars. We stayed warm the best we could, and when our feet got too cold, we took off our shoes and rubbed our feet warm with our hands. We wished we had our rubbers, but they were in the trunks. We had not expected it to be so cold this time of the year in Italy.

In Milan

Milan (Milano) lies between five and six thousand miles straight east of Portland. At 2:30 we arrived in Milano and, as we were really hungry, we went to a buffet and got a good dinner for ten lire (forty cents). Restaurants at the stations are first, second, and third class.

In third class there was so much smoking, swilling, and fighting that we could not even eat there. Even the rail cars are divided into three classes. Second class is maybe about as good as an ordinary commuter train in America, but for the most part, dirtier.

We succeeded in getting a room with heat at a hotel near the station for about fifty cents a day per person. It was really lucky for there was a lack of rooms in the hotel as we found out later.

The next morning there was still snow remaining on the roofs, and it began to snow again before noon. We got ourselves underway to go see the sights in the city, and first we came to the Duomo cathedral, which Giovanni Gallezzo began building in 1386 and is the largest church.[57] It was built in the Gothic style and covers an area of 126 square feet, 485 feet long and 356 feet high. It has two thousand statues on the outside and seven hundred on the inside, plus a number of paintings. It is built of granite and marble and is regarded as the most beautiful church in the world. And there is much that is splendid and expensive to see. On a lower floor, the body of San Carlo Barronet[58] is preserved in a casket of silver and gold, and you can see it for a lira. He has been dead for over four hundred years and the teeth of time have begun to gnaw on the old dead body, although they have tried to patch it together and hold onto it as long as possible, for the church makes money from it. It's said that the church has a nail from Jesus's cross and many other wonders. We also saw St. Ambrosius' church, built in 1835, and the St. Eustorgias and Virgin Mary church, where *The Last Supper*, painted by Leonardo da Vinci in 1494, can be seen. That church was used as a stable by French soldiers in the Napoleonic War.

We saw much grandeur in the royal palace. We even saw the bed slept in by President Wilson.[59] He is expected to return in January 1921 and sleep there once again.

The city of Milano is quite old. The Romans took the city in 221 B.C. The city has seen highs and lows. In 452 A.D. it was destroyed by the so-called Huns under Attila, and in 569 by the Goths and in 1169 by Germans. In 1179 it was conquered and built up anew. From 1535 to 1706, it was controlled by the Spanish, and that was a time of poverty for the citizens. In the 1700s it was under Austrian rule, and in 1796 it fell to Napoleon, but in 1811 it was retaken by Austria who held it until 1859, when it was incorporated with Italy. It has been successful since then and counts now 599,200 residents. It is situated in northern Italy in the middle of a fertile plain, with the Alps visible in the distance.

On Wednesday it rained all day, just like it does in Oregon, and the snow eventually disappeared. We walked and rode around the city and took in more of the remarkable sights, which mostly consists of Catholic churches and their grandeur, and museums with statues and paintings by the Old Masters.

In Venice

We traveled to Venice on November 4. We traveled over the plains, which were well cultivated and irrigated, for despite that it now rained and snowed, as was said, a month too early, the summers were dry and hot. Many fruit trees of different sorts, such as apples and pears as well as grape vines and so forth, are planted and well-tended, and alternate with small patches of corn, wheat, hay, etc. After a couple hours travel, the land became hillier, and when it cleared up we could see the snow-covered Alps in the distance that reminded us of the Cascade Range in Oregon and Washington.

Gradually the land became flatter and lower, and by noon our travels led us through low, swampy land with water on both sides of the tracks. Arriving at Venice, we got off the train and a little steamboat took us to the Metropole hotel where we got food and lodging for thirty-seven lire ($1.48) per day per person. We got a room on the third floor with a wonderful view over the Adriatic Sea. Many small islands were strewn before us. We found the Y.M.C.A., where we succeeded in getting an American woman to take us around and show us the sights in the city. She was a superb Cicero.[60]

What most distinguishes the city from other cities in Italy is that there are no trolley cars or vehicles of any sort, including bicycles, because the water canals flow through the streets and all traffic is by boats, which in general are rowed by two men standing with one long oar each. We saw ambulance boats, patrol boats, freight boats, and pleasure boats. We took a tour through the narrow, crooked streets in one of the last named, a so-called "gondola," rowed by a man with one oar. These boats are very long and narrow, like an old Viking ship. Smaller canals run in every possible direction and lively boat traffic goes on. Before a rower comes to an intersection, he shouts loudly, and if someone is coming to cross the intersection, he answers, and in that way they don't crash into each other. In the company of our guide, we wandered the narrow, crooked dry-paved streets. We went from one Catholic church to another and visited other places of interest.

The next morning was clear and beautiful. We got into the Bell Tower[61] elevator, which is three hundred twenty-five feet high, and from there we had an overview of the city and surrounding area. Then we wandered around the narrow streets in the company of our nice tour guide and viewed several old churches and an old prison from the 1400s and much more. The city even has a park, which lies beautifully along the beach, and we walked around in there. But all of the trees are fenced in and one must stay on the paths.

In Florence

At five o'clock in the morning on November 6, we got ourselves underway from the hotel to travel to Florence. We did not get a chance to get something to eat. It took fifteen minutes by boat to the station

and at six o'clock the train departed. In
Italy one ought to always be ready to
board a half-hour to an hour early, if one
wants to be sure of a seat. For several
hours the journey passed flat, well-cultivated lands. Then it got so hilly, passing
through one tunnel after another, that it
seemed like we were in tunnels more
than out of them and ever upward for

"Moving" in Florence

one long stretch. At last we were rolling downward, and the landscape looked a lot like Northern California on the south slopes of
Mount Shasta, but was, perhaps, a little more heavily wooded, with
little copses of oak, whose yellow leaves witnessed that it was fall
here too. The steep slopes were partly cultivated. Orchards, vineyards, and small vegetable fields alternated endlessly.

We followed a little river down, through a pretty valley that
widens more and more until it becomes a beautiful plain with
large orchards. In that beautiful valley lies Florence on both sides
of the Arno River, which flows in a northwest direction out to the
Mediterranean. We had expected a diner car to be part of the train,
but we soon found out that that was not the situation. At one station
there came a boy with food in bags. But when I took one, the girls
got to see that it even contained a bottle, and they said then that
they did not want it. I then gave back the bag with its contents,
but they came to regret it. We stopped in one town after another,
but there was no food to be had. At ten o'clock, we changed trains
and here was a diner car, but no food could be had before noon. A
little beforehand, I sent the girls to the diner car so that they would
be among the first. They soon came back with the explanation that
they had to wait for the third seating at the table because they had
not bought tickets beforehand. Orders had been taken before noon,

but they had not come as far as to us. It took an hour for each seating, so that meant a two-hour wait. During that time the train stopped at a station where food bags were sold. I bought two for six lire (twenty-four cents), and they contained rye-buns, ham, meatballs, grapes, and two bottles of wine. We ate our fill and gave the bottles to a woman next to us who said "*gracio*" and nodded cordially.

The city of Florence is almost ringed by heights on all sides. We walked up to a church that lies on a high hill on the edge of the city.[62] It was built in the 1100s and was encircled by high walls. Seen from there, the city spread out below like a beautiful painting and reminded us of Portland, Oregon, seen from Council Crest. It has nearly the same population, namely 232,000, but is smaller in area because it is more densely built. Most of the streets are very narrow with sidewalks sixteen to twenty inches wide, although they are shopping streets where all sorts of trade goes on. We had luck in finding lodging on the seventh floor of a hotel right in front of a piazza (an open area as big as a block), so we had a good view of it as well as over the city and the heights in the distance.

On Sunday there was an election of officials in the city of Florence, and there was some fear that there would be trouble, and many soldiers were in the city to maintain order.[63] We sought out a Scottish Presbyterian church and attended services there. It was good anyway that there was some Protestant activity in that land so filled with Catholics. Sunday night there was trouble in the city, and late at night and from our room we heard several shots, and the next morning our host told us that two had been killed and thirty injured. We stayed in Florence for four days and saw much of interest. This city is especially famous for its sculptures and paintings, both old and new. We met some Swedes from Sweden who were here to study the Great Masters' paintings. They were very amusing. We had interesting conversations about Sweden and

America and toured the Uffizi gallery, which is regarded as having the best collection of paintings and sculptures in the world. One afternoon we traveled by trolley a little way out of the city to a high hill, where an old town was located, and from there we had an excellent view over the city of Florence.[64] It reminded us of Portland as seen from Mount Tabor.

In Rome

The train to Rome should have left at 7:30 A.M., but was delayed almost an hour, so we had plenty of time. When it came everybody rushed in. With the help of an American soldier, we succeeded in getting in and finding seats. The morning was clear and chilly, and there is no heat in the rail cars in Italy. Our route led south along the river, over and under hills and mountains, and through a number of tunnels. Here too the countryside looked like northern California.[65] In the afternoon we came into Rome through one of the gates in the old city wall, and there was much of interest within and without these walls that were laid down in 564 B.C. The first to meet our gaze when we stepped out of the station were the old ruins of the Diocletiani bathhouse that is said to have been built by Christian prisoners in the second century A.D.

We sought out the Y.M.C.A. to secure a guide for the next day, but as they were all engaged, we set off on our own. We went first to King Victor Emanuel's palace and had the opportunity to see the large and expensively decorated building. On the outside it did not look like much except for having a large area. After that we went

The statue of Victor Emanuel in Rome

to St. John's church, which for a time was the foremost church in Rome, if not in the world, and was for several centuries the Pope's seat. Nearly all of its original splendor has disappeared through devastating wars, earthquakes, and fires. It was built on the high ground of one of the seven hills on which Rome was first built. Right across from that church is a chapel where at one time stood the Pope's palace. There is the so-called *Santa Scala* (holy stairs), which is said to be the same as the one in Pontius Pilate's palace, where Jesus walked when he was sentenced to death. The steps are of marble and said to have been brought from Jerusalem. They are now covered over with boards. That was done so that they shouldn't be worn out or so that they wouldn't be so hard on the knees when one crawls up the twenty-eight steps. It is hard to say. It is supposed to be a very good deed to crawl up them on one's knees, and Catholics devoutly pray a prescribed prayer for every step and kiss the stone. As we remember, Luther crept up these same steps on his visit to Rome to ease his conscience, but in vain.

Many crawl up these same stairs yet today. No one may walk up them and the steps are very worn from all the crawling. I crawled up them too, to experience what Luther did (not as a good deed), and my knees were pretty painful before I got up, although I crawled faster than the Catholics in my company. Indeed, I wanted to get to the top of the stairs to see the image of the Savior. It is said to be the same that remained on the cloth that a woman reached to him to dry the sweat from his face when he carried the cross.[66] But I was disappointed, for it was closed up in a cabinet and shown only on certain days of the year. I wondered how I would get back down since I could not walk down the stairs. I was informed of another stairway a little farther away that I could walk down on.

The next day we visited the Pincio Garden. That park is situated on a high hill in the northwest corner of the old district and within walls that were built in 220 B.C. These walls, however, have been repaired since then. This park offers an excellent view over Rome. Here is a general gathering place for Rome's population, in particular on Sundays. There is nothing there for entertainment, except for a band that plays there sometimes. Below the park lies the Piazza del Popolo. In its center is a fountain and an obelisk that is eighty feet high that was brought here in 30 B.C. We returned to the city wall and followed it to Salira, near which Victor Emanuel with his troops made a breach in the wall, and thereafter succeeded in taking the city in 1870. We also visited the Palatine Hill. It is there, according to legend, that Romulus laid the foundations for Rome. There, in bygone times, stood great palaces, and now there are only old stone and brick walls. Through excavation in later times it has come to light what large, rich buildings stood there long ago. Below the Palatine Hill is the so-called Forum and not far from there lies the Coliseum, begun in 72 A.D. by Vespasian and completed by Titus in 80 A.D. It was inaugurated with gladiator games that lasted one hundred days, when five thousand animals and many gladiators lost their lives. After that it became a showplace where Christians were cast before wild animals to be torn to pieces. The building is round and 1,848 feet in circumference and 65 feet high with three galleries and a capacity of 100,000 people.

Not far from there is Titus's triumphal arch. That arch was raised to the memory of the destruction of Jerusalem. One sees the seven-armed candle holder and other things from Jerusalem's temple depicted on that arch. Not far away are the ruins of Nero's golden house and also Constantine's basilica and a temple of Venus.

The fortress of St. Angelo was built in 136 A.D. by Emperor Hadrian to be his tomb. In the 1500s it was converted to a fortress and during the Catholic persecution of Protestants, there were incredibly many who were tortured and killed for their belief there.

We went down and viewed the underground dungeons where those who were accused of heresy were incarcerated. No light and no air could penetrate down there. Also displayed were knives and other tools that were used to behead those condemned to death. As the fortress is situated along the edge of the Tiber River, there was a hole in the stone floor for the blood to run into the river. There was even a water channel into which the dead bodies were thrown and washed down into the river.

One day we rode a few miles out of the city by horse-drawn wagon on the so-called Appian Way, which was laid down between Rome and Brindisi in the year 312 B.C. by Appius Claudius, to St. Calixtus catacombs, which consists of underground passages. These were used by the Christians during the first centuries, partly as crypts and partly as meeting places during the Roman persecution of them. There they held services when they were forbidden to hold them in public places. Guided by a monk, who, for a fee, gave each of us a candle, we headed down into these several-miles-long, dark passages, where, in some places, we saw caskets with glass lids, in which nearly completely decomposed corpses lay, and here and there human bones in niches. These niches are graves which had been walled in, but had been unearthed and opened. It felt almost as if we had been in a sanctuary. We had vivid memories of the story of them from the little book, *Light from the Catacombs* or *Stars in a Stormy Night*, which can be had from Augustana Book Concern and ought to be read by everyone who has a chance to.[67]

St. Peter's Cathedral and the Vatican

We also visited St. Peter's Cathedral, which is the largest in the world, and there was much that was precious and beautiful to see. It is 619 feet long, and has 245 pillars, 396 statues, and 45 altars and is 440 feet high. We climbed to the top of the dome by way of a circular staircase and then an iron ladder. From here one has a remarkable view of the city.

The Vatican lies adjacent to St. Peter's Cathedral, and is the Pope's home or "prison," for he may not leave his holy domain of eleven acres. But he has room enough to wander in the two thousand rooms there and in the surrounding gardens, and he is just one lonely old man. It took several hours to walk through all of the many grand halls, hung with silk, silver, gold, and precious stones. In the treasury there are great riches which belong to the church.

There are opportunities to see the "Holy Father" on Thursdays and Sundays. One must have written permission, and that is not easy for those who are non-Catholic. Our guide, who was Catholic, promised to request for us to see the Pope, provided we would bend our knees and kiss the ring on his finger. We couldn't go along with that, for it would have been a "Judas Kiss." It is not easy to have any respect or reverence for the Pope or the Catholic Church when one is reminded daily of the much evil they have done to Christ's true believers.[68] So, we had to skip the visit with the Pope.

The Waldensians

On Sunday we visited the Waldensian church, and although we could not understand the language, still it was a joy to see these confessors of Christ and their children assembled for evangelist Sunday school and church service. It was moving to see with what humble love and respect they met together. It reminded me a lot of our little congregation in America and, not the least, in Warren. May we never as evangelistic Lutherans lose this spirit of brotherly love! They even shook our hands and showed their joy over seeing us there. It felt encouraging for us foreigners to be received when, in most places on this side of the Atlantic, and even in some churches in America, we did not get such a loving reception, which, to a high degree, was the hallmark of the first Christian congregations. If anyone who reads this does not know the story of the Waldensians, I will say that they probably originate in the first Christian congregations in Rome and other places in Italy during the Apostles' time. After the institution of the papacy, they separated from the church and withdrew to northern Italy's mountains. In the course of years they spread to all parts of Italy. In the thirteenth, fourteenth, and fifteenth centuries, attempts were made to annihilate them and they were persecuted in the most horrible ways because they would not recognize the Pope. Despite the wars of extermination, they persisted, and now they are found in almost all parts of Italy.[69]

We also visited the American Methodist church in Rome and were met very cordially by the pastor and its members. We had previously met the pastor at the Y.M.C.A., which is on the Piazza Barbarino, and is a wonderful meeting place, especially for American travelers, where one can get all the information and help that a traveler needs in a foreign land. Among all of the Y.M.C.A.s we visited, the one in Rome best fulfilled its role as a reliable source of help, even though its staff is Italian.

We also wanted to visit the church of Santa Maria, which is built over the old house where the Apostle Paul sat captive and where many of his letters were written to the Christian congregations. After much inquiry, we found the little church on a narrow, hidden-away street. After searching for a while, we found a monk who took us directly to the sexton, a friendly old man, who opened a door to a staircase, down which we walked to the little room in the basement level where the Apostle Paul sat as a prisoner. We could see badly deteriorated paintings on the stone wall. They are said to have been painted by the Apostle Luke.

Behind and nearly hidden by the statue of Victor Emanuel[70] stands the old capitol on the highest of Rome's seven hills. Although it has been through a lot, the main part of the building, built before the birth of Christ, is still in fairly good shape. Narrow stone steps lead up to the bell tower, where an old clock, run by heavy weights, still shows the time. Higher up are two big bells that cannot be swung, but by rope the clappers are pulled back and forth so that they strike the sides of the bells. From the tower one has, perhaps, the best view of the city and surrounding area.

We have now stayed in Rome for ten days and hurried the whole time to see the city and the many antiquities that are told of in Rome's earliest history. Naturally there is much remaining that we have not seen. We have tried to see most of what has historical value. In short, Rome is a city of extremes. It has great, fine buildings, palaces and four hundred churches. But also there are the ugliest, small, dark, dirty holes under the city walls and houses where people live.

One sees narrow, stinking alleys, and next to highest luxury and stateliness are the poorest, the cripples, the blind, and old who sit or stand on almost every street corner and beg for coins. Most transportation is by donkeys, mules, and horses of all sizes drawing little two-wheeled carts. Very few automobiles are in use. Most of the horses are small and thin and are often tormented inhumanly by their drivers. The city is quite filthy. The smaller streets are very smelly this time of the year. What it must be like when the weather is warm!

People are rude in many ways and modesty is in short supply. But it wasn't much better in Paris. If anyone acted like that in America they would be arrested immediately. One can guess how clean the food is by the way it is handled. There is no overabundance of food in the hotels. For breakfast it's a cup of coffee or chocolate and two little rye buns. It doesn't seem like much for us from America, who are used to more. For lunch and dinner it might be anything from cabbage leaves and such, to meat and potatoes, which is seen as a real celebration. They use a lot of macaroni. They ruin it, though, with stinky cheese which they grate and sprinkle on if one does not stop them. One never sees butter, but that is probably for the best, as it is really bad in Italy. One never sees mush, pancakes, or syrup, and sugar is rare. There is no pie or other fruit dishes. However, grapes, figs, mandarin oranges, and apples are eaten for dessert.

To Naples

On the morning of November 20, we traveled from Rome to Naples. The hotel clerk had ordered a cab to take us to the station, about five minutes away. I asked the driver the price and he answered fifty lire (two dollars). I offered him twenty-five, and he refused to accept it. Then we called another, and that one asked ten lire (forty cents) and he got a tip to go with it.

The trip by train led through generally flat, fertile country, but then became hillier and then passed through a mountain range with many tunnels. We arrived in Naples at 3:00 p.m. and suc-

A peculiar team: horse, ox, and donkey in Naples

ceeded in getting rooms in a hotel that lay beautifully by the beach. From our windows we had the most wonderful view of the sea. We stayed for eight days, saw the city and made trips to nearby places of interest. One day we took a trip to Pompeii and Vesuvius.

The American Y.M.C.A. has an office in Naples and a guide who went along with us. First we took a cab to the fairly distant station and then took a trolley two hours to Pompeii.

Pompeii and Vesuvius

The volcano Vesuvius is visible most of the time with a cloud of smoke and steam rising from its crater. We passed along its foot, partly over lava fields, and traveled through Herculaneum, which is said to have been inundated and destroyed by lava at least twenty times, the last being in 1906, but was rebuilt. They make cameos from lava there.[71]

The excavation of the city of Pompeii, which was buried in ash, sand, and glowing hot stones which the volcano emitted in 79 A.D., and for centuries lay hidden and forgotten under twenty feet of ash, began in 1748. The excavation has continued since then so that now half of the city lies exposed, and we wandered now on the stone-paved streets where Roman wagons, said to have been hauled by slaves, wore deep ruts in the pavement. We saw many now-roof-less buildings of every kind in which there is everything possible which had been buried: human bodies, and even food that had not moldered away but had been preserved so long by the ash that so completely covered them. On the walls there are paintings and stat-ues, and all of them show that there went on a life of drunkenness, gluttony, luxury, and high-living, just as in Sodom and that the city came to a similar end. That city is said to have been a vacation and entertainment place for the Romans.

After two hours wandering in the old city, we ate a good dinner in a hotel at the station and then made the return trip by trolley. At Puchano, at the foot of Mount Vesuvius, we got off and rode up Mount Vesuvius on a cog railroad belonging to the English tourist company of Cook and Son. That cog railroad is similar to the one on Pikes Peak in Colorado, but much steeper with a 42 percent rise near the top, where steel cables are used to draw up the cars. Arriving near the top, the cars stop and we continued a piece on foot through thick, strong, nearly suffocating sulfurous smoke. We made it through and we suddenly stood at the rim of the crater with the red-hot boiling mass of lava before us, which, from time to time, cast fire balls into the air. It is now fourteen years since it last burst out and covered several small cities at the foot of the mountain with lava, ash and sand carried by the wind all the way to Naples, where a three- to four-foot-deep layer fell, and people fled the city in terror. The volcano subsided and has been somewhat calm since then, but it is said that it is becoming more and more active, and it is uncertain when it will erupt again.[72]

Pozzuoli

On another day we made a trip to Pozzuoli (Puteoli), the place where the Apostle Paul stepped ashore on his trip to Rome to appear before the emperor and stayed with Christians before wandering the one hundred fifty-seven miles to Rome. Puteoli was in its heyday then and had here, as in other places, large theaters, bathhouses, temples, etc., the ruins of which are still in good condition.

Near Puteoli is the crater of an old volcano which is not extinct, but from which smoke and sulfur fumes still exude. In the crater are caves where people used to take hot steam baths to treat rheumatism, and it did not take long before we began to sweat in there. A little over a mile from Puteoli is a round hill (Monta Nuova), four hundred fifty feet high, which unexpectedly arose from the ground one night in 1538.[73]

From Pozzuoli we went by boat, rowed by two men, each standing with one long oar, to the town of Baja, three miles across the bay. It took an hour and cost seventeen lire (sixty-five cents). Here too were ruins of old temples, bath houses, and cisterns to provide water for ships during Rome's heyday, but which were destroyed in the 800s by Saracens. We went to another little town called Bacola. We wandered through the narrow streets to reach an eminence from which we had a re-

The old amphitheater in Pozzuoli

markable view of the surrounding area. In the doorways of the little rooms that constitute an entire family's home sat women doing different kinds of hand work. The narrow streets swarmed with children of all ages. A girl gave Anna a flower and got a coin in return; a boy quickly came and gave Signe flowers, but we had no more coins at hand and he followed us, and soon we had a troop of twenty or more noisy children who followed us through the streets. Their mothers called them but they seemed to pay no attention. At last they tired and gave up. The little town seemed poor in everything except children, of which there was an abundance. We returned that night to Naples.

Back to Naples

The city of Naples is built at the upper end of a bay of the same name, a part of the Mediterranean Sea, and has a beautiful location. It lies on the slopes by the bay but stretches up a steep hill on whose top lies an old fortress and prison.[74]

Cable cars go up the steep slope to near the top of the hill, from which a wonderful view of the city and the bay on whose shores little villages can be enjoyed. The newer part of the city is built on the top of the hill. An electric tram also goes up to the top, but has to make many sharp turns to get there.

In Brindisi

On November 29, we traveled to Brindisi. That city is located in southern Italy on the Adriatic Sea (a branch of the Mediterranean Sea). The rail line follows the Bay of Naples close by Pompeii where it crosses a peninsula which is very mountainous and hilly. We passed through a number of tunnels even here and at the city of Salerno we came to a bay of the same name, but soon left it and crossed the southern end of Italy over and under a stretch of hilly, mountainous land to Taranto on the Bay of Taranto after which we traveled over a low tongue of land to Brindisi. The ship on which we were to sail, the *Corinthia*, belonging to the Lloyd Triestino[75] steamship line, previously of Austria, but fell into the hands of the Italians after the war, was to arrive December 2, but was delayed so that it did not arrive before December 5.

Brindisi, Italy, has a population of twenty-three thousand and a beautiful location on a little bay of the Mediterranean Sea and has a first-rate harbor. It is a lively port city, visited by many ships. There are no trolleys and quite few automobiles. Transportation is mainly by horse and donkey. Goats are to be seen on all of the streets, in particular in the mornings and afternoons, when they go to and from their pastures after they are milked. There were no cows to be seen.

On Sunday we tried to find a Protestant church, but had no luck. We had no desire to go to a Catholic church, as we had visited them so often and got little or no use from them. So instead, we held services in our room. At 7:00 P.M., an interpreter from Cook's travel bureau came rushing in and said that our ship had arrived and transportation stood by the door to take us to it. There was now a big rush to get our luggage in order and get going. They had told us previously that the ship would not land before Monday, so we were completely unprepared for such a hasty departure. However, we were glad to begin our Mediterranean voyage to Palestine, where we all longed to go. When we got to the dock, there was frightful yelling and noise to the highest degree. But, in good time we came aboard and everything fell into order. Early the following morning, while we lay fast asleep, the ship left Brindisi harbor.

Now that we have left Europe's coast after spending time in three of its countries, we wanted to take a little look back. France has a climate and vegetation a little like Washington State's, but not such high mountains or such large forests. The residents are lively and talkative. The difference between rich and poor is greater than in America. Those with money go in for more luxury and finery, and the poor are ragged and filthy, and live simply and cheaply. A worker gets $1.00 to $1.50 per day, and food is about the same price as in America. The cities, not the least Paris, are dirty, and the people are crude in their habits. Also, their morals seem to be at a low standpoint. Men and women drink wine, beer, and cognac, and smoke cigarettes. Most of them call themselves Catholic, but seldom go to church.

Switzerland is much like the western half of Oregon, but is somewhat colder in the winter. The people are more genteel and progressive in general, far more than France. The conditions are a lot like those in America. The morality is higher than France, and there are more Protestants there. Italy is like California in climate and production. Irrigation is used where water can be had. The people and conditions are a lot like those in France with, perhaps, less politeness. People indulge in strong drink and cigarette-smoking there as in France. In matters of the church it is much like France, but the religiosity is perhaps greater. However, none of the people have much faith in the Pope and his cronies.

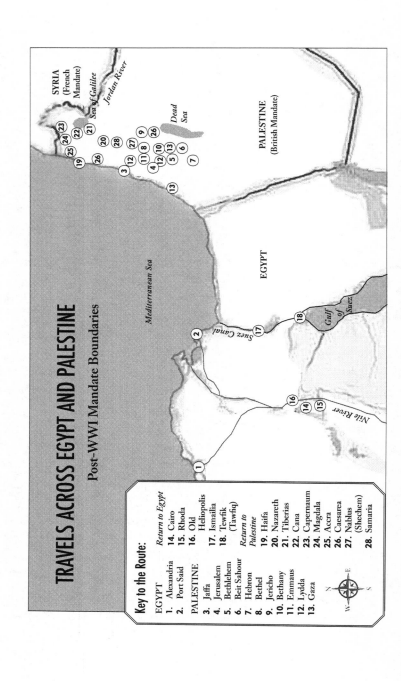

TRAVELS ACROSS EGYPT AND PALESTINE
Post–WWI Mandate Boundaries

Key to the Route:

EGYPT
1. Alexandria
2. Port Said

PALESTINE
3. Jaffa
4. Jerusalem
5. Bethlehem
6. Beit Sahour
7. Hebron
8. Bethel
9. Jericho
10. Bethany
11. Emmaus
12. Lydda
13. Gaza

Return to Egypt
14. Cairo
15. Rhoda
16. Old Heliopolis
17. Ismailia
18. Tewfik (Tawfiq)

Return to Palestine
19. Haifa
20. Nazareth
21. Tiberias
22. Cana
23. Capernaum
24. Magdala
25. Accra
26. Caesarea
27. Nablus (Shechem)
28. Samaria

EGYPT

When we awakened on the morning of December 6, we were a good piece on the way. The ship had departed at 1:00 A.M. from Brindisi, and at daylight we saw the coast of Albania in the east. As most of the passengers had gotten sick during the night because of the high swells, which caused the ship to rock, the sight of land was very welcome, for in most cases, the sight of land eases the seasickness. Heavy, gray clouds concealed the sun, and as the day progressed it began to rain. We were now in the shipping lane where Paul, as a captive on his way to Rome, was subject to such a strong storm that they had to let the ship drift in the wind until they came to the island of Melita [Malta], where they were shipwrecked. If we had been on one of the sailboats of those times, it might have gone a similar way for us. But now our iron-clad steamer cleaves its way through the frothing billows and sails proudly against wind and waves, which can do no more than make it rock.

Along the Coast of Albania and Greece

We followed the Albanian coast all day until four o'clock, when we drew in to Corfu, on the island of the same name, to unload merchandise. Those who had been seasick had gotten better and the eating tables, which that morning had been nearly empty, were, in the evening completely filled with passengers. Six o'clock the next morning, we continued our journey. Everyone had gotten a calm night of peace and rest, and was now hale and hearty. The morning was clear and promised a beautiful day. We were now following the west coast of Greece.

The coasts of Albania and Greece are, in general, steep and stony. There was, however, some farming. We noticed mostly vineyards and orchards on the steep slopes, where there was even one and another little town to be seen. How meagerly and simply those people must live! No railroads, trolleys, or automobiles, but all traffic is on donkeyback, now as it was three thousand years ago.

During the day, we passed many small islands. At nearly three o'clock in the morning I was awakened by a crack of thunder, and I saw out the porthole one lightning flash after another. I got dressed and went up on deck. I wanted to see a thunderstorm on the sea. The sky was clear with one black cloud, when there was a lightning bolt to be seen to the north. A strong wind blew from the south, and as we were sailing in an easterly direction, the wind and waves struck the ship broadsides so that it canted significantly. A lighthouse could be seen to the right, which showed that we were passing an island. The ship slackened speed and proceeded carefully, for we were sailing through a narrow, crooked passage. After a while, we could see a band of light, meaning that we were headed for a town, and at dawn the ship landed at Kalamata, on the southern end of the coast of Greece.

As the ship was to lie here until 5:00 P.M., we took a rowboat to shore to see the city. There was little of special interest to see here.

Like all of the other cities in this country, the buildings are built of stone with tile roofs. Grapes, figs, currants, and olives are cultivated on the slopes around the city. The first rain of autumn fell that day. The climate is like that of southern California: nine months of the year without rain and three months of winter when it rains several times. At five o'clock, we continued our voyage.

At Crete

The night was stormy and rainy, and the boat rocked considerably, so that the next morning many complained that they had not been able to sleep. At daylight on December 9, we entered the harbor of Chania, which lies on the north side of Crete. We departed from there at 8:00 A.M. and arrived at Kandia, on Greece's Peloponnese Peninsula, at 2:00 P.M., where some passengers disembarked and some boarded. Some goods were unloaded and others were brought aboard, wine barrels in particular. At 8:00 P.M. we weighed anchor and continued onward. On the morning of December 11, when we came out on deck at dawn, we saw nothing but water on all sides and a low cloud bank surrounding on the horizon. Gradually it took on an edging of gold and in a while, the sun's glittering beams broke through over the clouds and promised a beautiful day. What a gorgeous sight! A fresh wind blew from the north and as it was from the side, the ship began to rock with the wind. The interesting thing about the sea when the billows fly and the ship rocks, after one gets used to it, one does not get seasick. That morning we saw something in the distance that looked like treetops, but at closer range proved to be a sailing ship with five masts, with all sails billowing. When we got closer, we saw that it was loaded with lumber. I told the girls that it was probably from the Pacific coast and they cheered with joy. Afterward we found out that that was not the case, and they weren't so joyous. It is true that when one is far from home, anything that comes from there comes as a fond greeting.

On a voyage one meets a motley crew. In first class there were Englishmen (among others, one who had lived in Cairo for many years and had been on a visit to England), Frenchmen, Italians, an American priest on his way to Jerusalem to work in the mission service, who had previously lived there for many years (during the war he had been forced to escape with his family), and some women in the same group. In second class it was the same mix: an English Episcopalian minister and his wife who lived in Haifa and had been home to England, and three Swedish-Americans. The variety is even greater in third class with Austrians, Bohemians, Slavs, Jews, Greeks, and Arabs, plus one old American from Washington, D.C., who, like us, wanted to see Palestine and celebrate Christmas in Bethlehem. First- and second-class passengers have it pretty good; good food and clean rooms with good beds, but in third class, the conditions are pretty miserable. No food is served, and the passengers must get by the best they can. Some of them brought bags of food along onto the ship and eat sitting or standing. There are no tables, chairs, or kitchenware for them. Some of them can buy a meal from the galley, but the cook seems not to want to trouble himself with that, so few even try. Also, there is no place to lie down, except on deck or in the hold. Some have bedclothes with them; others have none, but lie down where they can, like swine—men, women and children piled up together. However, they were not discouraged. They sang and were happy, except for those who were seasick.

In Alexandria

What does one do on a sea voyage? Well, the most of them talk with their fellow passengers, and if one cannot make himself understood any other way one signs with gestures. Conversations cover different subjects such as politics and religion, and conditions in different countries are discussed and compared. I wrote and read a great deal of the time, and others did the same, more or less. In that way, time flies fairly quickly, and now we are arriving in Alexandria, Egypt.

As the ship was to lie here for a couple of days to unload, we had a chance to go ashore and have a look around the city, after our health condition and passports were checked. What did we see in this city located at the northern end of Egypt? Well, nearly everything was different from what we had seen before. People of different skin color and strange clothing crowded each other in the crooked streets. We saw Turks with red caps and barefoot Arabs in clothes that looked like nightshirts in many colors, and a cloth wound around their heads. Everything possible is bought and sold both indoors and out. Shoemakers sat in the streets fixing shoes and making a sort of a shoe that consisted of a bit of wood for a sole and a strap over the foot. Many of the poor begged for a coin, and filth and uncleanliness were everywhere, especially in the narrow streets. We went and saw the Pillar of Pompeii, which is the largest pillar carved from a single piece of granite in the world, eighty-eight feet high and nine feet in diameter.[76] Underneath it there are three levels of catacombs carved into the stone. They are burial chambers dating from the first and second centuries. The city of Alexandria was founded in 331 B.C. by Alexander the Great, who lies buried under the Nebi David mosque.[77]

We stayed over in Alexandria Sunday and went to church services at the American Presbyterian church in the morning and in the evening. The pastor gave a good sermon on the subject: "Choose today whom you will serve." It points out that every person feels a need to have a god, and thereafter, that one has a God, and that is what one holds dearest. But only God, the creator of heaven and earth, is the God who can help and give happiness and joy now and forever, and therefore we should let Him be our God, the one we worship and love above all others. About forty to fifty English sailors in their blue uniforms were present. They listened with the greatest attention and reverently bowed their heads during the prayer, a good custom, which ought to be observed by every church-goer. It is a custom that is much neglected in America, even within our own synod, particularly by the young folk. How indifferent it appears when churchgoers sit with their backs and necks straight and stiff and, perhaps, even look around the church during prayers! How few are we not who call ourselves Christian Lutherans and who have the True Light, yet blush when we see how serious other believers are. How many of them, are there not, who, in the bustle and noise on boats and trains, still have their prayer times, and are not embarrassed by it wherever they are? And we, who have the True Light, should we be shy or neglect to profess before other people which God we worship? May God not punish us by taking the Light away from us.

That evening we heard a sermon by Pastor Thompson from America, a fellow passenger on his way to Jerusalem to work in the American Mission Service. He had his family and some co-workers in his company. He was stationed in Jerusalem for several years before the war, but when it broke out, he fled from there with his family and stayed for that time in America. He, too, gave a good sermon. It is God's great blessing that such a congregation exists here in these benighted lands which once had been enlightened by the evangelists, but because of sin and faithlessness had sunk to such a low point. On the streets of this city, there is no visible difference between Sunday and any other day. The same business goes on with few exceptions, and in the way things are here, no real Sunday observance is possible. The Muslims observe Friday, the Jews observe Saturday, and the so-called Christians,

Sunday, and we fear that the latter are the most indifferent with respect to the day of rest.

Past the Suez Canal to Palestine

On December 13 at 5:30 P.M., we left Alexandria harbor just as the sun was sinking into the western sea, and the next morning we landed at Port Said at the mouth of the Suez Canal, where stands a statue of De Lesseps, the canal's creator. It is about fifty years since the canal was dug and the city was founded at the same time. Here, too, the ship lay over for two days, and so we went ashore to see the city, which, in general, was like Alexandria. Many third-class passengers boarded here and most of them were Jews from every corner of the earth, who had come on other ships. One could almost say that here were "Jews and proselytes, Cretans, Arabs, and those who live in Mesopotamia, from Asia, Phrygia and Pamphylia, Egypt, and Libya," most of them headed to Palestine. Many Jews travel there these days to see what it is all about. On the evening of December 15, we set out from Port Said, and the next morning at daybreak we saw a lighthouse and a dark streak on the horizon that soon proved to be land. The land that we now saw was Palestine, the land of my longing ever since my childhood, but which always seemed so distant and shrouded in darkness. During this entire journey, I have harbored a fear that something would prevent us from getting there. Now we were so close that we could see it, and I thanked God for His goodness and mercy that He led us here and that He, in mysterious ways, helped us many times when we were ignorant and at a loss.

We were not the only ones who were thankful. A bunch of the Jewish passengers had assembled on deck, and at the sight of land they lifted their voices in a heartfelt song of praise. I did not understand a word, but I understood their feelings. Many of these Jews had lived in Palestine previously, but had to flee their homes during the war and lived in other places. Others had never been there before, but felt it was their homeland, because it had belonged to their forebears, and they were of the belief that it would become their homeland once again. In a while, a city on a hill could be seen before us, and just as the sun raised its glittering gaze over Jaffa, our ship docked in its harbor.

PALESTINE

Jaffa

The sea was still and calm, something that is not always the case, it is said, and when it storms, landing is very difficult because the water is shallow with many rocks and only a narrow inlet for small boats to squeeze through. Now it was not the least difficult.

The city of Jaffa is beautifully situated on a height above the seashore and has about fifty thousand residents, including twelve thousand Jews, ten thousand Christians, and the rest Muslims. Jews have established a new community to the north of the old town which is excellently built. There is a German colony also. It was begun sixty years ago and was successful until the war began, and they had to flee,

The harbor at Jaffa

71

and lost much of their property. Some of them are returning now. They also have several other colonies outside the city and in other places in Palestine, where they carry on farming and fruit-growing. Among the charitable institutions whose purpose is furthering Christianity and education among Jaffa's diverse population, may be named Miss Arnott's school, which the noble English woman began alone in 1863 and which does much good for the city's people.[78] Much good work is done by the English hospital, which was founded in 1882 by Miss Newton, and which, at her death, was left to the Church Missionary Society.[79] Also there are several Catholic institutions.

We stayed in Jaffa until the next morning and during the day we walked to Simon the Tanner's house by the sea and up onto the roof where Peter was when he, in ecstasy, saw the cloth lowered with the animals inside and heard the voice say "Peter, slaughter and eat" (Acts 10: 9). Then we wandered through the city's narrow streets and beyond them, between orange trees with their golden yellow fruit glittering between the greenery. Our guide also took us to an orchard where we could have, for free, all the oranges we could carry. Big, sweet, and delicious were these Jaffa oranges, and a lot of them are exported to European countries from here. We met one camel caravan after another loaded with oranges, which they carried on both sides of their backs, eight crates on each camel. After an hour's

An orange transport

An orange grove near Jaffa

wandering, we came to Dorcas's house, where she lived and died, and where Peter revived her (see Acts 9:36–43), and where she is buried. There is a Russian Orthodox church there now whose tower offers a beautiful view of the orange groves, Jaffa, and the sea. To the east, spread the Plains of Sharon and farther to the east the mountains of Judea. The day was clear, mild and pleasant, and all of it made the best impression on a stranger.

On the Way to Jerusalem

The next morning, December 17, we went by train to Jerusalem, fifty-four miles distant. We needed to get our three trunks to the station, and that evening I asked the hotel manager how we could have them driven there. "Leave it to me," he said. "The dragomen will carry them there first thing in the morning." In the morning a black Arab came and took two of them on his back, one hundred pounds each, and in a while another one came and took the third, weighing one hundred and fifty pounds, plus a suitcase weighing fifty pounds. We followed him to the station, and he walked at a steady pace about ten minutes without resting. On arriving there was a terrible row between the two men, and for a while it looked like there would be a fight. At first we wondered what the problem was, but we realized that the first wanted to carry it all and the second had come between-times and deprived him of the work. He would have made fifteen piasters (sixty cents) for taking them to the station. When I understood how it was, I gave them ten piasters (forty cents) each, and they calmed down.

From Jaffa to Jerusalem, our journey continued by train in an easterly direction, first through orange orchards, then through olive groves, and then through the Plains of Sharon, where they mainly grow grain. Farmers were now busy with their fields. Seed is sown

Jerusalem

by hand and turned under with a little crook, which makes a little scratch in the ground. The implements are drawn by a camel, a pair of oxen or cows, or a pair of small donkeys. When the crop is ready at harvest time, it is cut with a scythe or sickle, threshed by trampling by oxen, and cleaned by tossing in the wind as in olden times. On that plain we passed the little town of Lydda where Peter was when word was sent to him to come to Dorcas's house at Jaffa. In a while we passed Ramla, said to be the place where the city of Aramathea was and where Joseph, who buried Jesus's body, lived. Also we passed the place where the city of Ekron lay, mentioned in the Book of Joshua (see chapters 13, 15 and 19). Soon we passed Sedia, mentioned in the story of Samson (see Judges 16:4).

The landscape gradually became hilly and stony, and to the west a cliff with a cave was visible, which is the one to which Samson escaped after he slew the Philistines with the jawbone of an ass (see Judges 15). The tracks now followed a stony, winding valley that got steeper as we went, and the train went slowly puffing upward until, at the top, one could see the new city quarter outside Jerusalem's walls, and soon we were at the station. Here there was a lot of hurry-scurry, but soon we got a cab that took us to the Hotel Olivet, outside the walls, a good distance from the station. It cost $3.00 a day per person. The next day we moved to another, where for $2.00 a day we got more food. At the first, we could hardly eat our fill.

In Jerusalem

Sunday, December 19, we went to services in an American church, which belongs to the "Christian Missionary Alliance."[80] This

74

organization does not belong to any certain association, but only to Christians who work together for Christianity and true enlightenment among the people in Palestine and other countries. Dr. Paul Raider[81] from Chicago is president of the alliance and president of Moody's Bible School as well. He was here in Jerusalem on a visit and was making, in the company of his wife, a trip around the world, visiting the different mission fields.

He preached to an audience of about three hundred attendees with very different appearances and stations in life. A third of them were Americans and Europeans; the rest were Arabs. A number of these were dressed like Europeans; others had very badly patched clothes with cloths wound around their heads. They were dressed in clothes that looked like night-shirts, some white, some red or black. There seems to be no difference in rank here. Those who were well-dressed sat on the same bench with the worst-dressed Arabs. The speaker pointed out in a powerful way that there was no difference. Everyone sat and listened with rapt attention. In the afternoon Sunday school was held, to a great extent in the Arabic language. Dr. Raider spoke for a while to the Sunday school through an Arabic interpreter. In the evening, services were held again, when Dr. Raider preached in English, which an interpreter translated to Arabic. They assembled on Monday and Tuesday evenings. The Christmas program was held on Wednesday afternoon because there was a problem with having it on Christmas, when a number of the schoolchildren, who live in different places, travel home to celebrate Christmas. Sunday school, daily school, the girl's school, and the young men's school were all present and participated in the program with declamations and song. The Sunday school told the story of the birth of Jesus in unison. Around two hundred children and some older people participated in the celebration. It was moving to see these children's faces, radiant with joy though dark-skinned, and hear them read and sing of Jesus, the world's Savior, in this city where he was carried up to the temple at the age of eight, and at twelve asked and answered the rabbis, and where he then wandered the city's streets and in the temple, doing good and helping everyone who came his way, and where he then had to suffer and die to save a sinful mankind. All of the children had little bags filled with confections and nuts and a Bible picture.

In the evening, church services were held in English, where Dr. Raider preached on the great and plentiful evidence that Jesus was God's son, which is denied by Mohammedans and is the greatest hindrance to the spreading of Christianity in these countries. On Thursday a Christmas party was held at a German Templer church in one of their colonies near the railroad station for children studying at a school at the Christian Missionary Alliance. Germany had had this operation before the war, but subsequently had to abandon it, and the Alliance took up the work. Here, too, the children performed declamations and songs. Again the audience was made up of a mixed group. In the evening they held a prayer meeting where prayers and songs were in English and Arabic languages. Clearly this mission carries out blessed work. It has many chapels and schools where Arabs and Jews get Christian and secular education, and that is something these people so very much need to be lifted up from Islam's delusion and oppression.

Christmas in Bethlehem

We celebrated Christmas in Bethlehem. We had, as it happened, become acquainted with a Syrian widow who lived in Jerusalem but had lived in Bethlehem before the war, who had there a few furnished rooms for rent. She invited us to stay there while we were in Bethlehem, and as there was no hotel for Americans or Europeans, we accepted the offer with gratitude.

We hired a boy with a donkey to carry our belongings to her place in Bethlehem. After we got the donkey loaded with our things, the boy climbed on top of it all and hurried off.

Bethlehem

We thought and talked about how Joseph and Mary, 1,920 years ago, had had to pack up their necessities and load them on a donkey to go to Bethlehem to be taxed. We hired a cab and rode the six miles very comfortably while they, on the other hand, had probably had to travel the long road of fifty miles from Nazareth to Bethlehem on foot or, in the best case, on donkeyback if they could afford it.

Arriving at our refuge, we entered into a proper house with three-foot-thick stone walls, a stone floor, windows with iron bars and thick wooden casements, rough and heavy doors with big strong locks and hinges so that no thieves or robbers could ever break in. After spending a little time putting things in order, our little abode seemed fairly inviting, while Joseph and Mary had to make do with a donkey stall in a rock cave. By four we had everything in order and went for a walk, first through the city of Bethlehem, which lies on the eastern slope near the top of Judea's mountains and claims eight thousand inhabitants. We passed the so-called German Lutheran Church, which lies high and beautiful in the western part of the city, and then to the church of the Nativity, walking through the narrow, fairly steep shopping streets, where everything possible is for sale, to a great extent, in the open air. We continued then down the north slope of a mountain ridge below the city to the approximately one-and-a-half mile distant little town of Beit Sahour, which would have been the shepherds' home.

Christmas Eve in Bethlehem

Through the little town's narrow, filthy streets, we walked to the east, where a beautiful valley with cultivated fields spread out for our gaze. These are the fields of Boas, where Ruth picked spikes of grain (mentioned in the book of Ruth) and where now, as in Boas' time, barley and wheat are grown. On the slopes of the heights all around, which are fairly stony, fig and olive trees are planted between rows of crooked stone walls. Also, grapes are cultivated on the hills. We followed a road through the fields to a little garden on a somewhat elevated stony ridge. Here the shepherds kept watch over their flocks at night. There is a grotto in the mountain that was, in the 400s, made into a Greek temple and is said to be the place where the shepherds were when they saw the light and heard the angel's message that the Savior was born in Bethlehem.

In the Shepherds' Fields

Twilight had fallen, but the moon shone brightly over the area, and its gleam on the white rocky heights around the valley made it yet brighter. Everything was still and peaceful, and we lingered awhile to enjoy its beauty and to ponder what once had taken place here. There was almost a sense of expectation that the angels would come, and we raised our voices in our simple way, "There were shepherds abiding in the field." Then we wandered up the winding mountain path to Beit Sahour, where we, at the urging of our hostess, who was along, entered the town's richest and most venerable house. It was a low stone house with a flat roof, a dirt floor, no windows, a fire in the middle of the floor and some rugs lying around where the house's barefoot residents sat or lay. We were very well-received and were regaled with dried figs from their garden, and wine, which we turned down with the explanation that we, as Americans, never drank wine. They invited us to stay while they prepared a meal. When we, unfortunately, could not stay, we had to promise to come to dinner another day. Our host felt honored by our visit and showed us a portrait of their son and his family in southern America.

We went then to our quarters and cooked rice pudding which, together with pickled herring (instead of lutfisk),[82] cheese, bread, and tea, constituted our evening meal. Then we went to church, which is built over the cave, and saw the manger that had been Jesus' bed. The Roman Catholics held church services, or Mass, from 10:00 P.M. at night until the next morning. Many ceremonies alternated with songs and bell ringing, and they carried in a box with a picture in it that was supposed to depict the Christ Child. We stayed until two, but left then to get a little rest.

We were up again early in the morning and went to the church, where the Catholics were still holding services. The Greek Catholics were having their early-morning songs in another part of the church. We soon left church and walked down the slope to the shepherd's field to escape the hubbub and have some quiet to ponder. A herd of sheep was grazing on the green grass on the slopes. A typical Levantine shepherd with a staff in his hand and wearing a mantle sat on a wall watching his sheep. It was just before sunrise. I thought, "Probably this is where David watched his father's sheep and maybe sang 'The Lord is my shepherd,' and other verses." When we came to the fields of Boas, we met a bunch of Arabs coming from the chapel in the grotto. They had celebrated early-morning services there. It was the time of the morning, according to the course of the sun, that we usually came away from early-morning services at home, although it was eleven hours earlier at home, and we remembered our friends there and wished them, in our thoughts, a joyous Christmas.[83]

We picked some flowers from the fields of Boas and returned to Bethlehem and got to the so-called German Lutheran church in time for the Arabic services there, led by a Syrian Lutheran priest. It felt good to hear, in the quiet and simplicity, the word proclaimed and the familiar psalm-melodies sung, although we could not understand the words. This work was begun by Dr. Schneller of Germany.[84] During the War, the Germans had to leave for a time. We met the pastor after the services. He was very friendly and invited us to his room, where we regaled with Christmas pastries. He and his wife spoke fairly good English and we had a lot of interesting conversation with them about their operation and the War, etc.

I had bought a little hen for Christmas dinner, which weighed two and a half pounds, alive, and cost $1.40, and potatoes, which are expensive here, too, at ten cents a pound. And so, we celebrated Christmas in Bethlehem, and it was truly interesting. The weather was clear and pleasant, a little cooler than in Jaffa, since Jerusalem and Bethlehem lie twenty-six hundred feet higher.

In Hebron

One day we traveled on horse and carriage to Hebron, situated sixteen miles south of Bethlehem and in the same mountain range. A few miles from Bethlehem, we passed Solomon's reservoirs, which, when they were in good repair, held great quantities of water. Solomon laid down an aqueduct of stone from them to Jerusalem. They still exist but are no longer used, for pipes have been laid from a spring in the mountains to Jerusalem. Solomon brought the water from them to the reservoirs.

Hebron is a little town of fifteen thousand inhabitants, in a depression between two rocky hills. It was here that Abraham bought the fields of Machpelah and the cave where he interred his wife, Sarah, and where he himself, and his grandsons are buried (see Genesis 49: 29–32). Above that cave there now stands a Mohammedan mosque, and it is difficult for Christians to gain entry, for the Mohammedans guard it carefully, and we were not allowed in. A short distance away is Mamre's oak grove. This is where Abraham lived in a tent when the Lord visited him, and it was over these stony heights that he wandered. We returned to Bethlehem and stayed there eight days. One day we walked to Herodium, some miles from Bethlehem, also called Frank Mountain. This hill is round and two hundred feet high and looks as if it was partly shaped by human hands. At the top are ruins of Herod the Great's castle, where Herod was said to be buried. There is a remarkable vista of the landscape round about, from that height, and you can even see the Dead Sea. A short distance from here lie Adulam's caves, where David and his men hid out from Saul's persecutions (see 1 Samuel 22). We returned to Jerusalem on the eighteenth day after Christmas and attended services at the American Mission Church. Near the road, a mile from Bethlehem, is Rachel's grave (see Genesis 35: 16–20) and by the road a well, where it is said that the Wise Men again caught sight of the star that they then followed to Bethlehem.

On our return to Jerusalem, we rented two rooms in St. John's Hotel for two dollars a day and cooked our own food, which seemed cheaper, and we could fix it when we wanted it. People here use a lot of sheep and goat tallow and olive oil in almost all of the food, and we are not used to it and we did not find it tasty. We got into a little dispute with the woman in whose house we had stayed in Bethlehem. When we traveled there, she would not tell us how much she wanted in rent, just saying we could pay what we wanted. When we returned to Jerusalem she didn't say anything about it, but wanted us to rent a room from her there. Then, when she came to Jerusalem, she wanted $66.00 in rent for eight days, and we had taken care of our own meals and even fed her. We could not go along with that. I went to the American Consul and asked him for advice. He and other prominent men who I asked said that I should not pay it, but give her the customary rent, which I did, adding 20 percent. She accepted it, but was unhappy and threatened with a lawsuit. We heard nothing more except that she sometimes wrote threatening letters. We heard later that she was a very difficult person, who used guile to bring harm to her relatives and others with whom she had business. However, such business practices are much used by the people in these countries, especially to make money from Americans.

In Bethel

One day we traveled by automobile to Bethel, where Jacob saw the "stairway to heaven" in a dream (see Genesis 28), located eight or ten miles north of Jerusalem and on the same mountain ridge. It is a filthy little town of mud shacks. The inhabitants are all Arabs. Three fairly proper stone houses were being erected by Arabs who had been in America for a time and had earned a great deal of money. They praised America. I asked why they did not stay there. They answered that they had their property and their families here and had to return. They intended, however, to return to America if they could sell their property. Otherwise they must leave their families here and travel abroad to earn more money. I mentioned that many Jews were coming to Palestine now, so it should be easy to sell their property. They answered that they would never sell to Jews. Arabs hate Jews and, to a nearly higher degree, Englishmen, because they give Jews entry and let them crowd out the Arabs in many areas. Right next to a hill are the ruins of a medieval church on the place where Abraham had his tent and built an altar and called upon the Lord's name (see Genesis 13: 3–4). It is said that nearby here, two bears came out of the woods and mauled forty-two boys who taunted the prophet Elisha (see II Kings 2:23–24). Much else occurred in this place, of which one can read in the Books of Kings.

At nine o'clock in the morning of January 5, we left Jerusalem by cab from the Jaffa gate and rode north to the northwest corner of the city wall, then east along the wall past "Gordon's Golgotha"[85] and Solomon's quarry. One passes the place where Stephen was stoned, east of the wall. A little Greek chapel is there now. So leads the road over Mount Kidron and through the garden of Gethsemane and, two miles from Jerusalem, through the little town of Bethany, where Jesus revived Lazarus. Here the road leads down a steep mountain slope into a valley where

Bethel

we pass a spring that is called the Apostles' Spring, where it is said that they rested on their way to Jerusalem. Then the road bears upward until one reaches the top of an eminence where there are some mud houses that are said to be the Good Samaritan's refuge. Then the road heads down steep hills, which were very rocky. On the way we passed road workers who were carrying stones and gravel in baskets on their heads. Most of them were women and children. Others were bringing stone from a more distant quarry on donkeyback. Then we met camel caravans and donkeys loaded with wheat and oranges on their way to Jerusalem or Jaffa, carrying them two or three days' journey from the east side of the mountains of Moab. Others were carrying wood and twigs for fuel, mostly for baking, some on camels, others on donkeys, and we met groups of women carrying large faggots of twig on their heads for several miles. A flock of sheep and goats grazed here and there on the green slopes watched by a shepherd. There were many jackals in these tracts, and they would scatter and kill the flock if there were no shepherd to guard them.

The road continued downward until we came near Jericho, which lies on the west side of the Jordan Valley, about three thousand feet lower than Jerusalem. Here there was real summer weather in the month of January. It looked beautiful. Oranges hang ripe between the green leaves and half-grown bananas in the lush groves, and everything is so wonderful and pretty. At Jericho, which is now just a little village of mud huts, we stopped and ate dinner, which we brought along, while the horses were fed corn and hay.

At the Dead Sea

We continued our journey over the plain about six miles. There was no vegetation, only plains of clayey, salty soil. It was hot and sweltering in that depression in the earth, which is, indeed, the lowest point in the world, which is to say thirteen hundred feet below sea level. We wandered for a while on the shores of the Dead Sea, into which the Jordan River ceaselessly empties its water, but never gets fuller although it has no outlet. It was somewhere here that Sodom and Gomorrah once stood, and somewhere by this sea that Lot's wife was transformed to a pillar of salt. The water is so enormously salty and bitter that no fish can live in it. If any fish come down with the Jordan River's water, they die. The Dead Sea is 46 miles long, 9 miles wide, and 1,080 feet deep at the deepest place.

The Jordan River

The journey continued along the Jordan River and after an hour's travel over naked clay flats, we came to the Jordan Valley itself, which is overgrown with dense brush and reeds. Here the Bedouins graze their camels. In a little while we arrived at the Jordan River at the place where it is said that the Israelites crossed, dry shod, when Joshua divided the water (see Joshua 3: 14–17). It was here too that the prophet Elijah struck the water with his mantel so that it was parted (see II Kings 2:8), and it was to the Jordan River that Naaman was sent by the prophet [Elisha] to be cleansed of leprosy (II Kings 5 :14). It was also here that John preached and baptized, and it was probably here that Jesus was baptized (Matt. 3:5–17). The Jordan River is eighty to one hundred sixty feet broad and varies greatly in depth at different times of the year. It is deepest in April, when the snow melts in the mountains of Lebanon. The Greek Orthodox come here annually at Easter from Jerusalem and other places in great throngs to bathe here as they see that act as bringing great blessings.

We returned to Jericho at twilight, and just before we arrived we passed a herd of grazing camels. Our driver seemed troubled, and when I asked him why, he answered, "Bedouins bad," and urged the horses to do their utmost, and all the while he watched carefully in the direction of the camels, as he feared that the Bedouins would suddenly rush out, which sometimes happens in these parts. But none were seen, and in a while we arrived in Jericho, where we found refuge in a simple but clean hotel.

The next morning we were up early, and after we had a little food, our honorable host informed us of the way to Elisha's Well (see II Kings 2:19), where a considerable stream of water flows forth from under a hill. That water irrigates beautiful grain fields and lovely orange orchards. The weather was as mild and soft as a June morning in Oregon, and we had never seen such a beautiful sunrise as on that morning. On the hill above the well are a number of old ruins of stone and sun-dried mud, where the old city, whose walls fell to the Israelites, was situated (see Joshua 6:20), where foundations and parts of the old wall are visible since they have been excavated in recent years.

After we wandered around for a while and viewed the interesting sights, we returned to the village and climbed into the wagon, and turned back toward Jerusalem. The return trip went fairly slowly for the road was very steep and stony. We got down and walked, and the horse could hardly draw the empty wagon. It became necessary for two Arabs and me to push, and I gave them a few coins for the help. It reminded us of the trip through the Rocky Mountains the previous summer, when we had to push the automobile where it was very steep. At midday we came to the Good Samaritan's refuge and ate dinner there.

At Lazarus's Tomb

Toward afternoon we arrived at Bethany and stayed there for a while and visited Lazarus' grave. By climbing down twenty-five steps, one comes to a little room cut into the stone. It was from here that Lazarus, at Jesus' command, threw off his shroud (see John 11). A short piece from here, one can see the old walls of the house where the three siblings dwelt. Above that place is an old tumbled-down tower where Simon the leper lived.

It was from Bethany that Jesus sent two of his disciples to Bethphage for the donkey on which he rode into Jerusalem (see John 12 and Matthew 21). Bethphage lies between Bethany and the Mount of Olives.

On the Mount of Olives

From the Mount of Olives, which lies a little higher and to the east of Jerusalem and a river called Kidron, there is a lovely view over the surrounding area, and Jerusalem looks beautiful from here. We were there one evening when the sun sank down on the other side of Jerusalem, and it was a glorious panorama. Sunrise and sunset are often unusually beautiful in Palestine. Jesus and his disciples often walked up onto this hill. Here lie two churches, one Roman Catholic and one Greek Orthodox. It is said that Jesus arose to heaven from this hill, and in the Roman Catholic church, a stone can be seen with a mark on it from Jesus' feet.

The weather had been the nicest one could wish for while we were in Jericho, but the next day it rained like it does in Oregon sometimes in winter. The winter weather is much like Oregon's. The summers are drier and hotter.

The Temple Garden in Jerusalem

Jerusalem, as it is now, covers an area of 210 acres and is surrounded with thick stone walls 35 feet high. Thirty-five acres make up the Temple Garden, a nearly level, elevated plain in the southeast part of the city, surrounded by thick, high walls which are 1,601 feet long on the western side, 1,530 on the east, 1,024 on the north, and 921 on the south.

It has seven gates and the one on the western side is the most used. Here is the Mosque of Omar, which stands in the middle of the Temple Garden on the place where Solomon's temple once stood. Right at the top of Mount Moria, where Abraham sacrificed Isaac, is a great block of stone which is said to be the one on which Abraham built his altar. The mosque is richly and expensively decorated; the southern half of the Temple Garden is paved with smooth, white stone. Before one may enter this mosque, like all the others, one must take off one's shoes or

The Mosque of Omar in Jerusalem

cover them with big slippers, which the Mohammedan guards are very quick to bring out. They cost five piasters (twenty cents).

In the Church of the Holy Sepulcher, which is said to have been built over the hill of Golgotha, there shows a depression in the stone where the cross would have stood. Also there is a cave cut into the rock that is said to be Jesus' grave, or, more rightly, the grave that Joseph of Arimathea had cut into the rock. It is doubted by many that this is the right Golgotha, and a hill outside the city walls is seen to be the right Golgotha. Below that hill is a cave carved into the rock that is said to be Joseph's grave, where Jesus was laid, and that place better agrees, by my judgment, with the Bible's story than the other one.

In the Garden of Gethsemane

When Jerusalem was destroyed and thereafter was under Roman and Turkish control for a thousand years, all of the biblical places became so destroyed and altered that it is difficult to recognize them for sure. However, the valley of Kidron and the Garden of Gethsemane, east of Jerusalem, could not be changed, but are surely recognizable. Gethsemane is right next to and begins at the stream of Kidron, and stretches up the slope of the Mount of Olives. There are many very old olive trees. A little below, where stone slabs protrude from the ground, is believed to be the place where Jesus sweated blood for our sake. Here the Catholics have built a chapel, but they have left the olive trees untouched. On the opposite side of Kidron's stream, between it and one of the city gates, is the place where Stephen was stoned, and where also a chapel has been raised. Inside that gate is

David's Tower and Castle

the Pond of Gethsemane, where the water was touched by angels. The pond is fairly large and one must descend about thirty feet on stone steps to reach the water. I walked down the steps, and, as the light was dim, happened to step down into the water before I knew it. The pond of Siloam, where Jesus sent the blind man to wash himself, lies a bit

At Bethesda Pond

below the city in the valley of Kidron. The valley of Hinnom, which is quite deep with steep, stony slopes, lies to the south of Jerusalem, and on the hill on the other side stands a weatherbeaten tree that is said to be the one on which Judas hanged himself. David's tower and castle still remain, although the original walls are broken down, so are the newer ones that were built on the old foundations, and in certain places the large, old stone blocks that David had laid down there are still visible. Not far away is the room, on an upper floor, where Jesus instituted the Holy Communion. Kaifa's palace is also in the neighborhood. Pilate's palace can be seen also, as well as the jail where Jesus was held near Bethesda pond.

The streets within the city walls are very narrow and crooked. They were laid down by the Romans, for after the destruction in the year 70, they rebuilt the city. In many places there are stairsteps, because of the city's steep slopes. Only two streets are drivable, one of them being David Street, on which one comes through the large gate. It lies next to the Jaffa gate and was made in 1898 by tearing down part of the wall so that Kaiser Wilhelm could ride into Jerusalem. The original gate was built so that it was difficult to drive through. The Kaiser, on the other hand, did not like for the wall to be torn down for his sake. The other streets are traveled only by pedestrians, donkeys, and camels. In many places there are arches that constitute a roof over the narrow streets. People and animals crowd together past little shops, where everything possible is for sale. The streets are swept every morning. To the right of the entrance to the temple garden on Christian Street is the Jews' "Wailing Wall." Here they stand at the old wall surrounding the Temple Garden, which Solomon built, and weep and wail loudly over the destruction of their temple and that their religious rituals have been prevented by heathens.

Swedes in Jerusalem

A substantial city has grown up outside the old city walls on the western and northern sides with better and larger buildings, and broader streets. In these parts live mostly Europeans and wealthy Arabs. The American church is located in the northwestern part and the American colony is in the northeast. This colony has a shopping center just inside the Jaffa Gate on David Street and Thomas Cook's office is close by. The American colony, which was founded about ten years ago by a company of Americans from Chicago under the leadership of an attorney named Spafford, was based on Christian-Socialism, but was, perhaps, a little peculiar in some respects.[86] Later a group of Swedes from Chicago and a group from Dalarna, in Sweden, attached themselves to the American colony. They number about one hundred persons. They invited us to visit. We went there on New Year's Eve and were given tea, which is served to all who are there in the big, comfortable hall on the second floor, which is their assembly venue. It was pleasantly warm in there, something we were not accustomed to. All of the other places we had been since we crossed the Atlantic had been without heat. We had tea and cakes and were very well-received and had interesting conversations about their colony, the War, and so forth. During the War, they had had a soup kitchen for the poor and in that way had helped many, both friends and enemies.

They invited us to church services the next day, which was a Sunday, and so we went. There were good songs and Bible readings, prayer, and a short sermon as well as singing by a well-rehearsed choir. After services the choir also sang two numbers in Swedish for us. The children sang also for a while, and then we were served tea and baked goodies. We were invited to stay for dinner, and we had the best meal we had had since we left America. All of the colony's members who wish to, eat together in a big dining hall on Sunday evenings. They work and operate their businesses and all of the income goes into the same pot of which each gets his share. They seem to live in love and harmony. If anyone is unhappy and wishes to leave the colony, he gets something from the common fund, how much I don't know. They have their own school and educate their children in all useful subjects. They even have an orchestra and play very well. They managed the best of all the colonies and societies during the War. Because both Germans and Swedes belonged to the colony, they were very helpful to the Turks so that they were inclined to be friendly to them in return. However, after the English came into power, they got protection from them. All of the Germans had to leave the colony, although many of them were over fifty years old.

Prayer Week was observed in the American church every night, just as we do in Warren, and we, therefore, had the joy of getting to observe it in Jerusalem. The English Episcopalians also have a church near David's Tower, and the English soldiers mostly go there. There is a hospital for lepers near Jerusalem, and it was established and continues to be run by Germans.[87] It is a good establishment and deserves support.

Emmaus

One day we rode donkeys over stony mountain paths to Emmaus, a little town ten miles northwest of Jerusalem. It was an interesting

On the road to Emmaus

trip. An African boy walked behind and drove the donkeys. We hadn't laughed so much in our entire journey as we did that day, as the little donkeys were so funny. They are good to have, though, when it comes to getting around on such difficult and stony paths.

The goat, the donkey, and the camel are the animals that are most reliable in these lands. The goats are milked and the hair has many uses. Coarse cloth is woven from the goat hair for sacks, blankets, mantles, tents, etc. The hide is used for bags in which one carries milk, water, oil and so forth, and it is even made into gloves. The meat is for food. Donkeys are used in the fields, to carry loads of all sorts, and for riding. Camels carry heavy loads long distances, especially in the desert, and they are also used for plowing. Horses are used for light transportation within and between towns and are ridden by English officers. There are a lot of them here and also a number of soldiers from India among the English troops.

To Cairo, Egypt

We traveled by train to Cairo, Egypt, by way of Lydda, on January 18. There we changed trains and went south, then over the plains some miles east of the Mediterranean Sea. The Philistines lived here before the founding of Israel, and the land fell to Judah and the tribe of Simeon. Most of the land between Lydda and Gaza is cultivated, and beautiful fields of grain stretch toward Judah in the east and to the sea in the west. Gaza is an old, poorly built little town, where the houses are built of mud bricks and roofs of straw. Here there are verdant orchards of oranges, figs, olives, and almond trees. Then the railroad nears the sea, and eventually one sees only sand on both sides of the tracks. At four in the afternoon we came to Kontara at the Suez Canal, on the border between Palestine and Egypt. Here we stepped off of the train to walk over the canal bridge to the customs house to get our passports stamped and the contents of our baggage searched.

AGAIN IN EGYPT

And so we are back in Egypt. We board a new train and ride first through sand desert, and then through the land of Goshen. By now it was dark so that we could not see anything, although we wished we could. We arrived in Cairo at eleven o'clock at night. The hotel agents and the "dragomen" raised a terrible ruckus, and all of them wanted us to go with them, but we could only follow one.[88]

Cairo

Cairo is a big city with a population of six hundred thousand, located on the eastern side of the Nile River. East of the city one can see mountain-like heights, and upon them are the walls of destroyed cities. A few miles to the west, the great sand desert begins and stretches across Africa.

The flat, several-miles-broad Nile Valley, which is watered by the Nile, is well-tended and productive to the highest degree.

Here they cultivate grain, corn, rice, cotton, alfalfa, and root vegetables, and also certain types of fruit such as oranges, lemons, olives, dates, and almonds. The first day we visited several consulates to get our passports in order, and the health department where they wanted to check to see if we had any diseases. We got off easy there. We also visited the Swedish

The travelers in Egypt

consul W. A. Unander,[89] a very outgoing and interesting man, and the only Swede we met in Egypt. The different districts of Cairo distinguish themselves from each other, just as most cities in these countries. The western part of the city is inhabited mostly by Europeans and the more prosperous Egyptians, and here there are modern buildings and broad streets. In the northern part live the poor, and the streets are very narrow and filthy, and people live in miserable hovels and caves. The eastern part is the marketplace itself, with narrow, dirty streets and little rooms packed with wares, with the merchant in the door and customers out on the street crowding their way between the donkeys and camels. There are many poor people in that part of the city who go about shabbily dressed and barefoot, and the blind and lame who beg for coins are to be found everywhere. There is a surfeit of "dragomen" (as guides and porters are called here). One can never go anywhere in peace because of them as they hang along after and try, in some way, to get some money. I asked a young man, who complained that he had no money to buy food, why he didn't try some other occupation when the income from "tour guiding" was so bad. "Oh, this is my business," he answered, and so I had to give him enough to buy a meal.

At the Nile River and the Pyramids

The next day we directed our course to the pyramids, followed by a dragoman who wanted a dollar a day (an ordinary laborer gets forty cents). We traveled by trolley in a southwest direction over two branches of the Nile River and along a large city park and the zoo, where many animals that live in these countries can be seen. Then we crossed the Nile valley's well-cultivated plains, and far away, where the sand meets the valley's greenery, we see the pyramids, the highest of which is four hundred fifty-one feet high and another nearby that is nearly as high. They are built of stone and are nearly solid, with only narrow passages and vaults in the middle.

One enters through an opening on the north side and follows a narrow passage to the middle of the pyramid where the tombs are situated. The highest pyramid, called Cheops, was built during the fourth dynasty, 2000 to 3000 B.C., to create tombs and

At the top of the Pyramid of Cheops

monuments for the pharaohs. It was a gargantuan undertaking. We climbed the pyramid, which is a tedious ascent as the stone blocks that serve as stairsteps are three to four feet high. We were followed by no fewer than nine Bedouins, who tried every trick to get money from us. Indeed, we had to pay them for their company. One is afforded a magnificent view from the top. The Nile Valley spreads out to the east and on the eastern side is the city of Cairo. To the west and south are white sand dunes as far as the eye can see and far beyond. After we climbed down, we mounted camels that were waiting for us and rode the nine-mile-long road through the sand dunes to Sakkarah, where nine pyramids of various sizes rise from the sand.⁹⁰

At the Ancient Royal Tombs

Here are the ruins of ancient Memphis, buried in the sand since the time of the pharaohs. Some of the ruins have been excavated in recent years, and large tombs from long ago have been discovered. One of them is the burial place for the holy oxen, whose caskets are carved from huge granite blocks, and one wonders how such huge stones could be handled at that time when there probably were no powerful machines to do it. There are many great tombs where royal families and great men's bodies have rested for millennia. We returned to the first pyramids, but stopped on an eminence and picked up some beads that had been buried there for thousands of years, and first saw the light of day through excavations made in recent years. Then we came to the Sphinx, an image carved into a rock in the shape of a lion with a human face, fifty feet high and one hundred seventeen feet long. No one knows how old it is. A little in front of it is a temple of granite and alabaster, where the idol was presumably worshipped.

After we dismounted the camels, we returned to Cairo by trolley, and the next morning our backs were a little stiff after the eighteen-mile camel ride. We then traveled by trolley to Old Cairo, located a few miles to the south. That city was founded in 649 B.C. It has narrow, crooked, filthy streets, and the people looked very poor. On the heights to the east of the city are a number of old ruins where the so-called Babylon once stood. We went down to the river. There lay a lot of little sail boats loaded with wheat, barley, and corn to be carried down the river from the upper part of the Nile River to be sold. The grain was of good quality but badly

On the way to the tombs of the kings

cleaned. It contained a lot of dirt, for they thresh it this way: the grain is spread on the ground and they drive oxen over it hauling a machine with sharp wheels that grind the straw to pieces, but also churns up clods of dirt, which get mixed into the grain and are hard to separate by means of casting (into the air). We boarded a little boat that carried us over an arm of the Nile to Rhoda, on whose southern end is the place where Pharaoh's daughter found Moses in the bulrushes.

One day we traveled by train through well-tended, irrigated farms and orchards to Heliopolis, located about ten miles to the north of Cairo, where the Pharaoh lived in Joseph's time and where there remain ancient brick walls. The only thing that remains of Heliopolis is the oldest obelisk, erected in 2466 B.C. Not far from here is a very old sycamore tree, said to have shaded Joseph, Mary, and the baby Jesus in their flight to Egypt.

There is much to see in the Egyptian Museum. They have collected there some of the mummified bodies of Egypt's ancient kings and great men, and some of their caskets. Some of them were of stone; others were wood or metal. Many species of animals are exhibited there.

One day we traveled by donkey to the Petrified Forest and Moses' Well. Two black Egyptians came along to drive the donkeys. I protested, as I wanted, according to agreement with the donkey owner, to only have one along, for which I would pay sixty cents above the price of the donkeys, which was almost four dollars. But, at their insistent pleading, I let them both come and gave them an extra twenty cents. They said they were in great need of money.

After we came several miles into the desert, we saw a couple of troops of soldiers and cavalry who were out on maneuvers. I thought about how this is where the pharaoh and his army came through, pursuing the Israelites. Now England maintains many soldiers, to the annoyance of the natives.

Eventually we came to the Petrified Forest, but it was just a few petrified tree trunks lying in the sand.[91] Moses' Well, as it is called, is in a hollowed out place below a cliff. It had collapsed in a recent rain, so there wasn't any water to be seen. It is very doubtful that the children of Israel had ever been there. From time to time I let the donkey driver ride my donkey, but when the younger one wanted to ride, too, I said that the older one should ride. He replied that the older driver had shoes on his feet and he did not. When I asked why he did not have any shoes, he answered that he had a wife and four children to maintain, and there was no money left over to buy shoes. "They cost two dollars," he said. The older one explained that, although he was seventy years old, he had a wife and six children, the oldest being only eight years old. How many older children and how many other wives they had, they did not say.

Mohammedans have polygamy. They complained that the donkey owner took nearly all of their earnings, so that they got so little that they could hardly take care of themselves and their children. The dragoman who

The Virgin Mary Tree in Egypt

Elim, or Moses' Well

was with us at the pyramids complained over the great cost that was now connected with getting a wife. He had recently bought a second wife who had cost him $320.00. He had sent away the first, who had cost him $120.00, because he did not like her. Mohammedans have up to four wives and can reject one and take another when they so please. The Mohammedan teachings create cruelty, hardness, bitter hatred, and persecution of those who are not of the same belief.

Back to Cairo

During the three weeks' time we were in Cairo, we often went to church services and prayer meetings at the American mission, which belongs to the Presbyterians and was founded in 1854. They have 15,000 communicants in Egypt, 300 places of worship, 85 native-born pastors and 40 other assistants. There are 190 Christian schools with 140 for boys and 50 for girls, higher learning for both boys and girls with 16,500 students, 110 missionaries, two hospitals, and six American doctors. Twenty thousand women are under Christian influence and 70,000 Bibles have been handed out during the year, as well as other books, so it seems that their activities have been crowned with success. However they complained that it was slow work converting the Mohammedans. During the sixty-six years that they had worked in Egypt, they had converted only two hundred. They see the best way is to educate the children. The Mohammedans deny Christ's divinity and set Mohammed higher than

Poor Egyptian children

Christ, and that teaching seems to take hold under different names and forms in many countries.

We also visited the Episcopalian church. Quite a lot of people, mostly Englishmen, assemble here, for there are a lot of English soldiers. There is even a Scottish Presbyterian church as well as an English Wesleyan church.

From Cairo to the Red Sea

Cairo lies on the thirtieth parallel and has a climate similar to California's. At dawn we traveled through the Land of Goshen on our way to Suez. It is fertile land and is well-watered by the eastern arm of the Nile River. At Ismailia we changed trains and rode south along the Suez Canal, but there was only sandy desert here. The next morning we traveled by train from Suez to Tawfiq. It is only two miles distant and makes up the harbor at the canal's outlet at the upper end of the Red Sea.

We wanted to row across the sea and an English officer advised us to check in with the quarantine master. He was a Frenchman but spoke some English. When we explained our intent and that we were from America, he said he was glad to be of service for he had a daughter in America, where she had been treated very well. He engaged a couple of Egyptians who transported us across the water in a little sailboat. As we had a following wind, it took an hour and a half. We landed at the quarantine station and were warmly received by the guard there who saddled the one donkey they had, so the girls took turns riding through the desert to Moses' Spring, some miles from the sea, where, according to the Bible, there are twelve springs and seventy palm trees (see Exodus 15:27). Perhaps there are more trees now. It is a strange place in the dry sandy desert, and of its springs, the strongest running one is on a high hill.

From here one can see Mount Sinai very clearly in the south-east, and we would have liked to continue on to there, but it is deadly dangerous to travel in this desert, particularly after the war. Because the Bedouins attack travelers and kill and rob them, we had to put the idea out of our heads and be content with observing that wondrous mountain through binoculars from a distance. We then returned to the boat for the return voyage. But now we had a headwind which made for slow going, and it looked like it would be late before we could get back. However, the honorable Frenchman sent a steamboat to meet us, and then it was not long before we reached the harbor. We stayed at the Windsor Hotel during our stay in Suez.

We also wanted to see the other side of the Red Sea, where the Children of Israel were camped, at God's command, before they crossed the sea. We had seen from a distance the nearly vertical cliffs stretching almost to the sea, but we wanted to see them at close range. We set off, therefore, the following morning, and after a three-hour march of about eight miles, we were at the place where it is believed that the Children of Israel were camped when Pharaoh and his army caught up with them.

Whether they came from the north between the mountain and the sea, or if they came through the narrow mountain pass from the west, no one knows, but somewhere here, at that time, a strong easterly storm blew up. Maybe it was a cyclone that divided the Red Sea so that the water stood like a wall of water on both sides until the Israelites had passed through and the Egyptians were still in the middle of the sea, and Moses stretched out his staff and the water collapsed together over them. The sea here seems to be about three to five miles wide. We returned in time to catch the train at 5:00 P.M., and rode to Palestine over the same way through the desert along the Suez Canal to Kontara, where we had to change trains and go through the customs house, and then sit and wait until one o'clock in the morning when the train departed for Ludd [Lydda].

In Egypt the conditions are different from those in Palestine. The climate is drier and hotter, similar to southern California, so that the soil must be irrigated in order to produce crops. Most agricultural work is done by hand, particularly in the northern part of the Nile Valley. Much of the ground is worked with picks and shovels rather than by plow. The wages are low, forty cents a day. Here, too, the patient donkey is used, and heavy loads of 200 to 300 pounds are carried by the little animals. One rides camels, especially in the desert, and they carry heavy burdens. The Indian buffalo is also used as a work animal, particularly for hauling up water for irrigation where the water cannot be led up from watercourses. They are large and strong. The cows are much sought-after as milk cows. There are also ordinary farm animals such as sheep and goats, which are also led to the city to be milked. Cows with their calves, yes, even goats and sheep are led around to the milk customers' homes in the city to be milked in the street in the presence of those who buy the milk, probably so they do not have a chance to dilute it with water. On one occasion, I saw a baby laid under the goat to suck the milk directly.

Many are quite filthy about themselves. There is no lack of flies, and they suck unhindered at the eyes and mouths of little children as they sit by a wall by the street where their mothers sell small items or work or beg. In that way, many have bad eyes and countless Egyptians have bad vision, are one-eyed, or blind. We leave Egypt now and travel back to Palestine.

AGAIN TO PALESTINE

The trip to Palestine leads through sandy deserts, and at dawn we are at Gaza, where the fruit trees exude a pleasant scent and where green grain fields stretch toward the mountain heights of Judah. At nine we stop at Ludd [Lydda], and after a while we continue traveling north through the wonderful Plains of Sharon, where many beautiful flowers are in bloom and the grain fields promise a rich harvest. A great deal of the land was not cultivated, but covered with last year's weeds. I asked a fellow passenger, a pastor who could speak English, although he was Syrian, why that was, and he replied that the war had impoverished the people, so that they did not have enough plow animals and seed grain to use the ground. Another reason might be that great stretches are owned by rich Arabs, who do not tend the land themselves, but put it out for sharecropping, and the conditions are so meager that no one wants to do the work. Meanwhile it is a loss for the land and the people that such good, beautiful land should only grow weeds. Shortly

after one o'clock we pass a mountain ridge that stretches almost
to the Mediterranean. It is Mount Carmel. Immediately thereafter
we were in Haifa.

In Haifa at Mount Carmel

The city of Haifa lies by the Mediterranean Sea on the slopes of
the western end of Mount Carmel, which is, here, five hundred
feet above sea level. One day we walked up the mountain and
viewed the cave in which the prophet Elijah hid when King Ahab
wanted to kill him. The cave is located at the top of the mountain,
and a Catholic chapel is built over it. One must go into it to get
to the cave. Farther down near the sea are two larger caves, and it
is said to be here that Obadiah hid the one hundred prophets of
the Lord when Ahab wanted to kill them. A beautiful view of the
surrounding area and the Mediterranean Sea is to be had from the
top of the mountain. Down below is a German colony,[92] and the
grain fields are beautiful here, as the Germans use the earth here
better than the Arabs, who only sow and scratch around a little
between the thorn bushes. We traveled one day on horseback eight
or ten miles to the eastern end of Mount Carmel, where Elijah and
the prophets of Baal made sacrifice (see I Kings 18). The road runs
along the beautiful and fertile Esdraelon Valley,[93] where beautiful
grain fields flourish. We crossed Kison River twice and then followed it for a while until we came to the foot of the mountain. We
rode up a fairly steep slope until we had to continue on foot. We
found ourselves on the wrong road and had to walk cross-country
through brambles and stones until we came to the highest point of
the eighteen-hundred-foot mountain. It is regarded as the place
where Elijah went and prayed for rain. There is a remarkable view
in every direction: the Esdraelon Valley and Kison River below

the mountain to the north, in the east reigns Mount Tabor over the valleys that lie between, in the south we see Samaria's mountain range, and in the west, the Mediterranean. A little farther to the east and somewhat lower on another mountaintop sits another Catholic chapel, where the sacrifices are said to have taken place. On the first-named hill there are a good number of old stone walls, which perhaps served as fortresses in olden times. On the way down, we followed a fairly good road, and a little ways down from the top, we found a strong-running spring, which explains where Elijah got so much water to use in his sacrifices, something I had often wondered about.

We stayed in Haifa one Sunday and attended services at the English Episcopal church. We met a Swede by the name of Hamberg who had a store there and was interested in meeting another Swede and to get to converse in the mother tongue. He was the only Swede in Haifa.

By Horse and Carriage to Nazareth

After a few days' stay in Haifa, we traveled by horse and carriage to Nazareth, twenty-three miles northeast from Haifa. It lies between

Nazareth

hills on the slopes of a little valley. In the valley is an abundantly flowing spring with good water that is the main source of water for the city's nearly ten thousand residents. For the most part, it is carried by women in stoneware pots, four or five gallons each, on their heads, up steep stairsteps, which in many cases constitute the streets. I will here quote what a Swedish–American, who visited Nazareth, said about these women: "Strong and straight are they, and they hold their heads upright."

I thought: Our weak, bent schoolgirls should do that, and they would have good posture. It is said that the Virgin Mary was at this well getting water when the angel came and delivered the wonderful message. Joseph's workshop is seen as the place where Jesus in his youth would have worked. Also one can see the steep cliff from which the people in the synagogue tried to dash him (see Luke 4:29–30).

By Donkeyback to Mount Tabor

One day, we rode donkeys about ten miles eastward, over steep, stony paths, to Mount Tabor. That mountain lies isolated on the plains of Israel at the eastern end of the hills that encircle Nazareth and rises fifteen hundred feet above the surrounding plains and eighteen hundred feet above sea level. At the top of the mountain is a Roman Catholic monastery, a Greek chapel, and a number of ruins of cloisters and so forth. It is believed that this is the "mountain of declaration" (see Mark 8:12). One has a magnificent view over the surrounding area: around the mountain, the beautiful Israel Valley with green grain fields, in the northeast a glimpse of the Sea of Galilee, and farther north Mount Hermon raises its snow-covered top twelve hundred feet above sea level. In the east, one can just make out the Jordan Valley, in the south, the lesser Mount Hermon, and at its northern end, the towns of Endor (see I Samuel 28:11–14) and Nain (see Luke 7: 11–15) and to the west, Mount Carmel is visible. The weather was the most wonderful that one could wish for and we returned to Nazareth at twilight after an interesting day-trip.

We stayed in Nazareth one Sunday. The English Episcopalians have a church that we visited. In the morning services are held in Arabic. We did not understand a word of it, but we enjoyed seeing the church filled with attentive listeners and to know they worship the same God and Savior as we do. In the evening the services are held in the English language. Three-fourths of Nazareth's population is Mohammedan. The people of Nazareth are regarded as being fairly honorable, and the women are known for their beauty, and rival the women of Bethlehem.

The Sea of Galilee

We rode by horse carriage to Tiberias, which lies by the Sea of Galilee, twenty miles to the north. A few miles from Nazareth we passed Cana in Galilee, where Jesus and his disciples were at a wedding. The landscape is varied with heights and verdant valleys. Everything is gloriously in bloom this time of the year. Palestine seems to be richer in beautiful wildflowers than other lands. All at once we see a depression in the land before us, and soon the Sea of Galilee is like a mirror below us, and the green heights surround it like a frame. The road leads down steep slopes, for Tiberias and the sea lie six hundred eighty feet below the Mediterranean Sea. It is not large, only six miles broad and twelve miles long.

It is a strange sea, enclosed by mountains on all sides except the southern end, where the Jordan Valley, which is a few miles broad here, leaves an opening between the heights. It is also the lowest freshwater lake in the world and lies, as said, six hundred eighty feet below the Mediterranean, thirty to forty miles to the west. The surroundings are so different from what one otherwise sees in these lands. Ordinarily there is only white limestone on all the heights and mountains, but here it is gray-black, very hard basalt, and the formations show that this depression in the ground is the crater of a great volcano that thrust up the surrounding heights and then died and was filled with water from the upper Jordan River, whose fresh water constantly flows down into it from the snow-covered Mount Hermon. Here in this depression there is, so to speak, constant summer, although one can see the snow-covered mountain every day.

At the Sea of Galilee

That gives the shores around the Sea of Galilee a nearly ideal winter climate. It is rich in fish, now as in ancient times. There are hot springs on its shores, with temperatures ranging from 72 to 142 degrees Fahrenheit, so that one can have a hot bath at almost any temperature one desires. Many come here and bathe as a curative against different diseases. There is a very simple bathhouse at the hot springs, or one can go out in the open air to bathe. The area would be visited more if it did not lie so hidden away and were accessible only with great hardship. Now, very few make the difficult journey. For about fifteen hundred years the area has been populated almost exclusively by Bedouins, who come in the fall with their herds to this beautiful sea's shores to make camp for the winter. In the summer they move to higher, cooler ground.

The only city on the shores of Galilee now is Tiberias, with somewhat more than four thousand residents. Of these, three thousand are Jews, and the rest are Mohammedans and a few Christians. Tiberias was first built by Herod Antipas in 20 B.C., and became the largest city in the Galilee. Many beautiful buildings were erected here, which now all lie in ruins. Among these were a royal palace and an amphitheater. After the destruction of Jerusalem, Tiberias became a Jewish population center. Before that, Jews had avoided going there, as it is built over ancient graves. In the second century, the Sanhedrin moved here, and rabbinical schools were started, and some of the most important Jewish writings were presented here. After 500 A.D. the city was devastated, alternately by Arabs, Turks, and Crusaders. In 1837 it was struck by an earthquake and nearly half of its population died.

With regard to the Sea of Galilee, it may be remembered that Jesus chose to make His home at Capernaum on its shores, after He was driven from Nazareth, and that He chose His disciples from the poorest of Galilee's fishermen, and that it was around that sea that He wandered, taught, and worked His many miracles. It was on that sea that He walked, and stilled its raging billows, and from its fishermen's boats that He preached to the masses that had collected on the shores and on the heights that surround it. Here He held the wonderful Sermon on the Mount, and on some of these slopes, He fed the hungry masses in such a wonderful way. We got rooms at a hotel by the beach, where we heard the waves splashing on the shore, and from our windows, we saw when the fishermen came and sold their fish like Peter and his men did.

By Sailboat up the Jordan River

The second day we rented a little sailboat and set a course toward the northern end of the sea, where the Jordan River flows in. The weather was completely calm, and we had a remarkable opportunity to view these shores where our Savior wandered and worked. We rowed a ways up the Jordan River and landed on a beach, and ate the lunch that we had brought along, in the greenery near one of the Bedouin camps. The Bedouins are the least-civilized people in these lands. They live in tents made of goat hair and move around with their herds of goats, sheep, cattle, camels, and donkeys. Some of them practice agriculture, but they tend the soil badly. The women are, in general, facially disfigured with tattoos and are very filthy. The men dress in clothes that look like night shirts, with mantles of goat hair over them, and a linen cloth wrapped around their heads with a rope of black wool wound twice around their necks. They seem to be inclined to keep their heads and chins well wrapped up, but, in general, go barefoot and bare-legged in all weathers.

We boarded the boat and rowed back out into the sea. We would have liked to have traveled a little further up the river to Caesarea and Philippi, but our rowers seemed to be afraid to go further because of the Bedouins who are camped along the Jordan's banks. We followed along the western bank, and in a while we came to Capernaum and went ashore there.

Capernaum

Capernaum is now nothing more than old ruins. It was once a large town, but was laid in ruins by the Persians in the year 614. It had been blessed with the "White Synagogue," so-called because it was built of white stone that had been brought from a great distance. All of the stone around the Sea of Galilee is gray-black lava stone. It is said to be the synagogue that the king's men built (see Luke 6: 4-5), and where Jesus preached and worked miracles, as described in John 6. Although the Persians did not destroy the synagogue, it was destroyed in an earthquake in the year 670, so what Jesus predicted in Matthew 11:24 came to pass. The synagogue and other ruins that had lain buried under ten feet of earth and gravel has, in recent years, been excavated by a German scientific society, and now the great, splendidly carved stones that decorated the synagogue lie spread around on the surrounding site. But some of the pillars still stand, along with the stone floor on which Jesus walked,

Ruins of the White Synagogue at Capernaum

and walls a few feet high with stone benches remain to sit on. The building was seventy-four feet, nine inches long and fifty-six feet, nine inches wide.[94] A German Catholic priest who lives here showed us around. On the stones lying around are many well-carved symbols, such as the seven holy candles, David's crown, pomegranates, and Jacob's Star, among others. It is owned now by the Roman Catholic church. Jews have offered large sums of money for the place, but in vain. Capernaum was a substantial city in Jesus' time, but now all that is left are piles of stone.

We wandered up the beach to a height where, perhaps, Jesus fed the four thousand. From here one has a wonderful view of the Sea of Galilee. Directly across on the eastern side of the sea is a steep hill by the water where the herd of swine dashed themselves into the water when Jesus told the evil spirits to do so (see Matthew 8:28). Below us on the shore are the ruins of an old building where the town of Bethsaida once stood. A little farther to the west flow several strong, warm springs, from which an aqueduct of stone once existed. It is now destroyed, so that all the water is wasted. Nearby here a number of Indian soldiers were encamped. They stand in service to England and they seemed to enjoy splashing naked in the tepid water. A little farther to the southwest is a little bay, thought to be the place where Jesus preached from the boat, and where the fishermen still go to cast their nets as there are a lot of fish here.

On the beach there is now a German Catholic nunnery, where, before the war, all travelers were admitted and given shelter. Now it is full of English officers, so that now there is no room for ordinary people. That is the situation in all of Palestine; the English army takes up all such places, where travelers at one time could find refuge for a just compensation. But now there is no such opportunity to be had, and hotel operators charge travelers what they please. The nunnery has beautiful grounds, flower beds, and so forth, and has a lovely location by the lake. The Sea of Galilee's beaches are rather stony, but in many places one finds bright sand, which, to a great extent, is made up of tiny, beautiful shells. This is the case on the west side of the Sea of Galilee. We did not go to the east side, as the Bedouins are quite violent, so that it is not advisable to go there. Several acts of violence were carried out while we were in Tiberias. Among others, they destroyed a railroad bridge and robbed the train, and many were killed. We boarded our boat that was waiting for us at the nunnery, and steered straight across the bay that flows into Genezereth, to Tiberias. Here was a low plain about three miles long and a mile broad of beautiful, rich farmland, but it is now overgrown with thorn bushes. The wind had increased, and with billowing sails, the boat was driven rapidly onward. Our rowers could sit idly and smoke cigarettes, and seemed quite contented. In the evening, we were back in Tiberias after a very interesting day on the water. We hired a boat again that night and rowed out on the lake for a while. There was a full moon, and it shone so brightly on the glittering, rippling water, and we amused ourselves by singing some songs along the way.

In Tiberias

We stayed in Tiberias three weeks, starting February 21, and during that time we wandered around the Sea of Galilee's shores and climbed all the hills and mountains around it. Everywhere we went, the land was strewn with the most beautiful flowers you can imagine. Often I walked alone, although I was warned not to and was told I might be robbed by the Bedouins. However, they are not as bold now as before the war because there are now so many English soldiers here to keep them on a short leash. I went my way straight along and showed no fear for anything, as I had placed myself in God's hands. I merely greeted people politely in Arabic "*Halak sa'id*" in the morning and "*Sa'ida*" in the afternoon, and everyone politely greeted me back and gave me no trouble.

One day I walked two hours to a mountain called "The Horns of Haiten" which the Crusaders believed was the place where Jesus held His "Sermon on the Mount." The mountain lies between the Sea of Galilee and Nazareth, and is centrally located to all parts of the Galilee. It is the highest in these tracts after Mount Tabor, which lies father to the south. The mountain seems to have been a volcano whose top has blown off, leaving a depression in the middle with lots of stone blocks round about. It can be seen to have been suitable for people to have assembled there and that a stone block served as a pulpit. The heights that surround it and a little below it to the south are thought to be the place where the five thousand were fed (see Matthew 14:15–21 and Stanley's *Journey to Palestine*[95]). One feels deeply moved by those events and compelled, like our Savior, to kneel down on the mountain and talk with the Heavenly Father. One day we rode in the little gasoline-powered boat that shuttles between Tiberias and Samakh, which is a railway station at the southern end of the Sea of Galilee near the Jordan River's outlet from the sea. It is only a six-mile trip, and arriving there, we wandered down the beautiful, flat Jordan Valley, which is several miles broad here, until we came to the river several miles from the outlet and ate lunch by the murmuring water in its rocky bed. The Jordan River falls six hundred feet in sixty miles between the Sea of Galilee and the Dead Sea, and its bed is generally stony. We returned to Samakh in time to take the boat back to Tiberias.

There are a number of caves in the mountains near the Sea of Galilee, which we also visited. Some of them are natural, others were dug out, and all have, at different times, been inhabited by different sorts of people. A few miles to the north of Tiberias were Arbela's caves, where the robber, who was the terror of the district in olden times, had his hide-out. Herod the Great captured or killed them by having his soldiers lowered to caves in baskets; the only way they could be reached.[96] One day I bathed in a hot spring. The water was as hot as I could stand. Another time we washed our feet in a warm spring.

Magdala, which lies a few miles north of Tiberias at the southern end of the Plains of Gennesaret, is a little town of mud shacks along the shore. Mary Magdalene was born here, so it is said. Here there is a level, beautiful valley, a mile wide and three miles long. A Jewish colony now owns part of the valley and they tend it well, but right next to them the land is owned by Arabs, and they just scratch around a little between the thorn bushes, which take up a third of the land and constantly spread themselves if one does not try to keep them down. It is a shame that such fine, fertile land should be tended so poorly when so many need bread. Part of the plain belongs to a German Catholic society and is well-tended.

A Russian–Jewish Colony

One day we wandered along the sea to its southern end, where the Jordan River quietly flows out. When it comes a bit from the sea, the fall becomes stronger and it can be heard as it tumbles over great boulders.

Nearby is a Russian–Jewish colony. I saw here a huge haystack, which I had not seen in a long time, and I had to go and see what else they had. It looked so nice and reminded me of farmland in

America. I went to the gate, which was open. The farmyard was surrounded by a high, thick stone wall and a heavy iron gate as protection against robbers. That was necessary during the War. Inside the gate was a watering trough, from which one watered the domestic animals. It is filled by a pipe from a well. Good stables built of stone with red tile roofs and other outbuildings, as well as silos, took up part of the farmyard; housing was at the other end. It was just at dinnertime, and the workers came home from the fields with loaded mules, which were watered and put into stalls to be fed. Everything looked so American. I approached one of the men, but could not understand him nor he me, for he only spoke Russian and Hebrew. He called the foreman, who could speak some English. He had been in the English army. I was offered to eat dinner with them. I showed them that I had food with me, but to no avail. I had to sit at the table with the workers. About forty, along with the foreman, ate at long tables in a mess hall. We got a piece of coarse bread, fried cauliflower, mush, and tea for dinner, with neither meat nor butter. I thought that wouldn't do for farmhands in America, but they seemed pleased and happy and healthy. I offered to pay for dinner, but they refused emphatically to accept anything. We talked for a while and the foreman showed me seed, cows, mules, and so forth, and farm equipment. I asked if farming here was profitable, and he said they had a fairly good harvest of about twenty-five bushels of wheat, and sixty bushels of barley and oats, per acre. But, he bemoaned, they didn't really understand farming, for neither he, nor the other workers had done such work before they began here twelve years previously.

I went out and viewed the fields. The grain was fine; the barley was just going to seed (it was March 9), and the wheat was knee-high. They were just planting beans, but it took a lot of work because they did not have suitable equipment for it. The women worked at clearing the cabbage and potato land. They tilled the ground with four mule-drawn plows. The plows were of German manufacture and were laborious to control. I wished that they had a good American plow to work with. But they do the best they can, and these Jewish colonies, of which there are a good many in Palestine, look homey with their well-built stone walls and red tiled roofs and well-tended fields.

On the other hand, the Arabs' ill-tended fields, to a great extent, are overgrown with thorn bushes or have large stones strewn through them, which they bring up with their hooks, year after year, but never remove from the field. In the best cases, they live in low houses of sun-dried mud with nearly flat earth roofs. On every roof is a roller of stone that they roll over the roof right after every rain so that the rain won't come through with the next rain. The so-called Bedouins live in tents of black goat-hair and they move around and make camp wherever it suits them at the occasion. They till the ground in some ways, but mainly practice animal husbandry. They make a sort of yoghurt from goat and sheep milk, which the women carry to town in goatskin bags. There they sit on the street and sell it. They are so filthy that one can smell them from a long distance and they are disfigured with tattoos. They wear many shiny decorations on their fingers and arms.

There are good roads being built in Palestine, and the work is being carried out by Russian Jews who, in particular, immigrated there after the war. We walked past where they were working. Some were digging the ditches and doing the roadwork, others did blasting or crushing stones that were brought to the road in wagons or on donkeyback. They seemed to work really hard. Many of the men were naked to the waist to not get too hot (it was 60 to 70 degrees Fahrenheit). They live mostly in tents, and we walked by one of their camps on the beach. There were about eighty round tents, and inside each was a bed, a little table, etc., and it looked nice and clean. In some tents there sat a woman doing handwork or writing. Some women worked at clearing and hoeing in an adjacent vegetable garden, and everything looked well-tended. A fairly large, wooden building made up the kitchen and mess hall, where probably all of them took their meals. They seemed to be happy and joyous, and often you can hear them in the evening singing lively songs in chorus. Probably they feel glad to have escaped from the difficult conditions and the hard climate in Russia, to the mild, beautiful summer-land year-round.

Tiberias has narrow, crooked streets, and only two of them are drivable. Nearly everything is carried by men, women, children, donkeys, and camels. Water is carried, in great part, from the lake by women who carry it in stone crocks on their heads. Also, old five-gallon oil cans are used for that purpose. Some of it is carried on donkeys that carry four or five gallon containers in boxes on each side of their backs. Houses and shops are, mostly, hovels. Trade is conducted, for the most part, by Jews who sit or stand in the little stalls waiting for customers. There are a few small restaurants, where Arabian dishes are served. Cooking and waiting are done by a man who stands in the door and does his work. In the morning a dish they call "haleeb" is served, which is a kind of thin porridge with sugar. Bread, which is bought from one of the peddlers on the street, is brought in, and porridge and bread make up the entire breakfast, which costs sixteen cents. For lunch and dinner they have stewed potatoes and mutton, but only a little meat, beans, rice, and other Arabian dishes. One can almost always buy good fried fish in Tiberias for a suitable price. Also one can buy confections, eaten with or after meals. Oranges are plentiful and cost only two cents each. Other fruits are eaten in the fall, such as figs, grapes, etc.

There is a Scottish clinic in Tiberias, run by Dr. Torrance, a Scot who is held in high regard in the city and the surrounding area as a good doctor.[97] He is a Presbyterian and does Christian works and holds services in both Arabic and English in the waiting room of the clinic every Sunday. We attended these services while we were in Tiberias, and the doctor and his wife were very friendly toward us and twice invited us to dinner and tea.

Our hotelier was a Jew, and we went with him one Saturday to the Jewish synagogue. Synagogues are built square-shaped. A raised platform in the middle, three or four feet high, constitutes the pulpit. Several stand there at the same time and a lecturer reads from the Pentateuch on a parchment roll made from goatskin, and as it is read, it is rolled up on another roller. The men stand or sit around about, and the women have their place in a gallery.

We stayed in Tiberias for three weeks, and during that time the weather was calm and beautiful with a little rain sometimes. The normal rainfall there is twenty-five inches a year. Most of it falls in December, January, February, and March. That winter the rainfall was below normal, but they were expecting more. The day before we were to leave Tiberias, the wind blew freshly from the north and was a little colder than usual. The waves ran fairly high, so that no boats dared to go out on the sea with the exception of a little steamer that carried the mail to Samakh. The next day was stormy, too, and it seemed unsure if the little steamer would dare to sail. However, it came and lay to, and we stepped aboard. The trip went well although the little vessel rocked and was cast about on the billows.

TRAVELS IN THE MEDITERRANEAN
Post-WWI Mandate Boundaries

Key to the Route:

SYRIA	**TURKEY**
1. Samakh	9. Alexandretta
2. Bethabara	(Iskenderun)
3. Beirut	**CYPRUS**
4. Bhamdoun	10. Famagusta
5. Ba'albek	11. Larnaca
6. Rayak	12. Limaso
7. Damascus	13. Adalia
8. Tripoli	14. Rhodes

TURKEY	20. Piraeus
15. Smyrna	21. Athens
16. Constan-	22. Island of
tinople	Corfu
(Istanbul)	**ALBANIA**
17. Kavoka	23. Valona
18. Kavalla	(Vlore)
GREECE	*Steamship*
19. Thessalonika	*to Italy*
(Salonika)	

THE TRIP TO SYRIA

In Samakh we boarded the train and traveled down the Jordan Valley several miles to Bethabara, where John baptized, according to some. Here we crossed the rushing Jordan River and the tracks lead west through the Valley of Israel. The little towns of Endor and Nain at the northern end of the little Mount Hermon could be seen a bit south of the tracks and soon we saw Mount Carmel, whose foot we followed along Kidron River almost all the way to Haifa, which lies at the western end of Carmel on the Mediterranean Sea. Here we felt almost at home, as we had been here before.

When we left Tiberias, we had thought to travel by train from Samakh to Damascus, but the Bedouins had once again cut the rail line to Damascus, so no trains could go there. Therefore, we had to go to Haifa and try to reach Beirut by steamship. A steamer had arrived and was to depart the next day. However it was very stormy, so that the steamship could not be reached, as it had to be boarded from a rowboat. The harbor was not deep enough for the ship, so it had to anchor a bit out from land. Then, toward evening, we found out that we could go aboard. Our passports and luggage had to be inspected; we were thereby delayed so that the little rowboat that was to take us to the ship was full and set out from the harbor when we arrived. We were told to wait until it came back, and we stood and watched as the tiny vessel was cast about on the waves, and time after time it looked like it would be swallowed up by the sea. We felt glad that we were not on board and hoped that the wind would lie down until the boat came back. They succeeded in reaching the ship; the boat returned, and now we stepped in. It started to grow dark, and it seemed perilous to set out onto the raging billows. But what could we do? We had to go along, so we placed ourselves in God's hands. It was terrible to hear the boatman's shouts and curses, and we were amazed at God's great patience with man's ungodliness. A Bedouin sat in front of us and kept a vice-grip on the arm of another passenger's arm, and every time a high wave threatened to wash over the boat, he looked frightened to death. We had no fear, as our faith in God's might to preserve us was strong. The five men who rowed us did their utmost. One stood in the stern and steered. Luckily, we made it to the ship and, one after another, we were drawn up the ship's ladder and came on board. The girls had second-class tickets and were shown to a cabin and got good food in the dining room. I traveled third class for that short distance. It only took six or seven hours. I wanted to see how it was.

The ship did not depart that night because of the storm, but lay anchored until morning. I had brought along a little bread and a couple of oranges for supper. It was blustery and cold on deck. Below decks there was a mixed lot of third-class passengers, all Arabs and Egyptians. Some were shabbily clad and looked poor, while others were well-dressed with glittering rings and bracelets. Here were men, women, and children, families and individuals. Some had nice, fine bedclothes with them, and bedded down on the floor and lay down for a good night's sleep. Others did not have anything, but lay or sit on the floor however they could. I went back up on deck and sought to stay warm above the machine room, from which there arose a little warmth. I could not stay below because of the strong stink of the many goat skins in the hold. But, by midnight it was too blustery and cold to remain above, so I had to go below again.

Although the goat stink was unpleasant, it was better than freezing, and after a while I got used to it and did not notice it so much. I spread out on the floor the blanket that I had with me, and with a package under my head, slept fairly well until morning. I thought of the Apostle Paul's voyages on this sea. He probably had no better comforts, perhaps worse than I had that night, and he had to continue that way for months to convey the message of salvation to his fellow man. Just think! What he sacrificed, to serve others. How much do we sacrifice for others' wellbeing?

In the morning the wind lay down somewhat, and we weighed anchor and headed out to sea. The sun was shining, and it was right pleasant to bask in its rays. We followed the coast of Palestine, and we could see the cities along it; first Akka, which lay ten miles north of Haifa, and was once a respectable port city, then the old Tyre (now called Sur), which is a very old city and according to tradition was founded in 2750 B. C. It is mentioned in Joshua 19:29 and called the "fortified city" because of its position on an island nearly a half-mile from the mainland, and because it is enclosed by high walls which no enemy could penetrate until the coming of Alexander the Great with his army. It took a seven months' siege before they could enter the city, but first they had to build an earthen causeway to connect the island with the land, which still exists to this day. Alexander leveled the city and put to the sword all who attempted to oppose him, and had three thousand of the most prominent citizens hanged on the beach. Approximately thirty thousand were sold into slavery. Still, it was quickly rebuilt and regained its former power, according to Isaiah 23. In the New Testament, Jesus mentions this city and it is mentioned in the Book of Acts in connection with Paul's travels to Jerusalem from Ephesus (see Acts 21:3–6). Although it was occupied in the 700s by the Mohammedans, it was not destroyed. In the 1100s, it was captured by Crusaders and became a Christian city. In the year 1229, it was taken by an Egyptian sultan without resistance. It fell into neglect after that and by the 1600s, there remained not a single complete building standing. During the latter half of the previous century, it has been partially rebuilt and now has a population of about ninety-six thousand.

After that we passed Sarapeta, where the prophet Elijah lived with the widow during the long drought, when the oil in the crock did not run dry and the flour in the bin never ran low and where the prophet resurrected the widow's son to life (see I Kings 17:8–24). Then we traveled through the city of Sidon, which is regarded as being yet older than Tyre and was mentioned in Genesis 10:19. Even Jesus visited this city. It now has a population of about ten thousand, the greater portion of whom are Mohammedans. We passed a few other cities and at two, we arrived in Beirut.

SYRIA

Beirut is beautifully situated on high ground on the shores of the Mediterranean Sea and is the most substantial city in Syria, with about one hundred fifty thousand inhabitants. From here are exported silk, cotton, olive oil, and fruit. I cannot go into the long and varied history of the city. I just want to mention that it is known for its schools and charitable institutions. It has six hospitals, thirty-eight Christian churches, forty-two Christian schools for boys, twenty-five for girls and many mosques and Mohammedan schools. The so-called "American College," was founded in 1866 by Rev. [Daniel L.] Bliss with the name "The Syrian Protestant College" but recently changed its name to "The American University of Beirut" and has an outstanding campus on an eminence above the beach.[98] It has several good buildings and beautiful grounds and in general looks American. It is Protestant-Liberal and students of all faiths are accepted there. Instruction is based on Christian-Protestant principles and is given in Arabic, literature, mathematics, natural history, modern languages, commerce, biblical archaeology, medicine and pharmacology, and others. It is operated under administration in the United States. This school, with one thousand students, has brought knowledge and education to many people in these countries and we have met men and women in Egypt, Palestine, and Syria who received their schooling there, and all have been educated, honest, and devoted to Christianity. They hold the American people, who have done so much for them, in high esteem. The "British Syrian School," founded in 1860, is also a good school with education for the blind and disabled.[99] Also, there is a Jewish mission school which belongs to the Presbyterians and French schools and institutions, which are run by the Jesuits. Before the war, the Germans had an orphanage, school, and hospital but they are now occupied by French soldiers.

To Bhamdoun

Our next visit was to Bhamdoun in the Lebanon Mountains. While we were in Brindisi, Italy, and waiting for the steamship to take us to Palestine, I came one day down to the dock. A man of about sixty, who looked like an American, was walking there. I spoke to him and asked if he were American, and he answered "yes." I

Bhamdoun, Mount Lebanon, Syria; Anna Larson and Syrian girls

asked him if he were traveling and, if so, where. "I intend to go to Palestine as soon as a steamship lands that I can depart upon," he answered. I said that that was our destination also, and we expected one to land soon. "Are you a Bible student, too?" he asked. "I don't know if you can call me that," I answered, "although I have studied the Bible since I was a child." He said that he studied the Bible a lot. He was a Baptist and wanted to see if there was enough water in Jerusalem to baptize as many by immersion as it said to have been on Pentecost. He traveled third-class on the same steamer as we did.

In third-class on the Mediterranean, there are no cabins or bunks, nor is food included. One must lie on the deck in one's own bed-clothes, if one has any, and one must bring his own food or buy it on board. We set out from Brindisi in the evening. The night was stormy and the ship rocked so much that nearly all of the passengers got sick. Our American friend had not brought any bed-clothes, and when he became sick that night, he lay down on a cot that someone had left to go up on deck. In a while a young woman came and said that it was her bed, and asked him to get up and leave. He tried to speak to her in English and she understood a little and answered him as well as she could. In the morning I went out to see how our American friend was doing. He was a little better and said that he was doing all right, but he felt bad for the young woman, with whom he had become acquainted, for she was not accustomed to such living conditions and had no one with her, and felt very alone and dejected. He wondered if she could not keep company with my girls up on deck although they were not in the same class. I asked him to bring her to us as soon as it was suitable, which he did, and we became very good friends for the rest of the trip. She was from Germany and was on her way to Bhamdoun, Syria, where she was born and where her mother lived. For a time she had served with a Danish doctor, and when he went to Germany, she went with him. He had died just as they were about to return to Syria, and she had to travel alone. She had insisted that we promise to visit her in Bhamdoun, if it were possible for us to do so, and we now wanted to keep our promise.

We went to the train station in Beirut at six o'clock in the morning of March 23. The train was to depart at 7:30 but, as we knew that there would be a crowd, we left early. The train had not yet arrived, but there were many already there waiting for it. I left our bags and the girls in the care of a dragoman at the most suitable place to board the train, and he would help them get themselves and the luggage aboard. I went, then, to buy tickets. Many were crowded around the ticket booth, for everyone wanted to be first when it opened. I took a place with the group, and after an hour, the booth opened and the crowd got even worse. More had arrived, and the strongest pushed the weaker to the side to be first. I stood my ground, pushed no one aside, but let no one crowd me out, although there were several attempts, and eventually made it to the window and got tickets. I ran out to the train and saw the girls being stuffed into the only first-class car there was. The other compartments were either full or reserved for French officers and their ladies. I stepped into the compartment to squeeze in, but those who were ahead of me tried to keep me out. I let it be understood by my actions that I was coming in no matter what, and when they saw that I would not easily be dissuaded, they gave me a chance to crowd in. These compartments have seats for eight people. There were thirteen and a lot of large luggage and several big baskets full of household items, wine bottles, and so forth that took up almost all of the space. I managed with difficulty to find a place to sit, but I was glad to be there.

At first we followed a little river that wound between the hills, and eventually it got more mountainous and steep, so that the little locomotive was puffing hard and only with effort managed to pull the six little cars. After an hour the train stopped, and we were at the end of the line. The locomotive was uncoupled, backed into a side track, and now began to go backwards. We saw now that we were on a cog railroad like the one that runs up to Pikes Peak in Colorado and Pilatus in Switzerland. It now bore up a pretty steep height, and after a time we once again came to the end of the line. The locomotive was moved to the front of the train and we again began to move forward. We left the cog line, as we had come up the steepest part, and after an additional three hours, the train stopped in Bhamdoun.

Here was a little station building, a score of houses with some shops and a hotel, which was closed because there weren't enough guests in the winter months. We asked some men about Martha Schehin (the young woman we were there to visit). One who could speak English informed us that she lived in another town a half-hour away and offered to go with us there, as he lived there, too. We were allowed to leave our things at the station until later and wandered a winding path on a mountain slope above a deep valley to a little town of about six hundred people. Our guide led us to a little house where we met our friend Martha, who was busy teaching a class of little girls, who were sitting on little wooden benches. She was very glad to see us and took us to the matron, Mrs. Salibi, a Syrian widow of sixty-five, who received us very cordially and offered to put us up during our stay in Bhamdoun. We accepted the offer with gratitude. Also living with Mrs. Salibi were her twenty-five-year-old daughter, a daughter-in-law, and her three little girls. The son had been a doctor, but had died during the war and the women lived alone, and in the fall had opened a Protestant school for the town's girls in their home. Our friend, Martha, was entrusted with the smallest girls, and the daughter-in-law a class of the older. Most of the town's population was Catholic and had no school for girls. The older lady took pity on them and opened the school, for which she got financial support from a Miss Benton in America.

Around 1855 a Presbyterian missionary named Benton and his wife came to this town and successfully worked with the people, and through their work converted them from Catholicism and Mohammedanism.[100] With the persecution and bloodbath that the Druze and Mohammedans carried out against the Christians in 1860, this little town was the only one to escape those terrible deeds. It is said that when the Mohammedans marched toward the town, the missionaries went to meet them with open Bibles and said to their leader, "God Almighty says 'Thou shalt not kill, and he who spills human blood, his blood too shall be spilled.'" The leader then promised to spare the people. Around 1865 the missionaries returned to America for good reasons, and left the congregation in the care of a native-born teacher. In 1870 the Bentons' sent money to build a church on the land that they had acquired during their stay there, and has now served the town's residents and many tourists for over fifty years as an assembly place for God's word.

During the Bentons' missionary work, a man named Haddad and his wife were converted to Protestantism. They had previously belonged to the Greek Orthodox Church, but now raised their children in the Protestant faith. Mrs. Salibi is their daughter.[101] She is old now, but still active in the service of good. During the War, the people suffered great difficulty. Many starved to death, and others became sick and died from eating unsuitable food. Many ate grass and weeds from the ground, like cattle. Dogs and cats were eaten, and it is said that some ate their children. Mrs. Salibi's family avoided these difficulties as the son, who was a doctor, stood high with the Turkish general, who fixed it so that they got enough flour for themselves and a little left over for others.

The doctor died while serving the general, and so the women were left alone in their home. Realizing the need for schools for girls after the war, Mrs. Salibi wrote to Miss Benton in America about the situation, and she sent the means to start the previously mentioned school. Here the girls get a good Christian education at no cost.

Bhamdoun is situated on a slope on Mount Lebanon approximately four thousand feet above the Mediterranean Sea and only about ten miles away. It was the highest city that we stayed in on this side of the Atlantic, and Tiberias was the lowest at six hundred eighty feet below sea level.

The mountain slopes are planted in grape vines, which lie flat on the ground between stone walls that form terraces six to twenty feet wide. The soil is very rocky and, in the summer, so dry that grapes and a few other types of fruit are the only things cultivated with success. Some grain is grown, too, but the harvest is meager. In the early spring, the grape vines are trimmed, and the twigs are gathered by women and children, tied into bundles, and carried home by the women and men on their backs or on donkeys, to be used for fuel, of which there is very little because during the war the forests of Lebanon were, to a large extent, cut down and burned. A ring of tar mixture is painted around each branch of the vines to prevent insects from eating the blooms and fruit. The earth is plowed up between the vines with little plows or crooks pulled by cows. It goes slowly, but no one is in a hurry here. Then they set little stones under the vines to hold them up off the ground. Good grapes grow here. They are sold, some of them fresh to the cities and to the tourists who stay in the mountain tracts in the summer; some are pressed for wine or dried on smooth, flat stones. Others are boiled down to a kind of syrup called "*dips*," which is eaten with bread and tastes pretty good. Figs, olives, and walnuts are cultivated too, and mulberry trees are grown for the silkworms.

The silk industry is fairly widespread, and silk thread is sold to France and England to be woven or used in manufacturing. There are two factories here in the area in which the silk is taken from the pupae and wound into skeins, and many, mostly women and children, work there. The cultivation of these products is not very profitable, as the soil is poor and the methods by which the work is carried out are inefficient. The cost of living has been high since the War. A pound of flour costs thirteen cents, a quart of milk is thirty-two cents, meat is fifty cents a pound, and a cow is two hundred dollars. During the war, flour cost a dollar a pound and many had to sell their possessions cheaply to get bread. The people don't like Frenchmen, who are now in control, or their ignorant soldiers, but they are stuck with them.

The view is beautiful from Bhamdoun with the eight-thousand-foot Mount Sannine [Jebal Sannine] in the northeast, which is covered with snow this time of the year, and Beirut and the Mediterranean Sea in the west. The climate is similar to northern California's mountainous areas, and snow sometimes falls in substantial amounts although it is as far south as Los Angeles. The air is clean and thin and is regarded as being healthful, especially in the summer. People are fairly educated and very polite and mild-mannered. Also they are clean and better dressed in general than the people in other places we have visited on this side of the Mediterranean, if not on this side of the Atlantic, except for Switzerland. Arabic Protestant services are held in the church every Sunday, and prayer meetings in someone's home every Wednesday night. Attendance is not so great in the winter months, but in the summer, it is filled to overflowing because of the many tourists staying here. Also a Greek Orthodox church and a mosque are located here. Additionally, there is a sect called the Druze who hold some sort of worship services that no outsider may know anything about. It is said that they worship a calf or an ox. They are regarded as being barbaric and untrustworthy, and live mostly in their own villages.[102]

Ba'albek

On April 7, we took the train over the Mountains of Lebanon, as we wanted to go to Ba'albek and Damascus. We passed through a long tunnel and arrived at Boydar station, which is at the highest

pass the tracks cross. It lies about 5,000 feet
above sea level. Then the route bears downward through a long tunnel, and then we
catch sight of the Anti-Lebanon Mountains
before us, and the plains of Coele–Syria approximately 3,000 feet below us, and to the
left Jabal el Renish, 7,000 feet high, and to
the right Jabal el Barouk, 8,000 feet. The
course continued ever downward until we
reached the plain that spreads out so beautifully with its green grain fields between
the two Lebanon Mountain ranges. We had
to change trains at the little town of Rayak,
in the middle of the plain, in order to get to
Ba'albek. But, as we arrived at 1:00 A.M., and
no train departed from there before morning,
we had to remain there until then. There was
a sort of hotel there, where we got a room

Temple ruins at Ba'albek, Syria

and something to eat for an exorbitant price. We boarded the train
the next morning at 5:00 A.M. The journey now leads north over
the beautiful plains with Lebanon and Anti-Lebanon mountains on
either side. They were partly covered in snow.

After an hour's travel, we see Ba'albek's ancient temple ruins.
The temple was built around 220 A.D. by Elagabalus, son of Julius
of Emesa, for sun worship, and it is one of the wonders of the world.
There were three temples here of colossal dimensions. The great
temple of the sun is, to the greatest extent, in ruins except for six
granite pillars 75 feet high and 8 feet in diameter. The temple was
290 feet long and 160 feet wide and surrounded by 54 pillars. A
temple of Bacchus, surrounded by 46 pillars 60 feet high and 6
feet in diameter, of which 19 remain standing, was one of the most

beautiful in Syria. These temples exceeded in size and grandeur the temples of both Greece and Rome. Because of the expansion of Christianity, the construction was never completed. Part of the temple of Jupiter was rebuilt as a Christian church. At the beginning of Mohammedan times, the temple site was taken over by the Arabs. Most wondrous about these buildings are the immense stones in the walls. It is difficult to imagine how it was possible to transport and set in them in place and to raise the huge granite pillars. In the western wall are three stones, each over 60 feet long and 13 feet thick and set into the wall 20 feet above the ground.

We returned by train to Rayak that night and had to stay until one o'clock the next day, when we embarked for the trip to Damascus. We soon left the beautiful plain and climbed the Anti-Lebanon mountains until we reached the summit at 4,359 feet above sea level. Then we headed down the eastern side of the mountain. The scenery is varied and charming where the tracks wind down along the rushing river Albana, whose water the Syrian Naman regarded as being better than all the water in Israel (see II Kings, chapter 5) and on whose banks grow many trees of different kinds. Many were now in bloom. Suddenly the narrow river valley widens and Damascus lies below us.

Damascus

Damascus is surrounded by plantations that spread out for miles around the city and are watered by the river. There are two hundred forty-eight mosques with their minarets. Damascus is regarded as the oldest city in the world and was mentioned as early as Abraham's time (see Genesis 14:15). It is also mentioned in II Kings, I Chronicles, Isaiah, Amos, and Jeremiah, and Saul was en route to that city to jail the Christians when he was met by Jesus (see Acts 9). The "street called Straight" still remains, and the place on the wall where Paul was lowered in a basket, and Ananias' house (see II Corinthians 9:32 and Acts 9:25) can also be seen.

The Oriental Hotel had been recommended to us by an American, Dr. Allen, whom we met in Ba'albeck, and we found it to be comfortable and relatively cheap. We met several Americans here, among others one from Chicago and his daughter, who were traveling around the world. Also we met some teachers from an American school in Beirut.

We arrived in Damascus on Saturday night. On Sunday morning we directed our steps through the bustling city's narrow streets (business activity goes on here the same every day as many of the population are Mohammedans) to the Christian quarter in the eastern part of the city, to visit the Irish Protestant church, where Arabic services are held in the morning, and in English at 5:00 P.M. We were very cordially received and were invited to tea with the pastor in the afternoon, and then got to hear a good sermon in the church.

There are not so many Protestants in this city. They have often been persecuted and killed by Mohammedans, in particular in the painful year of persecution, 1860, when six thousand Christians were murdered by Mohammedans, merely for identifying themselves as Christians (see Colonel Churchill's account).[103] But the small Protestant missions that are to be found in these countries are seen as exercising a good influence and are much liked, especially by the Greek Orthodox members, and it seems as if even the Mohammedans have begun to be a little more responsive to Christ's evangelism. The sad thing, however, is that so many of the so-called Christian people live immorally in drinking and going to the casino and such, that it is a bad recommendation for us to these people who, according to Mohammedan teaching, never touch strong drink and are quite abstemious in other ways. It would be good if the so-called Christians demonstrated their faith by their deeds.

The great mosque covers an area of five hundred feet on the east and west, and three hundred on the north and south. Part of it is in disuse since it was destroyed by fire in 1893. The greatest part was rebuilt four years later. It was first built as a heathen temple. In the 300s it was converted to a Christian church, and over the south door, there is still an inscription from that time (Psalms 145:13) in Greek, which, despite Mohammedan fanaticism, still remains. It remained a Christian church for almost three hundred years, but when Damascus fell into Mohammedan hands in the year 634, it became available to both Christians and Mohammedans and then turned over to the Mohammedans entirely. The defenseless Christians were compelled to concede although they held a legal right to half. However, the Christians wait with patience for the time when Christian teachings shall disperse the Mohammedan delusions and the mosques become Christian once more. There is a sarcophagus in this mosque that is said to contain the head of John the Baptist.[104]

Damascus is a city of three hundred thousand inhabitants and is the trade center for Syria. Close by to the city, there is much cultivation of fruit and nuts, under irrigation, and further up the slope they produce grain. The climate and rainfall is similar to northern California. Grain is grown successfully without irrigation. The rainfall is eight to ten inches annually. Damascus lies just below a mountain ridge, and from its highest point, called Kassium, is the most beautiful view of Damascus and the surrounding area. The city, orchards, and grain fields spread out in a beautiful panorama at the mountain's feet. Although the climb is laborious, one feels well rewarded for the effort. We stayed in Damascus for eight days and wandered around in the bustling city's narrow streets. Many are covered over with stone arches and all sorts of trade is carried on. There are many shops where silk and other fabrics, tools and equipment, harnesses, saddles, sandals, wooden shoes, and wooden forks are made. All of it is done by hand. Beautiful furniture, which is very expensive and in high demand, are made from many different types of wood inlaid with ivory and precious stones. They are sold in all parts of the world. Also, we wandered out to the orchards that lie around the city. Here there were not only African fruit trees and walnuts, but also apples and peaches. Under the trees was heavy growth of barley, wheat, and alfalfa.

Jobar, a little Mohammedan town a few miles northeast from Damascus, is said to be the place where Abraham pursued the kings who had captured Lot. It was called Hobah (see Genesis 14:15) in those days and is also said to be the place where the prophet Elijah survived on the bread that was brought to him by ravens. Also, one can see here the cave that was the prophet's dwelling place. It is also said to be here that he anointed Hasael, king of Syria (see Kings 19:15).

Back to Haifa

On April 18 we took the train back to Haifa. The route leads in a southerly direction east of the Anti-Lebanon Mountains over wide plains that are mostly sown in barley and wheat. Closest to Damascus, the grain suffered drought, but further south it stood nicely, and the broad fields reminded one of the flat lands of eastern Oregon. Many railcars stood at the station loaded with grain, and great stacks of wheat sacks stood at the station as is usually the case in eastern Oregon. There were also great piles of loose grain on the ground. This area is said to be Syria's granary. We passed, from time to time, little towns of mud houses with flat roofs.

In the afternoon, our route took us down through narrow, winding valleys, where the tracks make many curves. Bedouin tents and herds of cattle could be seen here and there. So we passed over the arched bridge that was destroyed by Bedouins some time ago when they robbed the train. At three o'clock, we came down into the Jordan Valley with its green, level grain fields and the Sea of Galilee's enchanting shores to the right, and in passing, got to cast a parting glance to that remarkable sea. Soon we arrived once again at Es-Sakach, where the train stopped and a number of people crowded aboard. Then we continued the journey to Haifa by the same route we had come before. The grain had grown a lot and was forming seed-heads. It was April 18. At six o'clock we arrived in Haifa for the third time and now felt right at home there. We hurried to the post office and found longed-for letters and the *Oregon Posten*, which is always a welcome friend and always gives us good reporting on our homeland.

Samaria

We now directed our travels to Nablus [Shechem] to see how the Samarians would, in a few days, celebrate Easter. We had to ride the same way back to Afulie, where the railroad forked and one branch goes to Nablus. We crossed the plains of Israel, where many battles in the past were fought, and as we approached Samaria's rocky hills, we could see the old town of Dothan on top of one of them. It was here that Joseph came to his brothers, and they sold him to the Ishmaelites (see Genesis 37), and it was in this city that the prophet Elisha was surrounded by Benhadad's armies but was so wonderfully protected by armies of angels (see II Kings 6:13–23).

After an hour's travel, we pass the ruins of the old castle of Samaria, built by Israel's King Omri and which was the capital

for the ten tribes. It was here that King Ahab built a temple to Baal
(see I Kings 16:32–33). In II Kings 16:24–33 there is a description
of the founding of the city and in Kings 17:3–24 how Herod the
Great rebuilt the city and made it resplendent. It was to this city
that Phillip came and preached about Christ and that was a great
joy to the people (see Acts 8:5–8).

That once-so-proud city has decayed to almost nothing but a
pile of ruins with a miserable little Mohammedan village to one
side. The city, which was situated on a round hill, was encircled
by a carriageway about fifty feet broad with granite pillars on both
sides, of which many still stand or lie in the grain fields and olive
groves there, where lively activity, splendor and pomp held sway.
Now, only ruins remain of King Ahab's palace, Herod's temple,
and others. In John the Baptist's church, built in the twelfth century
but now a Mohammedan mosque, are the graves of John the Baptist
and the prophet Obediah as well as John's prison cell, where he sat
captive before his beheading (see Matthew 14:1–12). It is said by
many, however, that it never happened here, but in Herod's palace
Machearus, east of the Dead Sea.

At one we arrived in Nablus, the old Shechem, which got its
new name when rebuilt by Titus Flavius Vespasianus. This city
was once the capital of Palestine. When Abraham came here, the
Canaanites lived in this country (see Genesis 12:6), and this city is
mentioned in Jacob's time (see Genesis 33:34 and 44:5–7; Joshua
20:7; and I Chronicles 6:76). All of Israel assembled here in Joshua's
time (see Joshua 8:30–35), and it was here that the events spoken of
in Revelations 9 took place. A prominent stone block on the hill of
Gerizim is said to be Jotham's pulpit. Rehoboam and Jeroboam met
here when the land of Israel was divided and Shechem became the
capital of Samaria (see I Kings 12:1–25) and became the central point
for the Samaritans' idolatry after the return from captivity. In 132 B.C.

John Hyrcanus invaded the city and destroyed the Samaritans' temple. The city was rebuilt in the twelfth century, and now has a population of about twenty-five thousand, of whom about two hundred are Samaritans. The rest are Mohammedans and Greeks and a few Roman Catholics, Protestants, and Jews.

When the train stopped at the station, a number of half-grown boys rushed in and began to tear at the backpacks. They all wanted to earn some money and they were extremely assertive. We followed along to the only hotel where Europeans stay and got a room and a meal for three dollars per person per day, and it was bad.

The Samaritans' Easter Celebration

After we ate dinner we took ourselves up Mount Gerizim, at whose top the Samaritans hold "Passa" and eat Easter lamb.[105] An hour's wandering up the steep, stony path brought us to the top of the mountain, where thirty white tents were pitched on a somewhat flat area and here lived all of the Samaritans and celebrated the "Passa" holiday twenty-eight days after Good Friday. They leave their homes in town and all the men, women, and children climb the mountain, and pitch their tents and live in them, one family in each tent. They were one hundred fifty-six in number, and forty of them were priests who do no labor and are maintained by the others. This little group is all that is left of the Samaritan people, and are well the only ones who celebrate Passover in accordance with God's command to Israel's people (see Genesis 12:1–20). Jews abandoned it long ago, at least as a people. On the tenth of their month Ahib, which falls about twenty-one days after our Easter, seven white, flawless, year-old rams are chosen. They are washed and cleansed daily until the fourteenth of Ahib when, at

sundown, they are slaughtered and
scalded with hot water, after which
the fleece is plucked off. They are spit-
ted on a wooden skewer and lowered
into a heated pit, like a cistern, six feet
deep where they are left until almost
midnight, when they are lifted out and
the black-burned skin is peeled away.
Then the meat is eaten in great haste,
along with bitter herbs and unleav-

Samaritans' "Passa"

ened bread. The people are dressed for travel and the men form a
procession. Everything left over is burned up in a fire.

Mount Gerizim is twenty-eight hundred fifty feet above sea
level, and there are ruins of a church and a palace built by emperor
Seno in 474 A.D., and a castle that was burned by Justinian in 533 A.D.
There are also ruins of other buildings. A large, smooth stone slab
on the top of the mountain is said by the Samaritans to be the place
where Joshua set up the tabernacle, and a strangely formed stone is
said to be the altar where Abraham sacrificed Isaac. There is no evidence to support these assertions. It was in Siloa that the tabernacle
was raised when the children of Israel came to the land of Canaan
(see Joshua 18:1). And it was on Mount Moria that Solomon's temple
was built and Isaac's sacrifice took place (see Genesis 22:2). That
mountain is, as in Jesus' time, the Samaritans' holiest, and now, as
then, they say that is the place where one should pray.

The Samaritans treated us very well and showed us their codex,
which they said was very old and contained the Pentateuch. To the
north of Mount Gerizim, Mount Ebal rises somewhat higher on the
other side of the narrow valley, and we climbed it too. From here
one has a wonderful panorama of the surrounding landscape of rocky

hills, green valleys with fields of wheat and barley swaying in the breeze, and farthest to the north, the snow-covered Mount Hermon.

At Jacob's Well and Joseph's Grave

If one reads Joshua 8:33–34, one is reminded of what happened here, when the people of Israel were gathered here in the valley between these mountains at Jacob's Well, where Jesus sat and rested when the woman from Sikar came to draw water (see John 7). A Catholic chapel is now built over that well, but we were allowed to go in and see the seventy-five-foot deep well and drink from its fresh water, for which we gave a coin to the priest. A piece north of the well is Joseph's grave (see Joshua 27:32) and it too was overbuilt with a little synagogue, and Jews and Samaritans burn incense to thereby honor Joseph. A little farther to the north on the slopes lies the little rundown town of Sikar, and a little to the west of the well is the little town of Belata. There once stood the famous oak in Shechem (see Genesis 35:4; Joshua 24:26 and Judges 9:6). On a hilltop about twelve miles southeast from Nablus are the ruins of the city of Silo, mentioned in Joshua 18. The priests Eli and Samuel lived here where Joshua raised the tabernacle (see I Samuel 1–4), and after the Ark was removed from Silo, it was left a pile of ruins, because of the sins of Israel's kings (see I Kings 17). These ruins are located a few miles east of the road that runs between Nablus and Jerusalem, and we had to walk up there on a four-mile-long footpath through the wheat fields. We returned to Nablus late in the evening, and in the dim twilight passed through a tract where robbers often attack and rob travelers, and where three Americans were robbed two months previously. We returned to Haifa the next day to prepare for the sea voyage to the northwest. It had begun to get hot already at the end of April; the cornfields had begun to ripen, and the wheat stood in bloom. In some areas the crops were remarkably beautiful, but in others they suffered from drought. The rainfall had been below normal through the winter, and in the spring it seldom rains after March in this country. One day we traveled by train from Haifa to Accra.

In Old Accra

Accra is located ten miles northeast of Haifa on the coast and was, at one time, a heavily fortified city and the most important seaport in Palestine. The strong old city walls with their fortifications bear witness to the city's importance, and, at the present, there are ongoing excavations of a city that for centuries has lain underneath the present one. With the governor's permission, we were allowed to view the excavated streets and buildings.[106]

The road from Haifa to Accra leads along the coast through a beautiful plain that is divided by the Kison River. Accra is mentioned in Judges 1:3, and in Acts 21:7 by the name Ptolemais, in association with Paul's travels to Jerusalem and Caesarea. One day we took a one-hour train ride toward Jaffa, disembarked at a little station on the Plains of Sharon, and wandered a piece to the west, where there was a Jewish colony with good buildings and beautiful fields of vegetables, grain, and potatoes. We continued wandering toward the coast, as Caesarea lies by the sea.

In Caesarea

After a few hours' wandering, we arrived at the ruins of what had been a large city by the sea, with strong protective walls that now are mostly piles of stone. Part of the wall remains. We walked around and viewed the destruction that had befallen this once-so-proud Roman city. It was built by Herod the Great and named Caesarea after Augustus. This city is mentioned several times in the Book of Acts. Here lived Cornelius, who summoned Peter from Jaffa (see Acts 10:11); Peter came here from Jerusalem after the prison doors were opened for him (see Acts 12:19), and Paul landed here after his journey to Greece (see Acts 28:22 and 21:7–16). Later he was brought here from Jerusalem as a prisoner to be interrogated by Felix and Agrippa (see Acts 24 and 25) and he was sent from here to Rome on an Adriatic ship (see Acts 27:27). Now there are only a few who live in the mostly collapsed houses and testify to how impermanent all human works are. We returned after two hours' wandering. We had, that day, walked over twenty miles, and it felt good to board the train and sit down.

Mount Carmel

The next day we undertook a fifteen-mile hike from the west to the eastern end of Mount Carmel, and we walked the ridge, with the Mediterranean on both sides, along a winding mountain path and occasionally met someone riding or herding donkeys. Here and there were goats or sheep grazing on the slopes, and a shepherd with his staff watching over them. From time to time, a fox or a jackal hurried into the brush to hide. We got a longed-for drink of water at a spring under a cleft in a rock where a flock of goats were being watered, and at eleven we came to a Bedouin village where we got another drink of water from a woman, and shortly after noon, we arrived at the sacrificial place on the eastern and highest spot on Mount Carmel at 1,800 feet above sea level. The western end is 500 feet elevation. We had ultimately climbed 1,300 feet higher. Here in front of the Catholic nunnery building was a collection of Bedouins celebrating and performing a sort of dance. Only men were present. We could not find out what the festivities were all about, as the Catholic priests who were there did not speak English; they were Frenchmen. After we got some water and rested a while we began the return trip, after taking a moment to remember the events that took place here when the prophet Elijah and the prophets of Baal sacrificed for the people (see I Kings 18). We walked down to the Plains of Israel and soon passed the well that is probably where the water that drenched the sacrifice was fetched. Farther down in the valley, green with grain fields, the water of Kison River glitters where the prophets of Baal were killed. We had counted on riding the train halfway back, but when we came to the train station, we were told that the train did not stop there, and we had to keep walking. We arrived at Haifa at 8:30, pretty tired after walking more than thirty miles.

Now we have come to the end of our stay in this wonderful land that has so much of interest to captivate the mind and the gaze, and although we surely long to embark on the journey to our fatherland, knowing well that much of great interest is waiting for us, we leave Palestine almost with a sense of loss. We have stayed here over three months, but the time seems to have been too short to see and appreciate all that we wanted to see and should have seen. Although the living conditions were not praiseworthy, but were right difficult sometimes, and we often got food that we could not eat but paid dearly for, we never wearied of the country, and I believe that he who has once seen it, will long to return. We had to linger a few days in Haifa waiting for the steamship, and during that time we made some nice acquaintances, among them a Mr. Struve, Danish by birth, who served as American consul there, and his family, who were all very friendly.[107] We also got to know a Mr. Delbourgo, brother of the Norwegian consul in Beirut,[108] and several Syrian families who did what they could to make us comfortable.

In Egypt, Palestine, and Syria, there prevails much displeasure with the government and general conditions. In Egypt the people want to be free from England's rule, and it is said that England promised them their own government, but people do not much believe it. The Egyptians are mortified that Englishmen and Indian soldiers there should carry out what they themselves want to do. Arabs in Palestine hate the English, for they say that England gives preference to Jews in every area, and the result will be that the Jews will crowd out the Arabs. It appears as if the Englishmen in every country where they have control are threatened with defeat. That is the situation in Africa and India, and how long they can remain on firm ground is hard to say.

The French, who are in control of Syria, are criticized and hated by the Syrians. They are said to be hard and immoral, and they exert a harmful influence on the people and plunder the land. The people of both Palestine and Syria have chosen to come under the governance of the United States, and have 80 percent voted for it, but, they say that the English enticed President Wilson with concessions so that they could hold onto Palestine. I asked an Arab if they could run the country themselves and if Turkey would not re-conquer them. He answered that they have both knowledge and power enough to have their own government and that they no longer feared the Turks. I asked the former consul about the matter, and he gave the answer that if the Arabs acquired self-rule, they would immediately kill all of the Jews in Palestine. People in general seem to feel that America dealt them an injustice when they left them under England's power, and for that they blame President Wilson.

At the Shores of the Mediterranean

We departed from Haifa on May 4 and arrived in Beirut at five o'clock the next morning. We had bought second-class tickets ten days in advance in order to secure cabins, but when we came aboard, we found that there were none left, therefore we had to spend the night on deck in a sitting position. As the weather was balmy, it went quite well. In Beirut we were brought ashore by the

Norwegian consul, whose acquaintance we had made the last time we visited this city. He was not Norwegian but a Spanish Jew, a very friendly and outgoing man.[109]

The centennial of the death of Napoleon was being celebrated in the city that day and they had decorated trucks with flowers for the parade and competed for prizes like in the Rose Festival in Portland. Many beautifully decorated trucks participated, and quite a lot of people were there. Our host led us into a hotel and out onto a balcony where we had the best view of all over the whole thing. We departed at twelve the next day, when our journey continued northward along the west coast of Syria with the snow-covered Lebanon Mountains visible a great deal of the time.

At four o'clock we arrived in Tripoli, which had a beautiful location on the seashore on both sides of the Kadiska River. After three hours' stay in Tripoli, we continued on our way during the nighttime hours. At five o'clock, when we arose and went out on deck, we saw, nearby, a high mountaintop on the coast. We had, in the early morning, passed Latakia [Laodicea], mentioned in Revelation, and later in the morning passed Antioch, mentioned in Acts 11:19–27, and at ten we landed in Alexandretta and lay there until eight o'clock, when the journey continued.

On Sunday, May 8, we landed in Mersin at six o'clock. We did not go ashore because landing was difficult and expensive, so we stayed aboard during the day and had a couple of devotions in our cabins and spent the rest of the day in reading and conversation with our fellow passengers. Old Tarsus, home town of the Apostle Paul, is not so far from Mersin.

On the Island of Cyprus

From Mersin our course led nearly straight south toward Famagusta, on the island of Cyprus, where we arrived at six o'clock in the morning. Shortly before we had passed Salamis, where Paul landed on his mission to the island of Cyprus (see Acts 13:4–5). It had once been an important port city and strongly fortified. Its harbor was the best one north of Alexandria, so the ship could easily reach the dock. We disembarked here and toured the city, which has many ruins of old churches, built in the Middle Ages, which were now more or less collapsed since the Mohammedans took control here, too. A large, splendidly built church that was preserved in fairly good shape still existed, but had been converted to a mosque. The landscape around this place is nearly level. Great orange orchards, where unusually large oranges grow, lie close to the city, and a lot of them were loaded onto our steamship. Here, they are loaded in baskets which are covered with a piece of sackcloth. Also, part of the cargo was potatoes, which are successfully cultivated here. The orchards are irrigated with windmill-powered pumps. They also use waterwheels, like those in Egypt, which are driven by an ox or cow.

At midday we continued our journey along Cyprus' southeast coast, and stepped ashore at Lamaca. At midnight we continued on, and landed at Limaso at 5:30 A.M. After rounding Cape Gatta, we followed the island's coast in a northwesterly direction. We passed Baffo [Paphos], where Paul and Barnabas came after they wandered through the island of Salamis. Proconsul Sergius converted to Christianity after Paul struck blind the wizard Elymas (see Acts 13:1–13). We passed Cape Arnauti, the island's northwest-ernmost point, and continued northwest toward Adalia. We had now rounded the island from northeast to northwest. The Apostles had walked the entire island. Cyprus is 140 miles long and 60 miles broad and has two mountain chains running through it west to east, whose highest point is Mount Trodes, 6,406 feet above sea level.

Half of the island's surface is taken up by the mountains; the rest is flat land and part of that is good agricultural land, where grain is cultivated successfully without irrigation. The climatic conditions are similar to central California. The island's known history dates from 569 A.D. [sic],[110] when the Egyptian pharaoh conquered it, and it has since been the object of many battles and has been held by many different countries. It now belongs to England since Turkey lost its right to it after the war. The population is made up of a mix of Greeks and Arabs, and the number of inhabitants of the island is about 307,000, of whom 214,480 are Greek Orthodox, 56,428 Mohammedans, 1,073 Maronites, and a few Roman Catholics, Jews and Protestants.

The journey continued through the night, and at daylight we sighted land, with snow-covered mountaintops in the distance. In a while we entered the harbor at Adalia, where the coast is quite magnificent, with vertical cliffs above caves and glittering streams that heedlessly cast themselves over the clifftops. We could not dis-embark here, as it is under Italian martial law. It had, before the war, belonged to Turkey, but had since been awarded to Italy.[111] Attalia is mentioned in Acts 14:25 as the departure point for Paul and Barnabas after they had preached and worked wonders in Antioch in Pisidien, Iconium, Derbe, and Lystra, which are located to the north and east of the city (see Acts 14:1–23).

We had expected to stay here only for a few hours. The ship was loaded with wheat and a lot of cheese, and in the evening goats were brought aboard from lighter-boats, brought aboard the ship by means of rope tied around their horns or one leg, and lifted six at a time with a crane. The poor animals struggled and bleated in distress when they were swung upward, but it didn't help. One fell and broke its leg and had to suffer in the heat and over-crowding.

The next morning cattle were loaded in the same way, as well as some sheep that took up half the deck where the passengers would otherwise stroll. At three o'clock, they weighed anchor and the journey continued. We had had to lie at that town for thirty-three hours and used the time for reading, writing, and conversation with other passengers and crew.

We followed the coast of Asia Minor and in the evening passed Myra, where Paul and his fellows changed ships when he was on his journey to Rome (see Acts 27:5–6), and a little later Patra, and early in the morning we caught sight of Rhodes. At six, we laid to at the city of the same name. Those two cities are mentioned in association with Paul's journeys in Acts 21:1. The island of Rhodes belongs to Italy since it was taken from the Turks. Here, as in many places, a load of flour was unloaded, and upon close inspection we saw "Cascade and Portland Mills, Portland, Ore." in big letters on the sacks. It felt like a fond "hello" from our own city, and we were glad that our state's flour even found its way to these foreign shores and fed the many hungry who are here. But think how far it was transported. It probably came through the Panama Canal and was now at least nine thousand miles from its home, just like us. At 1:00 A.M. on May 13, we continued between Smyrna's up-thrust mountain peaks on the right, and one little island after another on the left. Toward evening we sailed past the island of Kos and the city of the same name, mentioned in Acts 21:1. During the night we passed Melitus, where Paul gave his remarkable farewell speech (see Acts 20:17–38), and a bit to the west the little island of Patmos, where John received Revelation (see Revelation 1). To the right, on the mainland, we saw Ephesus, where one of the seven congregations stood, whose "angel" received both encouragement and reproval (see Revelation 2:1–17), and to whom Paul wrote the wonderful epistle (see Ephesians).

We had also passed in the night Trogylium and Smos, and in the morning at daylight we passed Scio (see Acts 20:15), where the passage between the island and the mainland is fairly narrow. We gradually changed course from north to east and southeast, so that we would avoid the projecting Smyrna peninsula. The weather was pleasant and the scenery was splendid. At ten we pulled into Smyrna's calm harbor.

TURKEY

Smyrna is quite a substantial harbor city, and many products are unloaded here from many ships that call here. Among others there was a ship here flying a star-strewn flag that is so dear to all who come from its homeland. Here, on the dock, stood great stacks of flour from Portland, Oregon, and from Canada. From our boat they unloaded the goats that had sailed for three days without water and very little feed. The poor sheep had to travel yet further, starving and thirsting. We stuck some bread crusts in our pockets after dinner to give to them, but what good did it do for so many! We went ashore in Smyrna and wandered for a while in the bustling city along narrow, crooked streets that were partly taken up with vendors of various sorts. There was a little trolley line, whose cars are drawn by horses and mules, and several large grandiose mosques. The Greeks have been in control here since the war, but a sharp conflict goes on right now, one hundred fifty miles inland, between the Turks and the Greeks, and there is a danger that the Greeks might lose. It was to the "angel" of the congregation of this town that the encouraging letter was sent, that is found in Revelation 2:8–11, and Philadelphia and Sardis are located not far from here (see Revelation 3:1–13).

At 6:00 A.M. we resumed our journey, and during the night passed Thyatira and Pergamum, mentioned in Revelation 2:12–28, and the island of Miletus and the cities of Assos and Troas, which are mentioned in Acts 20: 6–38. It was in Miletus that Paul gave his great farewell speech that can be read in Acts 20:17–38 and following verses, and it was in Troas that he revived the youth who had fallen from the third floor and was assumed to be dead (see Acts 20: 7–12).

Through the Dardanells

At eight in the morning of May 15, we came to the mouth of the Dardanelles passage. It was here that three thousand of England's army, consisting mostly of soldiers from Australia, Canada, and India, fell in the fruitless attempt to storm ashore. On the heights can be seen many graveyards in which the fallen lie buried. One English and one French warship lie sunk outside the fortifications at the entry itself, and the fortress walls are badly damaged by shells and bombs. Yes, it was in truth a terrible and destructive war, whose effects we have seen in France, Egypt, Palestine, Syria and now even here. We sailed through the fairly narrow sound and saw then the beautiful yellow-and-blue flag floating from the stern of a steamer. It was the first we had seen on our journey, and it came to me like a whisper of my homeland and its beauty. It was at the fortress at the Dardanelles that in olden times, Leander swam the entry, over three-quarters of a mile, and the same feat was carried out again by Lord Byron about a hundred years ago.[112] The shores along the sound have natural beauty and the vegetation on the banks were more luxuriant than we had seen in recent days. The coast and the islands had, before, been mostly rocky and stony with little greenery. It was the second Sunday we had spent on this ship and we used the day for morning prayers and a period of reflection on the day's texts.

In Constantinople

We landed at Constantinople on Monday morning, but a thick fog hid the city from our gaze. After we disembarked, we hurried to find the American consul and received a friendly reception, and got our passports in order. That afternoon we couldn't get much done, as it was a Turkish holiday, but we went aboard the ship and saw them unload the poor sheep and cattle that had been without feed or water for five days. Some sheep had been trampled to death. The next morning we hurried to the Italian consulate to get our visas, for we had now decided to continue our trip on the same steamer to Trieste, Italy. We had hoped that we could travel by train from Constantinople to Germany to save time, but after inquiring with the consuls and the railroad station, we found that it was very difficult and expensive. It was really crowded in the Italian consulate, so it took a lot of time, for we had to visit four different departments to get our passports stamped. In the afternoon, we had to go to another bureau to get the right to leave Constantinople, and there were still worse crowds here and there. We stood in the crush for an hour, but had to leave to go aboard the ship. You see, it was to sail at three o'clock. It would pass through the Bosporus to Kavoka near the Black Sea and we wanted to go along and see the narrow passage between the Sea of Marmara and the Black Sea, highly praised for its natural beauty. Arriving onboard, we found out that the ship wasn't to depart before four o'clock. I hurried back to the office to get the right to depart. The crowd was frightful, and as I stood and got knocked to and fro, I became aware that my vest was open. I buttoned it quickly, and eventually my turn came to present our passports, whereupon I was asked where the photographs were. I showed that they were on the passports. "They are not enough," was the answer, "You must have one more to be left here. Come back tomorrow at nine o'clock and bring the portraits." I hurried out and ran to the harbor with the thought of sailing with the boat, but it had already set out. What could I do now? The girls were on the boat, two single girls and no other passengers. We had to be at the bureau with the pictures the next morning, and now both the girls and the pictures were gone. I stood there alone and could not do anything. I asked a watchman when the boat would return and he answered "Probably sometime tomorrow." "What time?" I asked. He made the characteristic Italian shrug of the shoulders and answered "Maybe tomorrow noon, maybe tomorrow night." With that information I became dejected in fear that we would have to stay another couple of weeks longer and would not make it to Sweden to the longed-for midsummer time, if the boat did not come back in time for us to get the passports in order. It was my intent to travel to Kavoka on another boat, but I stuck my hand into my vest pocket, where I had the steamship tickets to Italy, and found to my horror that they, that had cost $300.00, were gone. I felt to see if my wallet, in which I had our traveler's checks and about $700.00 in cash,[13] were gone too but it was still there, and that gave some relief, for I still had enough to reach our goal. I hurried immediately to the office where I had bought the tickets to report the matter. When I walked into the office, sweaty and hot, the clerk told me that they had just telephoned from the company's other office, that my tickets had been found on the floor, and if I went there I could have them. Naturally, I was delighted and hurried there and got them immediately.

Now I hurried down to the harbor, but was given to know that no boat was leaving Kavoka before ten o'clock the next day. I was taken up with the anxiety that we would have to lie in this wretched city for two weeks, but I was left alone and could do nothing. I wandered up and down the streets and did not know what to do. So, I came to an open, vacant area on a steep slope, and since it seemed to be some sort of historic place, I went that way. Here stood some individual trees and stones lay spread around. I found that it was an old graveyard and the stones were gravestones. Here and there was a dirty, ragged man sleeping, and a group of people were eating food they'd brought with them, between the old gravestones. I threw myself down on a little green patch and prayed God for help and advice, and that everything would turn out well. It calmed my troubled mind, and I sat for a while thinking of what the people who had been laid to rest in this ground had been, and what they believed. However, I had not much time to sit, sunken in these thoughts. The sun had sunk behind the hill and I had to seek some kind of refuge for the night. I went from one hotel to another, but either the price was too unreasonable, or they were full. I chanced, at last, to walk by the Y.M.C.A., and stepped in and asked for lodging. They said they had a room for $1.60 for the night. I was shown to a little room several floors up, with a little bed (cot) and a chair for furniture. I was tired and quickly fell asleep. At two o'clock I was awoken by a great noise. It sounded like hundreds of dogs howling all around. After that a loud report that was quickly followed by more, and I began to believe enemies had landed and had begun bombing the fortress. At four I went back to sleep and slept soundly until six o'clock. I heard that the Turks were having some sort of festivity, and were firing off the shots that I heard.[114] At nine o'clock I went down to the harbor, and, to my joy, our steamer came slowly gliding in. I saw my girls standing at the railing looking for me, too. I called out to them to hurry down as fast as possible and bring along the photographs. As luck would have it they had them handy and soon we were on our way to the passport bureau, but it was noon before everything was straightened out.

We were glad we could take the boat, where we still had our things, and we thanked God with all our hearts for His help and wonderful guidance in our hour of trouble. Many had to remain in Constantinople for many days before they got their visas.

The Bosporus

And how was the girls' trip up the Bosporus? We'll let them tell it themselves:

"The Bosporus is a narrow, sixteen-mile-long sound that connects the Sea of Marmara with the Black Sea. We left Constantinople at 4:00 P.M. and soon passed, among others, three American warships, and it was nice to see our beautiful, star-strewn flag in this foreign land. On a hill between green trees, one can see beautiful white buildings that are said to be the American Roberts College.[115] It is like the institution of higher learning in Beirut and is, and has been, of great use to seekers of knowledge in these lands. It has a very lovely location. The passage up the Bosporus is very narrow and winding. The sloping banks are decorated with green trees, and between them were big, beautiful houses. After an hour's travel we were in Kavoka, our destination, where we could see the Black Sea in the fading light. That night we laid ourselves calmly to rest, but awakened at four o'clock with coughing and stinging eyes and heard how people ran up the stairs and banged on our door and shouted that we must come out, which we did as fast as we could. The reason was that they were smoking the boat with sulfur, for there was word of contagious sickness in Alexandretta when the boat was there. It was cold up on deck, but we were glad to escape the awful smoke. In an hour we could go back to bed. In the morning the boat returned to Constantinople."

Constantinople is a city of over one million people and has a beautiful location around the northern end of the Sea of Marmara. Part of the city is sited on steep slopes. Unfortunately we had no time to see much of it, but we rode the trolley over the Golden Horn on the Galata Bridge to the St. Sofia mosque, formerly a Christian church, and it is said to be the largest and most beautiful after St. Peter's in Rome.

As it was a Mohammedan holy day, some hundreds of Mohammedans were praying, all the while assuming various body positions. In each corner of the temple stand two granite pillars, brought there from the temple of the sun at Ba'albek in Syria. In one pillar is a gouge where it is said that Mohammed chopped it with his sword, and Mohammedans stick their fingers in it and then stroke them over their eyes and faces. Another pillar is said to have healing powers, and the sick seek it for cures. We also went to the museum, where a number of interesting things are to be found, but were not allowed in because it was a holiday. We went up in the Galata Tower, located on a height, and from there we saw almost the entire city in a few minutes' time; a quick way to see Constantinople that otherwise would have taken several days.[116] In addition we rode the trolley through the Galata tunnel, which brings people to and from Pera, which lies on the highland and where the hotels and European office buildings to the greatest degree are situated.

We went to the Swedish consul, too, who met us very cordially and looked over our passports, which he found to be in good shape for entry to Sweden.

On May 19, we weighed anchor, and the trip to Italy had its beginning. When we came out through the Dardanelles, we set our course for Kavalla, formerly Neapolis, which is mentioned in Acts 16: 11, and we now followed the same route that Paul and Timothy travelled when they sailed from Troas to Neapolis. We passed the islands of Lemnos, Imbros, Samatracia, and Thasa, and came to Kavalla [Neapolis] at six in the evening on May 20. The boat lay there until the next day and loaded tobacco. Philippi, mentioned in Acts 16: 12–40, lies not too far from here.

GREECE

On Sunday morning, May 22, we entered the city of Thessalonika's calm harbor (now called Salonika), mentioned Acts 17: 1–9. We went ashore and first sought out the St. Sophia church, for we did not know if there were any Protestant churches in this city. A mass was going on, with reading, song, and ceremonies, among others the kissing of a lot of Saint's pictures [icons]. They celebrated communion, too, and those who wanted to participate went forth to the altar, and the splendidly dressed priest gave them bread but no wine. After it was done we went to another Greek Orthodox church where mass was going on grandly. There were a lot of ceremonies here too. A men's chorus presented some good singing. Then we went up the street a piece to the triumphal arch, one of the old gates in the city wall that is now embellished with beautiful artwork. We turned a corner where there stood a Greek Evangelist church and walked that way, and heard powerful, beautiful communal singing.[117] The church, which only had seating for about a hundred people, was tightly filled with attentive listeners. First there was a little Sunday school and after that song, Bible reading, prayer, and then a sermon. I had a Swedish Bible with me, and a nice man behind looked up the passages that were read so that we could follow along.

The city of Thessalonica sits at the upper end of the Thermaic Gulf [of Salonica], and the landscape around about is fairly level lowland. The city is fairly extensive and has a trolley system and is like an American city. We noticed that the red Turkish cap wasn't seen so much, and the churches seemed more pleasant when men bared their heads. The Greeks are, in general, shorter, thinner, and less robust than the people in Egypt and Palestine. In the afternoon we busied ourselves with Bible meditation, prayer, and song in my cabin, as I had it alone. We talked for a while with a Mrs. Tsilka, who, together with Miss Stone, were kidnapped in 1902 and held captive by Macedonian brigands.[118] A sum of $60,000, raised in America, had to be paid to get them released after six months stay among raw, ignorant people. During that time she became mother to a child. She praised President Roosevelt, who had recommended the collection of the ransom money, and even the American people for their readiness to help. Mrs. Tsilka had traveled to America in 1893, educated herself as a nurse and a doctor, was married in 1901, and returned to Albania in the company of her husband. She was kidnapped on a trip to Macedonia. Miss Stone was a missionary. For a time after her release, she traveled to America and gave a number of lectures.

In Old Athens

We left Salonika at 5:00 P.M. and followed the east coast of Greece. The following night we went ashore at Piraeus, and went from there to Athens. We rode a taxi to the top of the Acropolis, which lies five hundred feet above sea level. It had once been the capital for the Athenian kings, but since the time of Pericles, about 500 B.C., the Acropolis has been devoted to service to the gods. Of the sights at the Acropolis we want to name Propylaea, the gateway itself. A broad stairway of marble leads up the mountain to this gate, and just within is the temple of Nike. Built long before the time of Christ, it was restored in 1835. Stones, pillars, and statues are in a Turkish fortress, where the Turks took them.

After that we came to the remarkable Parthenon, the world's most beautiful building, so it's said. I shall not even try to describe this building, as it is all too magnificent. When Athens was at the height of its glory, a statue of Athena, the city's protective goddess, stood in this temple. It was made of gold and ivory, stood thirty-nine feet high, and was a work of Phidias, one of the ancient world's foremost sculptors. The Parthenon was finished in 437 B.C., and was in good shape until something over two hundred years ago. The Turks ruled Athens at the time, and they used the Parthenon as an ammunition dump. An army from Venice besieged Athens in 1687, and a bomb struck the Parthenon then. This wonderful temple that had stood for two thousand years was badly damaged. Even in its present condition, it is impressive, and its site is outstanding. It is the crown of the Acropolis. A third temple on the Acropolis is the so-called Erectheion. In the one part, the roof is supported by six goddesses instead of the usual pillars. Inside there was once a statue of Pallas Athena. It was made of olive wood, and, as no one knew where it came from, it was believed to have fallen from the sky. On the slopes below the Acropolis one can see the ruins of many buildings. There was a Bacchus theater and Odeon, and a Roman theater, not to mention others. Not far from here is the Dionysius theater. It was constructed of white marble and erected in 40 B.C., and had seating for thirty thousand spectators. Orator and legislator Lycurgus lived then, and Aeschylus, Sophocles, Euripides, and Aristotle educated the Greek people with their stage plays. Here the Greek drama reached the height of its heyday.

Not far from the Acropolis is the temple of Theseus. It is the best preserved of all the Greek temples, and still stands with walls, roof, and pillars in fairly good shape. It was already there in 500 B.C. Theseus was a legendary Greek hero who, later, was elevated to demi-god. On the slopes that lead to the Acropolis is Mars Hill or Areopagus, mentioned in Acts 17. Court proceedings were conducted here in the open air. It was here that Paul made a speech, and here, near the pagan temple, he said, among other things, "God does not live in a temple that was made by human hands." Paul was a bold man. Indeed there were not many who had faith in his words, but his words have gone out into the world, and nations have listened and listen to them yet today, long after the Athenian temple and gods have lost their glory and eminence. The Athens of today is well built and has good sanitation. All of the modern comforts are here and the Acropolis affords an outstanding view of the city and its harbor. At five o'clock, we set off once more, and that night we sailed close to the coast at Mount Olympus, and then followed the coast between islands and past headlands and skerries. From time to time we passed a little city or town lying on a mountain slope, or sometimes on the top of a high hill. Here and there we saw grain fields. Fruit trees, olives in particular, are commonly planted on the slopes.

Our journey continued, and after a couple of hours we came to the Corinthian Canal, completed four years ago. By passing through that canal we saved twenty-four hours travel time, and although it costs large sums of money for the steamer to sail through, it pays off in savings of coal and time. The canal is three miles long and cuts through an approximately one-hundred-meter high ridge. The canal's walls are mainly stone. It is about sixty feet broad. When we emerged from the canal into the Gulf of Corinth, we could see the city of Corinth to the south. We are reminded of the events that took place here during Paul's missionary journeys, spoken of in Acts 18: 1–18. Then we continued to travel along the narrow gulf via Patras to the Island of Corfu, which belongs to Greece. The city of Corfu is well fortified and has a beautiful location. Some miles to the south of the city is a house built for the Empress of Austria, and later belonged to the Kaiser of Germany.[119]

In Albania

The following day we came to Valona [Vlore] in Albania. We had now sailed around the coast of Greece and between the many Islands for many days. Greece is a beautiful, romantic country with alternating rocky shores and islands, but there are also lovely plains and valleys. They were just harvesting the grain, but the only harvesting equipment we saw were sickles, mostly used by women. We stopped for a few hours in Valona. It was here that the Italians tried to invade Albanian territory, but had to turn back in shame and defeat, for the brave Albanians were their equals.[120] However, the city of Valona was burned, so that on the hill where the city once stood there remained only ruins. A new city has been built below the hill. We sailed across the southern end of the Adriatic Sea to Brindisi, and for some hours we were out of sight of land. At four o'clock we landed at the excellent harbor of Brindisi, and we recognized it immediately. It felt like we were much closer to home as everything was much more like the cities in the western countries. Broad, straight, clean streets and merchants in shops and one went inside when one wanted to make purchases. In eastern cities, one mostly had to stand out on the street to do business.

ONCE AGAIN IN ITALY

At ten o'clock, or more rightly said, at nine, for we had to turn our watches back an hour, we continued our voyage, and the next morning sailed into the harbor at Bari. We disembarked and went to the St. Nicholas church, where they hold mass and communion. The communicants received bread only. The priest himself drank all the wine. St. Nicholas is buried in a crypt that once constituted the church. Above his grave is an altar, where the pious Catholics prefer to pray and receive communion. We wandered around in the city for a while and saw some of the broad, modern streets and houses, and everything looked clean and orderly. However in another part of the city it was old, narrow, crooked, dirty streets, and the people were ill-mannered in their habits. After a few hours we set out again, steered our course straight toward Trieste and sailed for twenty-eight hours without stopping (the longest at a stretch since we left Haifa), and arrive at Trieste on May 28.

In Trieste

Before the war, this territory belonged to Austria. We succeeded in getting rooms in a private home, for the hotels were overfull. We were a little sorry to have traveled away from fresh oranges, but we cheered up when we saw great mounds of cherries and straw-berries for sale at a cheap price. We bought some and ate them, and remembered Oregon and the good berries there.

The next day, which was a Sunday, we sought out a German Lutheran church and attended services there. It was a big, beauti-ful church, but only about fifty people had found their way there. Although we did not understand what was being said, we could hear that the pastor preached with fire.

Trieste is a modern city with broad streets and good buildings, and has over two hundred thousand residents. It is beautifully situ-ated at the northeastern end of the Adriatic Sea. We made a trip by trolley car to Opcina, a town located on a height a few miles from Trieste. The rail line there is, for part of the way, fairly steep and a cog-locomotive is used where it was steepest. The view from that eminence over the city, the sea, and the surrounding landscape is magnificent. The trees, grass, and farmland were so healthy and green after a recent, refreshing rain. It is so nice where it sometimes rains even in the summer, as it is so refreshing. We had to get our passports stamped in Trieste in order to travel through Austria and Germany; therefore we sought out the consulates for those coun-tries. They were very friendly and helpful, particularly when they found out that we were Swedish-American. They especially like the Swedish people and even want to be friends with Americans. The German consul lamented that he was required to charge so much to stamp our passports, but because America took so much from the Germans, namely $10.00, that Germany, therefore, took the same. Still, he knocked off almost nine dollars off of our three visas, but the Austrian consulate took full price.

At ten o'clock on May 31, the train departed to carry us to Germany, but it stood still more than half the time and we never found out why. Indeed, we were in Italy, where there was no hurry; one gets going eventually anyway. The trip over the Alps was beautiful. Its mountain ranges reminded us of some parts of Oregon; partly of the coast range on the way to Tillamook, and partly of southern Oregon's mountain passes and high altitude forests, and even of Switzerland's green heights and valleys. It rained a little bit during the day, so that the clouds concealed the mountaintops, but we saw many on which there was plenty of snow.

AUSTRIA, GERMANY, DENMARK

We only made it to Villach, Austria, the first day, so we stayed there overnight and continued the next morning, arriving in Munich the night of the second day.

We stayed in Munich overnight at a hotel for eleven marks per person (only twenty cents), and even the food was cheap. The following day we passed Leipzig in the morning and arrived in Wittenberg that night, stayed there over night until the afternoon of the following day, and saw all the sights there.

In Luther's City

In a square near the hotel where we stayed stood two big statues of Luther and Melanchton. The next morning we saw the so-called Luther House, that had been Luther's home and was yet unchanged and in good condition, although the floor was beginning to develop rot. The simple, old furniture was still there. We visited the All Saints Church, where Luther posted the famous ninety-five theses, which was the beginning of the Reformation. The pulpit from which Luther so many times proclaimed the Bible's truth still remains. Luther and Melanchton lie buried on either side of the pulpit.

In Berlin

Our journey continued from Wittenberg to Berlin, where we stayed for a few days and bought clothes, of which we were in great need, for we had nearly worn out our American clothes. Also, Germany is one of the cheapest countries where one can buy such things. The Germans are optimistic, although they had countless losses in the war. They are frugal and hard-working, and believe that in time they will come back on their feet again. Everything looked inviting and pleasant, and although the greater part of the people were simply dressed, they were clean and good-looking. The land is beautiful and bears good harvests. We also saw beautiful, well-tended forest tracts. Berlin is a large, well-built city with fine, broad streets and beautiful parks. The much-praised street "Unter den Linden" seemed very inviting.[121]

From Berlin to Copenhagen

After several days stay in Berlin, we continued on our way by train to Warnemünde, then by steamer to Zealand, and from there by train to Copenhagen. We traveled through fertile, well-kept fields with cows in long rows grazing on clover fields, and looking very contented. In Copenhagen there is plenty of milk, which had been in short supply for us for a long time. Milk was especially lacking in Germany, and there was even a shortage of bread. Germany must send so many cows to France in compensation, and could not buy flour from America for a long time. We traveled by steamer to Malmö, and were glad to be spared the worry and trouble with passports for a while.

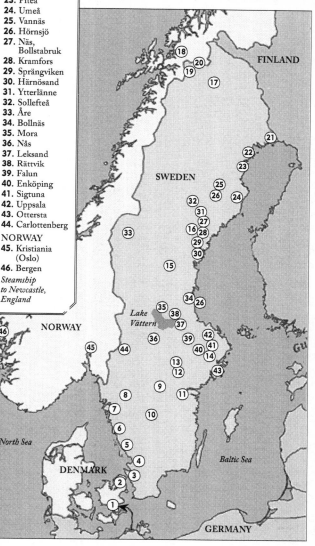

TRAVELS ACROSS SCANDINAVIA

Key to the Route:

Steamship from Germany to Denmark
1. Zealand
2. Copenhagen

SWEDEN
3. Malmö
4. Lund
5. Heberg
6. Frillesås, Halland
7. Gothenburg (Göteborg)
8. Trollhättan
9. Motala
10. Jönköping
11. Norrköping
12. Strångsjö
13. Katrineholm
14. Stockholm
15. Bräcke
16. Bollstabruk
17. Kiruna

NORWAY
18. Narvik

SWEDEN
19. Abisko Jokk
20. Torneträsk
21. Haparanda
22. Luleå

23. Piteå
24. Umeå
25. Vannäs
26. Hörnsjö
27. Näs, Bollstabruk
28. Kramfors
29. Sprängviken
30. Härnösand
31. Ytterlänne
32. Sollefteå
33. Åre
34. Bollnäs
35. Mora
36. Nås
37. Leksand
38. Rättvik
39. Falun
40. Enköping
41. Sigtuna
42. Uppsala
43. Ottersta
44. Carlottenberg

NORWAY
45. Kristiania (Oslo)
46. Bergen

Steamship to Newcastle, England

To England

FINLAND

SWEDEN

NORWAY

Lake Vättern

North Sea

DENMARK

Baltic Sea

GERMANY

SWEDEN

In Malmö and Lund

Malmö is a well-situated city with broad, clean streets and good buildings. The statue of Gustavus Adolphus, which stands in the square of the same name, evoked many strange thoughts, and most of all we thought of how he sacrificed his life for the sake of the Reformation.[122]

From Malmö we undertook a trip to Rydsgård, in Skåne, to deliver two paintings to the sisters of one of our friends in Stockholm, Kansas, who sent them with us. After one night's stay, we returned to Malmö and traveled from there to Lund. Here, we turned our steps toward the beautiful and impressive cathedral. The church's dome rests on eighteen pillars, and there are, in that church, a number of precious vessels, icons, works of sculpture, etc. It was built in 1080, but has since been added to several times. Underneath the cathedral there is the so-called "Crypt," where there is also a

Lund's Cathedral

well with the best water. Among the noteworthy things to be seen there are pictures of the giant, Finn, and his wife. According to an old monk's story, Finn signed a contract to build Lund's cathedral. He would have, in return, "the sun, the moon, or St. Lars' eyes," as long as he couldn't guess Finn's name before the church was completed. The day before everything was finished, St. Lars happened to walk past Finn's home, where his giant wife calmed her screaming children with these words, "Tonight the giant, Finn, will come home with the bishop's eyes and the sun and the moon." And when the bishop shouted to Finn, using his name, the giant and his wife came rushing down into the crypt in a rage to knock down the temple, but at St. Lars' word, they were turned to stone. According to another tale, the church will never be finished, and that was Finn's revenge.[123]

We wandered through the botanical garden, too, that contained a number of rare trees and plants. The journey continued, then, along the coastal route. In the beginning we saw flat, beautiful farmland, but farther north it was hillier and more forested. Everything looked orderly and homey, and people were friendly and courteous.

A Visit to Halland

We stayed for a few days at Hedberg, and visited with friends from Portland, Oregon, the Carl Bernsons', who came to Sweden eleven years ago to farm, and they seem to be doing pretty well. We got to eat strawberries and some good Swedish food. We went to the church on Sunday where a good sermon was delivered to a fairly large congregation. After three days' stay we continued on to Frillesås, Halland, where we, again, stopped and wandered out into the countryside for an hour along a beautiful valley with bare rocky heights to Joel Nilson's family home to convey a greeting to his aging father and brother from the son in America.

In Gothenburg

We continued on to Gothenburg [Göteborg], where we looked up Mr. Forsman's home. He is a brother of Mrs. Swenson in St. Helens, Oregon, and we conveyed warm greetings. We were very well-received, and Mr. Forsman accompanied us the next day on a tour through the city. It is a beautiful place and has much of interest for the traveler.

Through the Göta Canal

The next day we sailed on a Göta Canal steamer up the Göta River to Trollhättan, where several high locks raise boats to the water level of Lake Vänern. At that previously so rich waterfall there is now a large power plant, from which electric power is led to Gothenburg and other places. We disembarked and followed a path along the river in order to better appreciate the wonderful things to see. We even got to go in and see the power plant with its mighty machinery. The path we followed is called "path of love."[124] Toward evening we arrived in Vänersborg, where the Göta River begins at Lake Vänern, which we crossed during the night. At 2:00 A.M., we arrived at the first lock in the canal that connects Lake Vänern with Lake Vättern. Here we followed one lock after another, to a total of fifteen, and it looks really strange to travel through that canal that lies higher than the surrounding land. The canal is very narrow, so that the boat almost fills it to the brim. This remarkable canal was built about a hundred years ago and is truly a masterwork. It was a great undertaking for the small, poor country that Sweden was.[125] The surrounding landscape is fairly flat, and beautifully varied with fields, pastures, and woodland. It was already becoming full daylight by 2:00 A.M., and a cuckoo was heard in a nearby grove. We passed one red-painted, white-trimmed cabin after another, and now and then, a little town, and sometimes a drawbridge over the canal, rolled to one side with a crank turned by a man or a woman.

Motala and Jönköping

The next day we arrived at Motala at 4:00 A.M., went ashore, and looked up G. H. Ekström's mother, and brought greetings from her son in Warren.[126] After some conversation, we went our way on another steamer along Lake Vättern in a southerly direction to Jönköping. We left Motala at ten o'clock, and landed at Jönköping at eight in the morning. We went and found Miss Lönegren's lovely home, and were very cordially received and entertained. We had a few hours of pleasant stay in their comfortable home, in conversation on every subject, not the least about her brother, Pastor F. W. Lönegren in Portland, Oregon, and of his noble striving to disseminate a good and useful newspaper that spreads enlightenment to so many Swedish-American homes in the (as it seems from here) far distant west.[127]

Jönköping is a well-situated and beautiful city, with nearly thirty thousand residents. We travelled on by train to Norrköping, passing through Nässjö, Lindköping, and other places. The landscape is beautiful and varied with lovely valleys and forested heights. It was partly stony, poor land, and partly good flat land. We remembered the story of the heather in poor Småland, for it did look stone-bound and thin in many places. However, everything looked pleasant and well-ordered where there was a red-painted cabin in the woods. Here and there a little lake offered a pleasant change.

Norrköping

Norrköping, which is a significant town with over fifty-six thousand people, has rich access to water power that drives many factories. I had been to Norrköping with my father one time when I was seven years old. We rode the five Swedish miles [thirty American miles] from Strångsjö during the night to be at the square in Norrköping in the morning. I wandered now to that square and recognized the place, although several new buildings have been built around it. Now it is stone-paved where there had been only sand. I recognized the place where my father parked his wagon and sold potatoes and other produce, and I remember how poor women and children came and asked for something. My father let no one walk away empty-handed. An uncle lived in Norrköping at that time, and I tried in vain to find out something about my relatives.

The Old Childhood Home

From Norrköping we traveled to Strångsjö, got off of the train, and wandered into the countryside between forest groves and green meadows to Nästorpstugan, an old red-painted cabin that my father built and where I was born. Before I arrived, I recognized the road and the big stone block that lay next to it. Everything was the same, except that the cabin had been sided with boards since then, but inside it was just as in my childhood, and many childhood memories rolled out at the sight of the old childhood home. Many prayer

Nästorpstugan in 2015 was still painted red. (Courtesy Lars Nordström)

meetings took place here, and the neighbor children assembled here on Sundays for a Sunday school that my parents began and ran. It was the first in these parts. But then my parents were told to quit holding prayer meetings in their home, or move. They chose the latter and immigrated to America.

We travelled on to Katrineholm. It was Saturday, June 18. We stayed there over Sunday, and rode by automobile out to Stora Malm church Sunday morning, and participated in services there. It was in that church that I was taken into God's society through holy baptism, and it was in the yard outside that church that I, as a boy, heard Pastor Ahlberg hold a gripping sermon, to which thousands of people listened with rapt attention.[128] Now we got to hear a good sermon from the former Court Chaplain Beskow, who had care of this congregation.

On the Way to the Midnight Sun

The next day we traveled to Stockholm, where we made only a short stop, for we wanted to hurry toward the north to celebrate

Midsummer there, and see the Midnight Sun. We only visited a Mrs. Carlson, sister to the late P. A. Anderson in Elgarose, Oregon. The next day we resumed our trip to the north through conifer and deciduous forests, and green fields, and sometimes passed a clear lake or a gurgling creek. We rode through Uppsala, Sala, Krylbo, Okelbo, and at 9:30 in the evening, we arrived at Bräcke, where we stayed overnight to continue the next morning to Långsele. Here we changed trains, and after travelling for a while, we arrived at Bollstabruk at the line between Sollefteå and Härnosand. Here we stayed in the home of August Wedin, Signe Ekström's uncle.

The next day was Midsummer Eve. They hoisted the blue-and-yellow flag, and a festive atmosphere prevailed everywhere. That night we wandered out to a forest grove, where, on a cliff, overlooking a beautiful bay, sat and awaited the midnight hour and sang one song after another. It was so lovely and bright. On Midsummer Day, we sought out a church and quite a lot of people had assembled. The next morning, we traveled yet further north through Norrland's magnificent landscape. Near Sollefteå we passed over the cascading Ångerman River, and near Vännäs, the Ume River, and at Bastuträsk, the Skellefte River. Then we crossed the Pite River and the Lule River. At Boden the track divided and we traveled northward. We rode the whole night, but it was bright as day.

In Kiruna at the Arctic Circle

We passed through Gällivara and continued to Kiruna, arriving there at seven o'clock Sunday morning. We attended church services in the mid-morning, and at a mission house in the afternoon, and that evening we listened to a temperance lecture in the church presented by David Östlund, who had been in America for several years working in the Temperance Movement.[129] His lecture was outstanding. He described the Temperance Movement in America from its beginning until it finally won victory. His view was that the cause could be driven through just as easily in Sweden, if the same method was followed, namely that all of the Christian societies and other friends of Prohibition worked together. On Monday night, he once again gave a lecture in the Salvation Army hall, and that one was excellent, too.

In the course of the day we had gone to Kirunavaara and saw how the ore was dynamited out of the mountain, how it was then carried by tram to the crusher, which with unbelievable power crushed the hard chunks of iron ore, and how, at last, the ore runs down into railcars in which it is transported to Narvik in Norway, and there emptied into steamships that carried it mainly to Germany to be smelted and fabricated. A long train carrying ore to Narvik departs every hour.

At eleven o'clock at night we walked to Mount Lussevaara, which is an unimaginably rich mountain of iron ore, a half-hour from town, as we wanted to see the Midnight Sun from its top. It had been foggy and rainy the two days we had been in Kiruna, but now toward evening, it had cleared up. The sun shone so clearly! We were delighted now that we had reached the goal for our questionable expectations. The next day we continued onwards to Narvik, and as that is the end of the line, we could go no further by train.

Narvik is a city of perhaps five thousand residents, and their income derives from iron ore, freighted from Sweden's mines and loaded onto ships here. Huge docks and loading cranes have been erected here for that purpose. Narvik lies between Norway's mountains, and the landscape is absolutely desolate and wild with sparse vegetation. We returned to Abisko Jokk, the Nordic Tourist

Society station, a few miles from the Swedish border, and stayed there a day and a night. It was fairly expensive to stay here, namely $4.00 a day.

Lapp Camp at Torneträsk

From there we took a boat tour to Torneträsk, to a Lapp camp at Pålnovik, where nine Lapp families lived in the same number of "kåtor," (singular is kåta) which are built of timber stood vertically, round in shape with a hole in the top like an Indian "teepee." The smoke rises from the fire in the middle of the floor, with the family members sitting around it on a floor consisting of birch branches on the ground. Women, children and old men stay here and live a primitive lifestyle without furniture or household goods. Only a few cooking pots lie on the floor. The younger men were up in the Norwegian mountains, guarding the reindeer herds. Lapps are small and slim-built like Chinese, and go around dressed in tunics and pointed caps. They make small trinkets out of reindeer horn and reindeer skin, and sell them to the tourists. They live up in the north near the mountains in the summer, and when the snow has fallen and the lakes are frozen over, they set reindeer before sleds, into which women, children, etc., are stuffed, and drive them to milder tracts at Jockmock and Kvikjock, where there are churches and schools for the Lapps.

Toward Haparanda

Our journey continued then, back the same way we had come, past Kiruna to Boden, where the line branches. The one line goes to Haparanda, and we continued on that one. A half-hour before we got there, many people came aboard the train. They had different appearances and different clothing from what one usually sees in these parts. They crowded into the car and spoke a language we could not understand, but we learned then that they were Finns on their way to Haparanda for a big Laestadian meeting.[130] They were less refined in their ways, and both men and women were so given to smoking that the conductor had to speak to them quite sharply before they stopped doing it. You see, smoking was forbidden in that car. Later, we visited their meeting, which was held in a big warehouse that had been temporarily set up for it and had room for several thousand persons. It was completely filled with people. They mostly preached in Finnish here, that was freely translated into Swedish, sometimes by a woman, and sometimes by a man.

When the preaching had gone on for a while, a woman jumped up and began to shout and scream full-throatedly and clap her hands. What she said was unintelligible. Soon another one sprang up and began hopping and stamping and screeching, and it went on like that until ten of them made so much noise that you couldn't hear what the preacher said. At last, even a man jumped up and began to howl. The preacher finished his sermon, a psalm was struck up, and eventually the noise died down. Another speaker stepped up, and soon there was the same ruckus again. After the meeting I asked someone what it all meant, and they answered that it was God's Spirit that was working on them, so that they could not keep quiet and sit still. I referred them to the Apostle Paul's admonition to the congregation, in I Corinthians 14, that everything should go orderly at their meetings and when one spoke, the rest should keep silent. But they did not want to listen to anything but their own prattle, and I remember what Luther said to those who pretended that they were so strongly moved by the Holy Spirit, and so far as I could tell about these women, they really believed that they were extraordinary and wanted to show it.

I sought out the Lutheran pastor and had a talk with him on the matter, and he seemed to think the same as I did. A prominent Laestadian happened to be visiting the pastor at the same time, and he tried to defend the Laestadians, their teachings and their practices, and maintained that Laestadius, from whom they taken their name, was a good, pious, and zealous servant of the Lord, and did much good in his time, in particular in spreading the evangelistic light among the Lapps. The pastor agreed with that, but maintained that the Laestadians now diverged essentially from Laestadius and what he taught. I visited the meeting that night, too, and I wondered at how, when they preached in Swedish, which was translated to Finnish, they all held silent and still. Presumably, the Swedish sermon was so spiritless that it did not have any effect. However it sounded as if their works were doing a lot of good among northern Sweden's and Finland's people, and until Laestadius' time, the half-heathen Lapps. Lars Levi Laestadius was born in Arjeploug in 1800, became a pastor, and worked mainly among the Lapps. Through his strong preaching, he evoked a movement that lives on today.

By Steamer to Luleå

We sailed with a steamer along the Gulf of Bothnia's beautiful coast and happened to be there just as the Nordic Exhibition was beginning. The exhibition here was mainly old pre-Nordic objects, but there were also many of recent time's products, in particular hand crafts. Also displayed was a number of white mountain-cattle, which are mostly raised in northern Sweden as they seem to produce better than others in that climate. We saw some Norrland horses. They were not just large, but handsome and good. We stayed over in Luleå over Sunday, attended services there, and got to hear a good sermon by the bishop. In the afternoon the Salvation Army held a meeting in a little park. They took up a collection, and everyone was invited to go along to their assembly hall to a revival meeting. However, upon arriving there, one had to buy an entry ticket. Many turned around and did not go in. I thought, "Has it come to this with the Salvation Army, that they sell tickets for entry to hear God's word on Sunday?" Then I fear they are on the wrong track.

Luleå has a lovely location on a cape in the Gulf of Bothnia, and the harbor stretches on both sides of the city. We continued by steamer from Luleå to Piteå, and quite unexpectedly met our friends the Leonard Eriksons from Portland, Oregon. It was a wonderful surprise and we had pleasant times in their company. They were living here temporarily, but intended to move farther south or return to Oregon. Also, we looked up Mrs. Leander Johnson's parents' home, a little ways from Bölebyn, where Mrs. Johnson's brother now lives.

From Piteå we once again traveled by steamer along the coast of the Gulf of Bothnia to Umeå, where we were to call on a brother of P. J. Anderson in Warren. However he had traveled away. However, it happened that Sweden's king and queen had arrived there on Saturday, so we got to see them and be there for the festivities held in their honor. Regimental music was played and speeches were held in the park. On Sunday we visited the church where even the king and queen attended.[131] They travelled then to Piteå, and from there to the exhibition in Luleå.

Umeå is a beautiful city of over seven thousand residents, on the Gulf of Bothnia, and it was the cheapest place to stay that we had encountered in Sweden. In a so-called "people's kitchen," run by an association, simple but good food can be had for three kronor per day for three meals. In other places it has cost seven to twelve kronor per day.

At Ångermanälven (Ångerman River)

We took the train from Umeå to Vannäs, where we stayed a couple of days and visited relatives of Mrs. Ekström in Warren. We got off of the train at London and Hörnsjö stations, where the relatives of Mrs. Ekström reside in the countryside. They were harvesting hay. It was thirteenth of July. The harvest was quite good. These homes were located in the woods and surrounded by them. Our trip continued onward to Långsele, where we changed trains and travelled down the beautiful Ångermanälv to Näs, Bollstabruk, where we made a halt for several days in Mr. August Wedin's home at the beautiful Näs at Bollstafjörd. The fjord stretches a ways into the land from Ångermanälven, and forms beautiful, rich valleys, where all sorts of farm produce are cultivated with the greatest success.

After a few days we took the train, on Sunday morning, to Kramfors, where we called on Mr. Erik Wedin, and brother-in-law of G. H. Ekström. Also, we visited the church, where a large number of people were assembled; mostly older folks, as it was Old Folks Day. Communion was held, and many stepped up to the Lord's Table. That congregation consisted of thirteen thousand people, but some of them were not Lutherans and didn't come to church.

The next day we continued on to Sprängviken, Signe Ekström's hometown, where she met many friends, in whose hospitable homes we were well-received, and over a week's time we went from house to house and had interesting conversations about our travels

View from Middagsberget, Sprängsviken

to different countries, about America and its situation, and the Prohibition movement, crowned with such great results, and many expressed the hope that Sweden would follow suit. There was no lack of music and song, for most homes had musical instruments and singers. There was no lack of food and drink, either. But during the war they had been in short supply. There was no strong drink to be seen among these folks for, as a rule, they were God-fearing, sober people. On Sunday we took a motorboat ride on the beautiful Ångerman River to Sandö, where Mission meetings were held all day, and where quite a lot of people were assembled, although it was a rainy day. We returned to Sprängviken, and the next day took the train to Härnösand after one of the most enjoyable week's stay among these honest and hospitable people.

Härnösand, with a population of about ten thousand, has a beautiful location by the Ångerman River, a little above its outlet into the Gulf of Bothnia. It is especially rich in trees along the streets, and it has beautiful parks. We took a steamer up the beautiful Ångerman River to Bollstabruk to our temporary home with August Wedin.

Ytterlänne's old church, built in the 1300s and situated behind the vicarage, is an interesting old church, where the congregation has met for worship from that time until 1860, when a splendid new church was built nearby. The old church was very small at first, was expanded later to twice its original size. Then a gallery was installed, and later on, another above the first. The pews were made of split wood—they were made before there were any saws in these parts—and in the gallery are benches without backs. Everything in that church spoke of olden times. An old Catholic painting of the Madonna, of wood, still remains, as well as a picture of Jesus on the cross.[132] On Sundays we attended the church at Näs while we stayed there, and became very well-acquainted with that honorable, friendly, and seriously God-fearing minister, F. Blixt, and his friendly and hospitable family. We had many dear times in their lovely home with interesting conversations, in par-

Ytterläne's old church, Ångermanland

ticular about the church's operations in both Sweden and America. They were very pleased with Augustana Synod's successes, and it meant so much to preserve the Lutheran faith and the Swedish language among the Swedes in America, and expressed the hope that it would continue to do so. We let them read several copies of *Oregon Posten*, and they were completely delighted and could not praise its editor enough for the great work he is doing in spreading good, useful information among the Swedish people in America, and for his interest in preserving the Swedish language among the Swedes in America.

We attended a youth meeting, held at the parish hall one Sunday afternoon, when candidate-minister Järnfors gave a heartwarming speech, testifying to a true fear of God, and the young people presented good song and reading. The Evangelical Fatherland Foundation [*Evangelistika Fosterlandsstiftlse*][133] held a big mission-meeting in Bolstabruk, and many of their preachers were there and presented interesting and uplifting truths in sermons and discussions. Pastor Blixt attended, too, with a very good speech. One Sunday we went to Gudmundrå church, also near Kramfors, and there met our friends, the Devalls from Clay Center, Kansas, and went with them to visit their brother who lives on Svanö. It

Hay harvest in Ångermanland

was a lovely trip by motorboat on the Ångerman River.

And so, five weeks had flown by while we lingered by the Ångerman River's beautiful banks. Haying had gone on all the while, and we had helped from time to time, so the arm muscles wouldn't get too flabby. The clover and timothy was good, and rye, barley, oats, peas, and potatoes were outstandingly beautiful. It was now August 25, and we had to get back on the road again so that the winter wouldn't set in before we could see something of beautiful Sweden.

To Östersund and Åreskutan

First on our itinerary was Åresund, so now we travelled up the Ångerman River to Sollefteå, a little town of 2,545 residents, beautifully situated on the banks of the river. As the river has a fairly strong fall here, the great water mass surges with headlong speed down to the Gulf of Bothnia, and the steamers that ply the river are not able to continue further upstream. We continued by rail via Långsele and Bräcke to Östersund. The way leads mostly through forested land with glacial ridges, lakes, and marshes. At Grimnäs there are two bridges over the Gällö Sound, and in a bay of Lake Räfsunda is the place where the people of Räfsund so bravely defended themselves from the Danes during the Gyldenløve feud of 1677.[134] We were to pass by Gällö, the home of Arnljot Gjillena, who lived in the time of Olaf II Haraldsson (St. Olaf). He is said to have been of giant-like size and strength. With King Olaf, he fought in the Battle of Sticklastad, was baptized, and fell in combat in 1030.

He is the hero of the epic poem, written by Björnstjärne Björnson,[135] and of Wilhelm Peterson-Berger's opera, *Arnljot*.[136]

At the top of Åreskutan

Later on we passed Pilgrimstad, where there once was a sacrificial well and was a resting place for pilgrims who were making their way over Jämtland to St. Olaf's church in Trondheim. At Brunflo we came to Storsjön's (Big Lake's) southernmost bay, and on the opposite side the slopes spread out in a beautiful panorama of fields, pastures, and well-kept farms. Storsjön is fifth-largest in size of Sweden's lakes. Although it lies more than a thousand feet above sea level, it is the middle of a bowl-shaped depression in Jämtland's highlands. The area, surrounded on the southwest, west, and north by mountains, possesses great natural beauty, with fertile soil, and was home to a settled population already in heathen times. It is now one of Norrland's most populous districts. No fewer than twelve churches lie on Storsjön's shores and islands. Östersund, which has a population of twelve thousand residents, is a modernly planned city with straight streets and cross-streets, and good buildings. It is somewhat sparsely built and resembles a newly built American city. It has a beautiful location on the shores of Storsjön.[137]

Our journey continued onward along Storsjön's northeast bay. Right across from Rödösund there spreads out a stately landscape that, however, gradually changes to uniform forests and bogs. We travelled, then, on through constantly changing scenes of forests, highlands, lakes, and rivers, and at 12:30 we arrive at Åre station at the foot of Åreskutan, towering regally above us.[138]

It has rained all morning, and we felt a bit disappointed in the hope of being able to climb Åreskutan that day and maybe that week. But then the clouds began to disperse and the sun came out, and it started looking hopeful. At noon we met up with three people from Gothenburg, and struck up an acquaintanceship, and at two o'clock we directed our steps to the station of the rail line, on which a cable-car carried us up the mountain a little part of the way, after which we walked up the mountain slope on a stony, and often very steep path to the mountain's top, a distance of about four English miles and 4,612 feet above sea level. When we reached the top, a glorious vista spread out before us.

Around about us gleamed lakes and streams between green forests in the sun's happy beams. Farther in the distance toward the west rose Norway's naked mountains, and here and there lay a drift of new-fallen snow, so that we could amuse ourselves with throwing snowballs. There was a tourist hut at the summit, and we rested for a while, wrote our names in a book that was there for that purpose, and in the evening we returned to Åre. It was August 26.

At Tännforsen

The next day we rented a car for us and our Gothenburg comrades and drove one hour to Tännforsen, considered to be one of Europe's most beautiful waterfalls. It is created by Åreälven [the Åre River], also known as Indalsälven [the Indals River], here called Tännån [the Tänn River] which, at the outlet of Tännsjön [Lake Tänn], is funneled between the rocks and casts its entire mass of water into Lake Norn, lying below. The vertical fall is eighty-six feet. There is a rock in the middle of the falls, *Björnstenen* [the Bear Stone], so called because, it is said, once a hunted bear fled here, and from here crashed down into the falls. With a terrific roar the mass of water crashes in cascades between the rocks washing the projections, and everything whipped into a cloudlike mist, where the sunshine reveals a beautiful rainbow. The falls' magnificence is enhanced by the grandeur of the surrounding nature and is reminiscent of Yellowstone Falls in America, although these are much higher than that. We returned to Åre and spent a while viewing Åre's old church which was erected in the 1100s or 1200s. It was built of rough-cut stones and there is much of interest to see, among others is a speech by King Gustav III to "Rikets Ständer," dated August 21, 1772.[139]

We began the return trip on Saturday afternoon and arrived back at Östersund at 7:44, where we stayed over Sunday. We visited the city church in the morning, and the mission society's hall in the afternoon, and the Baptist church that night. There was an interesting youth meeting there, and quite a few young people were present. Several young ladies participated in the program and in the choir. As far as could be seen, not many young men take part in the Christian activities. What is the reason? Entry was free and no food was served. It was blustery and cold in Öresund, and the frost had already made its mark on the potato skins, which had begun to blacken. On Monday we continued back to Bräcke and Bollnäs, where we stayed overnight.

In Dalarna

The next morning we rode on to Orsa, in Dalarna. At the change of trains, we stayed for a while in Mora. The station lies a ways from town, and between the station and the community we saw by the road, a statue depicting Gustav Vasa, tall and stately, when, on a hill near Lake Siljan's shores, he spoke to the Dalacarlians,[140] challenging them to follow him into battle against the Danes. On the stone is inscribed the year 1520.

We walked a piece out of town to the Vasa monument, which is built over the cellar, where the quick-thinking Tomt-Margit hid him and rolled a beer vat over the opening, so that the Danish spies who were following him could not find him.[141] We, too, climbed down and saw the little cellar. Several old paintings were at the monument, among others, one depicting the events here. Not far from here there is an old Mora cabin, where much from bygone times can be viewed. Mora church, which was probably first built in the 1100s or 1200s, is now a big, splendid church that has been rebuilt several times. On the high steeple, stretching its spire to the sky, can be read in big letters *Gudi till ära, hafver Konung Karl XI år 1673 låtit bygga detta torn* [To honor God, King Karl XI in the year of 1673, had this steeple built]. Inside the church there are many old things, among them old chasubles and choir robes from the Catholic times.

From Mora our journey continued to Nås, in Dalarna. We had been asked by the honorable Swedes in the American colony in Jerusalem to visit and convey greetings to their relatives there. Nås lies by the beautiful Dalälven [Dal River], which flows through a broad, smooth valley of well-cultivated land, where rye still hung on the hay-fences. The barley was being harvested, mostly with scythes, but with one and another harvesting machine in operation. The oats were still green, but had started to mature somewhat. The harvest was good, but the weather had been cold and rainy, so that the grain had ripened too slowly. We visited Anders Mattsson, Ernst Mattsson, and P. Olof Larsson here, who received us very cordially and did all they could to make our visit pleasant. We had conversations about everything, but especially about their relatives in Jerusalem. Here, we shall include a narrative concerning the colony in Jerusalem and the Dala people who have lived there for over twenty-five years. It was written by a relative of theirs, Anders

Olsson, who is the editor of the *Mora Tidning* [newspaper], and appears in the July 22, 1921, issue:

The Dala Colony in Jerusalem

The religious character in the Swedish people's spiritual life is known and discussed as far as written documents illuminate our land's history. Not the least, this trait is seen in Dalarna's poor people. Frederika Bremer spoke rightly when she said, "As the Dala River runs through Dalarna—a great and bright light through a serious, tedious life—so runs religion's life-veins through the Dala people's hard-working lives, and centuries have passed without leaving any rust."

Everyday toil and holy-day rest have been, through the centuries, blessed by faith's warming inner flame, but seldom, if ever, has it flared up with such irrepressible strength, as when it enabled some tens of Dala men and women to leave their ancestral homes, their country and people to whole-heartedly follow the call of an inner voice to God's holy city of Jerusalem.

Tomorrow, the twenty-third of July, it is twenty-five years ago, and this could be a time for remembering the event, so much better than this. When it happened, it passed unnoticed, and it later gave rise to false representation of essential points. One such memory constitutes an interesting example of how the most disparate courses of faith can merge, penetrate to isolated rural corners, where no railroads or modern newspaper reporting reach, and shape human lives more wonderfully than fiction.

Who could imagine that a little boy, Olof Henrik Larsson, who lived in the 1840s in the Uddevalla area would become the Swedish central figure in a sect-movement that stretched its branches to Dalarna, America, and Jerusalem? He was born in 1842. His mother had a zealous nature and had come under the influence of the fundamentalist-revivalist movement by the age of confirmation. He went to sea, as Bohuslän[142] boys usually did, and, as it not-so-seldom happens, the religious imprint faded away. However, at a meeting in Boston in 1870, he was awakened to regretful insight on his fall from his childhood faith. After a time of tormented doubt, he felt infused with God's power, but still had no peace in his soul. He came back to Sweden, and for a time went to navigation school. He sailed to America once again and was active with a Methodist congregation as a Sunday school teacher. The congregation wanted a preacher also, but he found that he had to go his own way. He struck his name from the congregation's rolls, and walked alone for several years, but later acquired a few followers in his own little congregation in Chicago. Among the members of that group, who from the beginning laid principally less importance on questions of faith than on Christian life, who with little success work in Christian brotherly love, were individual Swedish servant girls, among others, Tilda Helgsten from Lindenäs in Nås, and Lisslasses Karin Larsdotter from Tyna, in the same parish. Larsson married Tilde Helgsten in 1889, after he lost his first wife in death. At the end of the 1880s, Lisslasses Karin traveled back to her home district and became Larsson's first zealous messenger. In proclaiming and baptizing there arose a spiritual movement that under the guidance of the State Church [Lutheranism] could have led in a different direction. Thus the ground was prepared when Larsson, after a short time, came there with his new wife and began to preach. Even here a flock closed around the foreigner, who, with hard words, broke the staff of sham-Christianity, and who demanded living deeds, where others were satisfied with words. Before the first fires had yet cooled, both Larsson and Lisslasses Karin turned back to their brothers and sisters in Chicago. The little congregation in Nås had previously been provided with a caretaker and was constantly supported with letters from their teacher in Chicago.

While these events were going on, something happened in another quarter that would be of decisive significance for the Larssonite congregations. A rich and respected American attorney, Horatio Spafford, married to a woman from Stavanger, Norway, who came with her parents to America at the age of three years, had suffered losses in the Great Chicago Fire, and had to use all her power to find a new home and regain her old standing. In the Fall of 1873 she sailed with their four children to Switzerland. The ship capsized with four hundred twenty people. Mrs. Spafford saw her children disappear beneath the waves. She could do nothing to save them, but she devoted her life to serving God, if she were spared the same fate. In some unimaginable way, she was rescued and her husband understood when she told him of her promise in the face of death. After her children were gone, she no longer had any interest in worldly activity. Even her husband longed for a higher goal in life. The couple started a little society in Chicago with the ideal in life of making Jesus' teaching a reality, with the motto "Love the next person as you do yourself." After a time, they decided to move to Jerusalem, to live there as the first Christian congregations did in the time of the apostles. In September of 1881, nineteen members of the society came to Jerusalem.[143]

And so, a period of time passed. A distinguished member of the American colony, the widow Mrs. Weriting, was forced, after several years, to return to America to stand responsible for taking her two children to Jerusalem and placing their proper upbringing at risk. That she not only defended herself, but got restitution from the judge, is a story unto itself. It can be said here, that the case against Mrs. Weriting directed the American newspapers' attention to the peculiar Christian-communist society in Jerusalem. When members of the Larssonite congregation laid eyes on these depictions, they went and heard Mrs. Weriting and her companion, when they preached during their stay in Chicago, and there was a tangible agreement between hers and their own beliefs, and on those grounds there came a closer familiarity with the messenger from Jerusalem, and that led to the Larssonite congregation being invited to come along to the Holy Land. One day in February of 1896, a letter came to the Larssonite congregation in Nås that said that the congregation in Chicago had met with a brother and sister from Jerusalem, and was thinking of following them to God's holy city soon. The congregation in Nås was invited to come too. The letter was received with an enthusiasm that can be more easily understood if it is also said that the Larssonites in Nås—where they were also called Larssoners, which, according to perhaps less believable information, would be a name-form that, because of sound similarity, found itself taken up after they rejected an earlier name "Nazarenes"—for certain reasons felt themselves ridiculed and persecuted. The letter was seen as a calling from above. It came on a Friday, and by the next day, it is said, some of them had begun negotiations to sell their farms. However the break-up took a little time. A new letter came that called for patience until the brothers and sisters in America got there, got everything in order and sent someone to guide them. In the middle of March of 1896 the congregation in Chicago traveled to Jerusalem, where they arrived after three weeks. Among the travelers may be noted the Larsson family, Lisslasses Karin, and a couple of groups from Mora (of whom there was one who for health and family reasons returned home after a while). Later, Sköttens Anders (Schelbourg) from Nås, married a sister of Lisslasses Karin, and their two children. That family returned later on to America, but the mother and children came back to Jerusalem, where one daughter died.

At the end of 1896 Larsson came to Nås, accompanied by a multilingual Christian Jew named Jakob Eliahu, a former teacher at the English mission school in Jerusalem and later adopted by Mrs. Spafford. Various illusions were crushed. From Mora came a worried father asking for his children, who had been lured to Jerusalem from America. Another had not been able to go along. But most of them made themselves ready, sold their property and auctioned their homes.

The break-up came on the morning of the twenty-third of July, a radiantly beautiful hay-making day. Twelve wagons carried the travelers and their goods to Vansbro. Among the parishioners, many were sure that the venture was in the hands of frauds and that they were on their way to their downfall. From their scythes and heritage, they walked to the high road and took their last farewell. Eyes filled with tears and children wept aloud. At a fork in the road they struck up with "We are marching to Zion." Sorrow was mixed with triumph, triumph of the soul's victory over that which is worldly. It is said that, when the troop left Nås, the travelers said fire and brimstone would rain over the district. Perhaps that is backbiting; such words fell on either side. It is true that when the group passed the parish line, a storm broke out like none other in human memory. From Vansbro they traveled by train to Gothenburg, and from there by ship via Hamburg and Antwerp, to Jerusalem, arriving on the fourteenth of August. Through the new addition, the American colony had all together, one hundred thirty-seven members, now it is ninety. Some of those from America belonged to the finest families. When the Dala folk came, it must have been an odd meeting. Several had never seen a railroad; none of them spoke anything but their local dialect. But they were accepted and they have lived like siblings for twenty-five years. Larsson, who died several years back, never became a leader out there. By the virtue of greater wealth, Mrs. Spafford remained the guiding force in the colony, until advanced age forced her to retire. Now it is "Brother Jakob" Spafford—formerly Eliahu—whose words weigh heaviest in the colony.

Larsson, Bother Jakob, and the following people followed along with the Jerusalem pilgrimage from Nås: Innkeeper Mats Matsson, his wife and six children; Tipers Lars Larsson and wife and two children; Möckelind Erik Eriksson and his mother, wife, and seven children; Widow Hol Brita Larsson and five children; Josefs Lars Larsson and wife; Hemmings Katrina Persson; Jugars Jon Olsson; Hanses Anna Persson; and Hollisbets Jon Jonsson. Of these thirty-four, fourteen are dead. Of the elders, only three are alive. One has returned to his home turf, when Jerusalem did not give him what his heart longed for. The numbers tell that our countrymen in that distant eastern country, whose fate in the last quarter-century cannot be covered here, nowhere avoided difficult trials. But they testify also of a faith that, in unselfish love and fidelity to the calling, defied death. The Larssonite Jerusalem venture may have been fanatic and fantastic; however, it was an act of religious assiduity, which, in grandeur went far beyond ordinary measure. As an added blessing during the war, these crusaders filled their lives with dedicated, loving deeds that it is an honor, if yet in the scattering with its danger of erasing the national character, to call them countrymen, the Dala people, who have gone farther than the workers attained in previous times.

And, although the Dala people in Jerusalem lived so far separated and under such different conditions, still there were the same character traits with them as with the people in Dalarna, namely hospitality, honesty, and open-heartedness, and our stay with the one or another were highly pleasurable.

Leksand and Rättvik

Now we must travel on, for we want to see more of Dalarna and of those people, who so valiantly aided Gustav Vasa in driving the Danes from Swedish soil, and we made our next stop in Leksand, which has a beautiful location by one of Lake Siljan's southern bays. We spent a Sunday here, and on the streets and in the church, one could see both the young and the old dressed in their traditional garb, the men in yellow knee-pants and white stockings with a long blue-black coats edged in red, and the women in black skirts and sweaters edged in red, with red and striped aprons in brilliant colors, and elegantly sewn caps on their heads. The church, which holds six thousand people, is beautiful inside, disproportionately to the outside.

Its globe-shaped steeple is reminiscent of Russian churches and it is said to have been built by a Karolinian soldier returned

The church in Leksand

from a Russian prison. The bell tower dates from 1630. A Junior meeting was held in the afternoon at the mission church, which we visited. Ten girls from Rättvik were present, in their traditional clothes with blue skirts, white sweaters and green embroidered sashes, bias-striped aprons in black, red and yellow and black, pointed caps on their heads. Good speeches were given, and song and music, and reading and dialogue of good content were presented. In the evening a youth meeting was held, and that was interesting, too.

Dala Museum

A collection of old things from these areas is preserved in an old-time house a short distance outside the village, and to get there one walks over the Dala River on the so-called raft-bridge, which lies floating on the water. The old house and the collection are of great interest.

Our trip to Rättvik continued along the eastern shores of Lake Siljan. Rättvik is in a very beautifully situated place on Lake Siljan, and at the church, which lies fifteen minutes away from the station, the view over the lake is especially beautiful. That church would be one of the oldest in Sweden, and is said to have been founded by the Norwegian king Olof Haraldson during his campaign through *Järnbäraland* [iron ore country] in the year 1030. There are a lot of things of interest in and around the church. The Vasa Stone, on a hill by the shore next to the church, was raised in 1893. That great stone block bears the rune-like inscription: "At Rättvik's church, Gustav Eriksson Vasa, in December 1520, appeared publicly for the first time, challenging the Dalamen to save the fatherland from foreign domination and oppression. In January 1521 they victoriously battled King Kristian's soldiers here. That achievement, which was the beginning of the War of Liberation, was carried out exclusively by Rättsvik men, who during all developments, remained faithful to Gustav. Hereby, ground was laid for Gustav I's achievements for Sweden's independence and development. Sweden's king and people raised this memorial."

The Vasa stone is surrounded by twelve smaller stones with names of men and women who helped him during his Dala journey.

On the first stone can be read Barbro Stigsdotter's name. When Gustaf succeeded in escaping from captivity in Denmark and was on the way to upper Dalarna and lay deeply asleep in the loft at Arndt Persson Örnflykt's farm in Örnäs, Arndt fell to the temptation to claim the price that King Kristian had put on Gustaf's head. He went to the sheriff in Säter to get his help in capturing Gustaf. Arndt's wife, Barbro, who was a good and warm-hearted woman, ran to help Gustaf and subjected herself to her husband's wrath. She awoke him from his deep sleep and let him lower himself on a rope from the loft to a sled waiting below. She then heard with joy the sled disappear into the night out onto Lake Runn, with Svärdsjö as its destination. Gustaf hid there for a couple of days, disguised as a farm hand, with the priest Jacob Jacobsson, whose name is also on one of the stones, and threshed for his keep. The priest took him then to Sven Elfsson in Isala, where he hoped to find a more secure refuge. But the Danish spies followed him there, too, and when they burst into the kitchen, Gustaf was standing there warming himself by the stove. Sven Elfsson's wife was busy with baking and when she saw the danger she struck Gustaf on the back with the baker's peel and barked harshly, "Why are you standing there gaping like you've never seen people before? Pack yourself out to the barn and thresh!" The Danes, watching Gustaf disappear through the door like a simple farmhand, "had their noses pulled" by that quick-witted woman. Matts and Per Olsson's names appear on a stone. They were also among Gustaf's protectors and transported him far into the Leksand forests, where a fallen pine tree afforded protection. They took food to him there and fed him for three days. Then they carried him in a load of Sven Elfsson's hay over the lakes to Gärdsö, and when the Danish spies stabbed through the hay with their spears, Gustaf was injured so that blood began to drip on the snow. Then Sven surreptitiously made a little cut on his horse's leg, so that the Danes thought that the blood came from there.

Another stone bears the name of Ingel Hansson, who cared for Gustaf until his wounds were healed. Then Gustaf hurried to Rättvik and challenged the parish men to shake off the foreign yoke. Then he removed to Mora, where he was rescued from the Danes by Tomt-Margit, Tomt-Matts wife, who, with the greatest haste at the Dane's approach, lowered Gustaf down into the cellar and dragged a big beer vat over the hatch so that he was hidden. So, they were foiled one more time by a Dala girl. For that feat, she got her name on a stone, too. Lars Olsson, "Björnram," a respected and tested soldier, and Inger Mikelsson in Nederby, an Upplander gentleman farmer, recounted to the Mora men the violent deeds that King Kristian perpetrated on the Swedish people, and that ignited their bitterness toward him to a high degree. They hurried then to send two good skiers, Lars and Engelbrekt Ketilbo, to bring back Gustaf. With Store Guldbrand from Sälen as a retainer, Gustaf made his way through Malung to Mora, where he was chosen Sweden's captain by the most prominent men of all the parishes of both Öster and Västerdalarna, and he assumed leadership of the water-drinking, bread-eating band of farmers. Thus the war of liberation began.

The Höök Stone lies right next to the church on the so-called Hög Mountain, and was raised in the memory of Johan Stjärnhöök, the father of Swedish law. Stjärnhöök is regarded as the actual founder of Germanic judicial studies. He was born in 1596, in the chaplain's farm located on Hög Mountain at the time. One reaches the lookout tower, Vidablick, on Lerdal's heights, after a forty-five minutes' walk, which is well worth the effort. From that height, thirteen hundred feet above sea level, the view is particularly widespread and magnificent, and surely exceeds every other height around Siljan.

Falun

The journey continued from Rättvik to Falun, where we made a halt for a day, and viewed the church, which was very beautiful. There was an old cabin here, too, where much from old times are preserved. Also we went up to the mines, where at one time much copper was extracted. Now it is mainly pyrite, used in the paper-pulp industry, that is mined here. Also a paint pigment is made from a type of stone that exists here, and there is a good market for it here in Sweden, for most houses and out-buildings are painted red, particularly in the countryside.

From Falun we went to Enköping, but stayed over in Ornäs for a few hours and went out to Torsång, located three miles from Ornäs by the Dala River. This had been the Engström family's home (who now live in Warren), and we visited the schoolteacher Thelin for a while, and some others who knew the Engström family. They were very interested in hearing about them. The landscape between Torsång and Örnäs is very beautiful and good farmland. Then we continued on to Enköping and here, as in most places in middle and northern Sweden, the landscape varies with forested heights and fertile valleys, and every so often we passed a lake or river.

In Enköping and Sigtuna

Arriving in Enköping, we went to the home of baker Kikonius and his wife (they are in-laws of P. J. Anderson, in Warren), and were received most cordially. They had expected us for some time, as

Anderson had written that we would come. We had to stay with them for six days. It wasn't possible to leave before that, and that was nice. We traveled in their company by car to Sigtuna, about twenty-seven English miles from there. It was a very interesting trip. The gravel road wound along between grain fields and green pastures on the level plains in Uppland, which, indeed, were interrupted by a stony forest ridge. Here and there lay big stone blocks in the fields. However, the harvest was good all around.

Sigtuna, which is probably the oldest of present-day Swedish cities, is situated on a rocky ridge on Mälaren's shore and was founded before the 1000s. Sweden's first coins were minted here, and in that time three churches were built, some of whose walls and spires still stand, namely St. Per, St. Lars, and St. Olof. Sigtuna was the center for Christian activity for a time, when Uppsala was the capital of heathendom, and Sigtuna was probably Sweden's largest city for a period of one and a half centuries. However, in 1187 Sigtuna was destroyed. Estonians, who had ravaged Mälaren, burned and plundered the city, after which its role as a trading city was superseded by Stockholm, founded in the 1200s. Sigtuna retained its churchly significance, and in 1246 a new church was consecrated and devoted to St. Mary, and it became the abbey church for a new Dominican monastery built at the same time, the oldest and one of the most venerable in Sweden. However, Sigtuna lost its standing through the Reformation, and declined into an insignificant fishing town, which, however, has recovered in later years and now counts more than six hundred inhabitants.

The "Maria Church," which is built of red bricks, has been repaired and is now quite a beautiful church where services are held every Sunday. The others are mere ruins, but in the time when enemies attacked the city, they had been fortresses as well as churches, built of heavy granite with thick walls. In and around Sigtuna, especially near the church and graveyard, there are many strange rune-stones. In 1915 an institution was founded here, whose mission is to support, and to provide homes for those who voluntarily want to work for the Lutheran faith and religious education in Sweden. We returned to Enköping, and stayed with our honored friends yet another couple of days, after which our journey continued to Uppsala.

In Uppsala

Uppsala, Sweden's foremost city of learning, has 28,100 residents, aside from the student body, which now numbers over two thousand. Uppsala is the seat of the archbishop and governor of Uppland's county, and is the country's oldest university-city. Uppland's infantry and artillery regiments and two squadrons of Skanian hussars are stationed there. There are many industrial plants, as well as foundries, mechanical shops, technical factories, brickworks, etc., that give work to the residents. Among the institutes of learning, besides the university, may be noted a variety of schools, including secondary schools for girls, home economics schools, the Fjellstedt school for priest candidates, elementary and pre-school teacher colleges, and others. Uppsala is on the Fyris River, which empties into Mälaren a few miles away, and is beautifully situated.

Old Uppsala, which lies two or three English miles to the north of the present Uppsala, was already a seat of kings, Thing [legislature] place, market place, and nexus of spiritual culture at the kingdom of Svear. In the 1100s, Erik the Holy [also known as St. Erik or Erik IX] founded a church here, and in 1164 was named its first archbishop. Before that time, the largest heathen temple lay here, the center of which images of Thor, Odin, and Frey were found. By the temple was a holy grove in which the bodies of those men, horses, and dogs that were killed at the great sacrificial rituals were hung. The temple was mentioned again around 1067, but was probably destroyed shortly after. Uppsala served as Uppland's administrative center for a long time, and as late as 1526 and 1531 Gustaf I called Uppland's farmers to meet at the Thing at Uppland's mounds. These royal burial mounds, three great grave mounds, 58 feet high and 195 feet in diameter, date from the Iron Age. The objects found in the mounds are preserved in the National Museum in Stockholm. Next to the burial mounds lie the Thing mounds, from which kings spoke to the people. The church next to the mounds was built in the 1200s and is said to stand approximately in the same place as where the heathen temple stood.

We returned to the new Uppsala and viewed the first and largest cathedral in Sweden. It is 384 feet long and 146 feet broad and has two steeples that are 834 feet high [sic].[144] They can be seen from a long way off, and are the tallest in Sweden. The church is very beautiful inside and has many tombs where some of the most distinguished men and women are interred; among others were King Johan III and his consort, the murdered Stures, Ebba Brahe, and St. Birgitta's parents. In the Gustavian crypt, are, among others, Gustaf Vasa and his family members, and Johan III and his consort. St. Erik's silver casket, containing his remains, is there in the church, too. In 1160, Erik the Holy fell at Uppsala in battle against the Danish Prince Magnus Henriksson, and he is revered in the Nordic church as a saint.[145] The university building is fine and large, with about fifty rooms. The university library contains about four hundred thousand volumes, among them fifteen thousand manuscripts. Its most precious of all is the *Codex Argenteus* [the silver book], which contains the translation, that Bishop Ulfilas commissioned of the four Gospels, to Gothic (the oldest known Germanic language). The book is written in gold and silver on red parchment, and bound in silver.[146]

On the highest point of Uppsala spreads the impressive red palace begun by Gustaf Vasa in 1549, and completed under Karl XI. The palace now houses the governor's residence, the county administrative offices, and stately council chambers. In the court-yard stands a bust of Gustaf Vasa, and in the palace parkland, an image of Gunnar Wennerberg.[147] Uppsala Biological Museum houses a good collection of wild animal species that exist in Sweden and are divided into different sections after the different areas where they live. One can see, in a short time, the wild animal life of the North. The beautiful Karolina Park, the botan-ical gardens and the cemetery is worth the visit, which with its stately lanes, many monuments, and famous men's resting places, is one of the most remarkable in Sweden. We stayed in Uppsala two nights and a day. In the evenings before eight o'clock there was life and movement, especially on one street (Ågatan), where the students stroll, most of them in white caps. After eight, the crowd dispersed.

We traveled by steamer to Stockholm, first down the Fyris River, which cuts through Uppsala and at the beginning is very small, but widens all the more as it nears Lake Mälaren. The nat-ural beauty is splendid along the Fyris River as well as through Mälaren's northeastern-most branch, which winds forth between forested heights.

In Stockholm

After five hours of pleasant boat travel we arrived in Stockholm, where our steamer docked at Riddarholm Bay. Now it was im-portant to look for a temporary home during our stay in Sweden's capital. Stockholm is a beautiful city with four hundred and eight thousand residents, located where the Mälaren meets a bay of the

Baltic Sea, and is built in hills, islets, and islands. I don't want to try to offer a detailed description of this remarkable city, which is nearly seven hundred years old, but shall only mention some of the most interesting facts.

Gustaf Adolf's Square is Stockholm's center, both geographically and as regards movement and street traffic. The square got its name from the hero-king's horse-mounted statue there, which is

Gustav Adolf's Square and Royal Palace in Stockholm

one of Stockholm's most beautiful public monuments. From Gustaf Adolf's Square, one crosses to the palace over *Norrbron* [North Bridge], which was built in 1787 over the North Channel and Holy Spirit Island. On the western side of the North Bridge lies the *Riksdag* [Parliament] building. There are beautiful planted areas in the space between the Riksdag and the North Bridge. Stockholm Castle rises high over many of the surrounding buildings, because of its location and its awe-inspiring size. It was built at the beginning of the 1700s, and is constructed of brick and sandstone.

From North Bridge, one climbs to the north facade across the *Lejonbacken* [Lion's Slope], so-called for the two bronze lions, cast in Karl XII's time, that decorate it. On the *Slottsbacken* [Castle Slope], a broad area [and street] to the south of the palace, stands an obelisk of carved granite, ninety-five feet high, to the memory of the burghers' fidelity and steadfastness during the war with Russia in 1788–90. West of the Castle Slope is the stately *Storkyrkan* [Stockholm Cathedral], begun during Birger Jarl's time in the 1200s.[148] At the church's eastern end stands a statue of Olaus Petri. All of the kings from Fredrik I's time onward have been crowned here, with the exception of Gustav IV Adolf and the king reigning now. Both in

Nordic Museum, Stockholm

the castle and the cathedral, there is much of interest to see. A short street, *Källargränd* [Cellar Alley] unites Palace Slope and *Stortorget* [Great Square], the capital's oldest square, scene of the bloodbath of 1520, when King Kristian of Denmark had eighty of Sweden's foremost men decapitated. As is well known, that earned Kristian the epithet, "the Tyrant."[149]

Riddarsholm Church is the second oldest church, and on Riddarholm stands a statue of Birger Jarl, Stockholm's founder. From Riddarhus Square one comes quickly and comfortably over the Vasa Bridge to Norrmalm, from where one has a splendid view over the city, Riddarholm, and Mälaren. The National Museum, which lies near the palace, contains a large collection of interesting objects from Sweden and other countries, including Egyptian mummies from the time of the pharaohs. The so-called *Djurgården* [zoo], which is made up of a naturally forested height at the city's eastern side and has many animals of different kinds, is quite beautiful. There is even a tower with an elevator inside, to the highest point in the park. Here one is afforded a beautiful, magnificent view over Stockholm and environs. The Nordic Museum holds much of interest, and the objects are well organized into groups from the different districts in Sweden, and for different time periods, so that one can get an idea of the lifestyles of olden times. The Biological Museum is worth seeing, too. Here one can learn about animal life in different areas of Sweden. The National Natural History Museum, one of Europe's most prominent, is one large, beautiful brick building, located to the north of the city. It houses ten large halls, which

are exceptionally well ordered, and it contains a large collection of
historical and modern animals and plants.

An Excursion to Vaxholm

We traveled to Vaxholm [Wax Island] on a steamer that sails from
southern Blasieholm Harbor. The trip takes an hour. A former pastor from Lindsborg, Kansas, Dr. J. Selen, after his return to Sweden
twenty-four years ago, has lived on Vaxholm Island, and our goal
was to visit him in person. I knew him from my youth in Kansas,
when he was chairman of the Kansas Conference, when I got the
best of all impressions of him. And when the first subscription for
the building of Bethany College in Lindsborg was being taken up,
he came to Brantford, where I lived at the time, and I remember
what he said when I participated with a penny, which was the first
money I had ever earned. He was now seventy-three years old, but
still healthy and spry. They were packing their things to travel back
to America and spend their remaining days in sunny Kansas, near
their children who live there. We conversed for a while about the
Christian situation in Sweden and America, and many old memories
from pioneering days in Kansas were renewed.

To Ottersta in Södermanland

We traveled on the steamship *Nya Södertälje* to Ottersta, Sorunda
parish, Södermanland. The reason for our visit was Mrs. Inga
Hellgren, an old friend from the Kansas days, who, with her husband, moved there twenty-six years ago. She had been a widow for
two years and was now seventy-four years old. The voyage passed
through Mälaren past Södertälje, and through the canal that unites

Mälaren with the Baltic Sea. It is that passage that the Göta Canal steamers follow. We landed at Rongsta docks, and an old eighty-year-old farmer named Larsson, who was still healthy and spry, was there to meet us and drove us the five miles of road that evening. The road wound forth between well-tended fields and forested heights, and the tract was quite beautiful. Mrs. Hellgren and a maid live in the comfortable house, which Mr. Hellgren built on a hill on his property. Mr. Hellgren sold his property before his death, but the house and its contents were hers so long as she lived. We stayed here for a few days and it was very pleasant.

On Sunday we went to the nearby church and a young Pastor Berggren preached very well. He attended to the congregation until the new pastor, Andreen, who had been pastor within the Augustana Synod, arrived here. We had met Pastor Berggren the evening before at the mission house, where he gave a lecture on the State Church's [Lutheran] many branches within the educational and charitable activities, in Sweden as well as abroad. There was a meeting held on Sunday afternoon, where we got to hear some good talks, song, and music.

On Monday we ventured partway through some partly forested tracts on a walk to visit an old couple who lived in a little cabin on a hillside. The man was eighty, and his wife was sixty-eight, but they were both spry. They had lived in that little cabin for fifty years, ever since they were married, and they were pleased and happy with their lot. Thirty-five years ago, he had lost a hand in a threshing machine, and when I expressed sympathy for him, he said that it was probably the best thing that had happened to him, as it led to his salvation. He followed us back through the woods, and despite his eighty years, he was as spry as anyone.

When we returned to Mrs. Hellgren that evening, there were several of her relatives assembled there, and more of them arrived afterwards until there were twenty of them. The afternoon ran quickly by in conversation of Palestine and other countries and about America, and its churchly and civil conditions. After a short prayer and singing of "*Gud var med oss tills vi mötas igen*" [God be with us until we meet again], we parted with the feeling that we would probably never meet again in this world. At home with God, though, remains a blessed reunion for all of Jesus' friends. We returned to Stockholm by train the next morning, and stayed there for a few more days. We went to services one Sunday at Stockholm Cathedral, where head pastor Beskow held a good service for a large group of listeners.

Back to the Home District

Before I left Sweden I had to make one more visit to my birthplace. I traveled, therefore, to Strångsjö and walked out to the little cabin in the forest that my father built. It was the afternoon of October 4. The sun streamed so clear and mild, and the color change in the trees' leaves testified to the arrival of fall, and they stood there dressed in yellow and red between the evergreen firs and pines. I got to spend the night in the cabin where I was born, and many childhood memories unrolled in my mind, such as getting a whipping for being disobedient. But it was good for me, and I never more overstepped my parent's commands of my boyhood years, so far as I can remember. The next day I looked up some old people who lived in the area and remembered my parents. The one was my father's cousin and childhood comrade. He was ninety years old and was now fairly feeble. Another, who was seventy-five years old, tended the cows and was healthy and spry.

That part of Södermanland is fairly wooded and stony, with one and another valley of well-tended farms, and a croft here and there in the forest. This tract is owned by the noble Bonde family, and those who cultivate the soil must lease from them. It cannot be bought, and so it has continued for centuries, so that the people who have lived here could never own their own home. Not too strange that my parents and many others longed to go to a country where they could be owners of their own turf, and their children could live in security and not fear homelessness if the owner so decided, as was the case with my parents, merely because they worshipped God according to the convictions of their conscience. They had, you see, become so-called "readers." They were not tolerated in those days, so they left for America. It was interesting to wander through these woods on this road as my parents so many times walked the twelve miles to Stora Malm church. It was so still and quiet in the woods and no one was seen on the road that day. The farmers were busy with threshing and plowing. However, a couple of beautiful deer showed themselves at the edge of the woods, a lynx ran across the road, and in a lake, the wild ducks quacked so that it wakened the old hunting lust. It was nearly evening before I came to Forsa mill, where I requested lodging for the night. But there wasn't any to be had, and they advised me to go to a farmhouse by the road, but there was no room there either. At the next farm it was the same, no room, so I had to continue walking to Katrineholm and arrived there just before eight, tired and hungry. I got a room at a smaller hotel, but they did not serve food there, so I walked to the railroad hotel to get a meal. I was met there by a drunken man who was so impudent that I went to another hotel to get something to eat. At midnight I was awakened by loud talking and swearing, for a drunken man had come in and insisted on lying there, and it was difficult to get him out.

Drunkenness is frightful here. Daily, one sees many drunken men staggering around on the streets, and some are really obnoxious and ask money from everyone they meet. One even took me by the collar and asked for money, but he did not get any. I have been told that many overload themselves now that they only get a certain amount (namely, two to four quarts per month). Now they buy the whole ration at once and drink themselves drunk.

Again to Stockholm

I returned to Stockholm the next morning to get passports and tickets in order for the trip home. We had to stay there a few more days and had then the opportunity to see a little more. From the *Katrinahissen* [Katrina Elevator], built in 1881, and by which one can ascend from Katrina Street, one hundred seventeen feet, and then cross a bridge to go directly to Mosseback Square, and in that way save oneself the tedious climb to that highly elevated part of the city. From that bridge there is a wonderful view over the lake that lies below with its many boats moored down there. The Mariahissen [Maria Elevator], which was built in 1861, is another shortcut, which helps one up the one hundred foot height of Bellman Street. It got that name because the house where Carl Michael Bellman[150] was born is located on that street just west of the Maria Church. We visited the Årsta Hospital and Deaconage, which own several good utilitarian buildings on Årsta Street, and from which a beautiful panorama spreads out over a great deal of Stockholm, its harbor and archipelago. On Sunday, we visited the Jacob's Church and heard Pastor Hammarsten, a serious but uplifting preacher, and despite his seventy-five years, his words rang clearly and distinctly to every part of the great church, which was filled to capacity with attentive listeners. It was interesting to see and hear the old "faithful servant," whose writings we read at home

to our great edification. We also had the pleasure of talking with
the beloved man for a while.[151]

From Stockholm to Kristiania and Bergen

After having said farewell to our friends, whose acquaintance we
had made during the thirteen days we had stayed in Stockholm, we
began our trip to Norway on October 10, as we wanted to see that
country, too. It was expensive to get visas, that is, ten dollars each.
We traveled by express train, which only stopped at the larger
places, and made the first stops at Södertälje and Katrineholm. The
landscape was varied, with forested mountain heights and well-cultivated valleys, and here and there a lake or river. Around Vingåker
is a large plain, but then it becomes more changeable again. Soon we
passed the border of Södermanland and Närke. At Laxå the tracks
wander north and then northwest to Kristinehamn, at the northwest
corner of Lake Vänern. The route continued along the north end,
over level lowland to Karlstad, and then in a northwesterly direction past Arvika to Charlottenberg near the Norwegian border,
where we arrived at 6:45 P.M. There we made a halt.

NORWAY

We had now transversed Sweden where it is broadest, in a little more than ten hours. The next morning our travels continued at 8:00, and we arrived in Kristiania at 11:00 A.M., where we stayed over to the next day and used the afternoon to see what we could of the city. The landscape from Sweden's border to Kongsvinger is very like northern Sweden. Then one follows the beautiful Glommen River, which is reminiscent of the Ångerman River, to Fetsund, where one crosses.

Kristiania is about the size of Portland, Oregon, with approximately three hundred thousand inhabitants, is a beautiful and well-situated harbor city at the upper end of Kristiania Fjord and is, as is well known, Norway's capital. It has a beautiful palace and parliamentary building, several large churches and

Eidsvold Square, Kristiania (Oslo)

other splendid buildings, and, in general, broad beautiful streets. From St. Hans fortress, which is located on a lofty hill almost in the middle of the city, and on whose top is a lookout tower, one has a remarkable view over the city and surrounding area. At 7:25 the next morning, our journey continued toward Bergen.

Through Norway

The tracks follow a deep valley depression upward, so that the train went very slowly. In a couple of hours we are up on Roa summit, and then we head downward with increased speed down to Hönefors, where Ronds Fjord is crossed, and again follow a valley up toward Hemsdalen. On those steep slopes stood one little home after another with a little patch of cultivated ground around them. We wondered how those who lived here could sustain themselves as these homes, built of logs and for the most part unpainted, looked poor. At last we saw no more houses, and it got farther between stations. The terrain got wilder and more mountainous; eventually the forest ran out, and one saw only bare rocks with a little lake now and then, and then snowdrifts appeared here and there on the northern mountain slopes. The snow increased more and more until one saw nothing but snowdrifts. We were now in the barest of Norway's mountains, over seven thousand feet above sea level and north of the sixtieth parallel, and everywhere we looked there was nothing but rocks and snow and little lakes with a little stream connecting them together. The tracks were, for the most part, overbuilt with snow sheds between the tunnels, which were very numerous, so that only for short periods we could see the wild nature in all its magnificence. It began, gradually, to bear downwards and the train picked up speed, but we were still passing through one tunnel after another, until after the day's travel we passed through over eighty tunnels. The longest of these, second to St. Gotthard's tunnel, is one and a quarter mile long. Almost a year ago we passed through St. Gotthard's tunnel in southern Switzerland. The snow now began to slacken and twilight began to fall, so that we could see more of the magnificent natural surroundings. Shortly after nine o'clock we arrived in Bergen, where we must linger for two and a half days waiting for the steamship *Jupiter*'s departure for Newcastle, England.

Bergen

The name Bergen suits this city well, for it lies surrounded by bare mountaintops, although it is a significant harbor city, where great steamships find their way through a narrow, winding passage. The city, which has about one hundred thousand inhabitants and was founded in 1075 by Olof Kyrre[152], lies around the end of a bay, and the high mountaintops rise right next to it. A cable tram runs up the steep incline to a height of 984 feet on a track with a 33 percent grade, and when we arrived at the top, the city below us looked like a beautiful painting, but yet higher mountain ridges rose above us. We wandered up these on a well-built road that was blasted into the steep mountain slope, to the top of the mountain, where

a wireless telegraph station has been built. From here we could see in every direction, and to the north, west, and east, there was nothing to see but bare mountaintops. Toward the southwest, one can see the narrow water passage outward to the North Sea, between rocky shores and islands. It was a splendid panorama of Norway's nature.

Bergen, Norway

In Bergen there are several old churches of interest and monuments to prominent Norwegian men, among others, one in a city park of Ole Bull.[153] The Bergenska Museum contains a remarkable collection of objects from many countries. We have had fine weather during the trip over Norway's mountains, and even on the first day in Bergen, when we saw as much as we could. However, on Friday it was rainy, and on Saturday it poured. We were lucky to get a clear day in Bergen, they said, for it had rained almost constantly all summer. And so it is the case every summer, as there is an average of seventy-two inches of rainfall every summer, nearly twice that of Portland, Oregon.

On the North Sea

The steamship *Jupiter*, on which we were to continue our journey, sailed on October 15. It wound its way through the Byfjord's narrow passage between cliffs and skerries, out to the North Sea, and the fairly talkative passengers viewed with interest the one rocky island after another. It rained and blew, and when we came out into the open sea, the steamer began to pitch up and down, and it rocked a lot sometimes, too. One passenger after the other began to feed the fishes,[154] and then hurried down to their cabins. At last it was just I and a Norwegian lady remaining on deck. We withstood it the longest on deck over the water. At last, I was alone. I feared, however, to go down to my cabin as the ship pitched so violently that it was difficult to walk, and so I was afraid of becoming seasick. At last when it started getting dark, I had to go below, but I became sick, and I knew the girls were, too. However, I could not go down and ask how they were doing. After a few hours I felt better, and slept fairly well through the night. The next morning I was able to get up and eat a little breakfast, but the passengers did not eat much that morning or the night before. The morning was clear and promised a beautiful day, for we had left Norway's rainy coast. The waves still rolled high, but lay down gradually during the course of the day. Some of the passengers started feeling better and came up on deck and even found themselves at the dinner table, but we did not see the others until we landed at Newcastle at five in the afternoon.

ENGLAND AND SCOTLAND

Newcastle, which has a population of over three hundred thousand, is a lively harbor city. The next day we continued northward—for we wanted to see a little of Scotland—and we rode in a nice express train that went forty-five miles an hour. It carried us over beautiful fields and pastures, and after three hours we arrived at Edinburgh, which is a beautiful city of over three hundred thousand inhabitants. On a rocky hill sits an old castle, which dates from the fifth century, although it has been rebuilt or restored several times. It has been witness to many hard battles between the Picts and the Saxons. It was called the Maiden Castle, because it was used as a refuge for the Pictish kings' and noblemen's daughters. It was strongly fortified and what happened in that castle in the course of the centuries constitutes a particularly interesting story. The castle offers a magnificent view of the city and surrounding area. A little chapel, sixteen feet long and ten feet wide, stands at the hill's highest point. The beautiful and pious St. Margareta, Malcom III's queen, had it built in the 1000s, and there she sent up many fervent prayers during her austere life within the castle walls. An old cannon, cast in Mons in 1485, weighing five tons, stands on a plateau within the fortress and has been used on many different occasions to bombard otherwise impenetrable fortresses.

In Aberdeen, Scotland

The next day we continued on to Aberdeen. We crossed over the River Firth on a very long iron bridge, and the route followed Scotland's east coast, with the North Sea visible a great deal of the time.

At Dundee is another long bridge over the Firth of Tay, and as we go farther north, the land becomes hillier; but it was green and beautiful as if it were spring, and the weather was remarkably mild and pleasant to be so far into October, and the leaves on the trees had not yet begun to yellow. Aberdeen is quite a beautiful city and one of the oldest cities in Scotland. It has almost two hundred thousand inhabitants, is built of granite and has splendid, broad streets. The University of Aberdeen, located here, is made up of one big, splendid granite building, and from a high tower one has a good view of the city. To a stranger it seems quite strange, because so many of the buildings look exactly the same, and are built one next to the other for entire blocks. They all have big chimneys on the gables with six to twelve clay pipes sticking up from them.

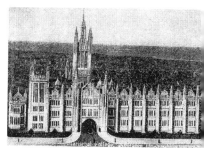

The next day we continued travel-ing to Inverness, in the northern part of Scotland, which had previously been the capital of the so-called Highlands before they were united with England. On an eminence, which affords a beauti-ful view over the city and the landscape

The university at Aberdeen

around about, lies the courthouse "Highlands," where Macbeth's castle once stood.[155] The landscape in northern Scotland is very much like central Sweden, but with fewer lakes. The many grain piles testified that a good harvest had been brought in, and people were busy digging potatoes and plowing. A number of sheep grazed in the green pastures. Also there were a lot of cattle. In particular the black Aberdeen–Angus breed was very common in northern Scotland, and they have even been brought to America from here.

In Glasgow

The next day our travels continued to the south toward Glasgow, which is a large city with more than a million people, located on the Clyde River. It is a harbor city, where Atlantic steamers arrive and depart to America and other countries. We visited the old Cathedral, built between the twelfth and fifteenth centuries. It is 300 feet long, 70 feet broad, and has a steeple that is 220 feet high. Nearby, on a high hill, is a graveyard and at its highest point stands a grand, stately statue of John Knox, who was a tool in God's hand to institute the Protestant teaching in Scotland in 1565. John Knox is highly honored in Scotland and called its reformer. The Presbyterian Church is the State Church of Scotland, and has carried out good work there as well as in other countries. A statue of Walter Scott, 80 feet high, has been erected in a town square. The landscape between Inverness and Glasgow is, to a great extent, very hilly, and great stretches are uninhabited. Hardly anything but heather grows in these heights. Great stretches of this highland are owned by Americans and used mainly for hunting grounds. Deer are the most common quarry, but there are also black grouse and partridges.

From Glasgow we traveled to Ayr, a pleasant city of over two hundred sixty-eight thousand residents, located on the Firth of Clyde. A monument to Robert Burns stands in a square near the station. Burns lived in this city for several years, and was born two miles away in Brig 'o Doon,[156] where one can tour the house where he was born. It is a small, thatch-roofed stone house, that his father built, and some of his belongings are preserved here. Nearby is the old arched bridge over the River Doon.

In London

Our travels continued, then, to London. The train departed at nine in the morning, and we arrived at seven in the evening. We had put about four hundred miles behind us, and we went so fast that sometimes we feared that the train would leave the tracks. As the tracks were fairly straight, everything went well. The landscape was varied, partly lowland and partly hilly. It rained during the day, and we feared that it would be rainy and foggy in London, for the city has that reputation. Arriving at the station, we asked after a hotel, which was mentioned on the time-table and asked if they had rooms for us there. The answer was in the affirmative. We climbed into a cab which carried us there for sixty cents, and we got good rooms and breakfast for about $1.25 per person, per day. We ate lunch and dinner wherever it suited us, for about twenty-five cents per meal.

On Sunday it cleared up and became beautiful. The rain that fell in the night had cleansed the air. We went to Westminster Abbey, which is a stately church, 513 feet long, 200 feet broad, and 101 feet high with a spire 201 feet high. A large number of great Englishmen are buried here, and a multitude of statues and memorials are placed around the walls. Services are celebrated by the Episcopalians, which is England's state church. A well-rehearsed choir sang remarkably well, but the congregation participated very little in the singing. A written sermon was read, but it was difficult to understand, as the preacher had a bad delivery. They need preachers with strong voices and clear enunciation to speak in such large churches.

Tower Bridge, London

We stayed in London for four days, and in that time we saw some of the sights. The Houses of Parliament cover a surface of eight acres, and there are many other large buildings in that metropolis of over seven million people. The city covers an area of seventy square miles. It has long been the world's largest city, but now it is said that New York has surpassed London in population. However, New York does not cover such a large area, for there they build unimaginably tall buildings, twenty-four stories and higher, when in London, seven floors is considered to be high.

London lies flat, like Chicago. We wanted to see a foggy day in London, for we had heard that it sometimes got so dark in the middle of the day, that one could not find his way down the street, but it was somewhat clear weather while we were there. True, it was always so smoky that one could not see far before him, and in the last days we were there we could not see a wagon from a distance of fifty meters. For a while the sun shone forth, and it appeared to our gaze like a red fireball, but it gradually became invisible and it got darker and darker. It burned the eyes and throat and it felt intolerable both outside and in, for the smoke penetrated everywhere. They burn a lot of coal in London in the many factories and in the homes, too, and when the air is still, the smoke settles over the city. If they then have a thick fog, as is often the case, it becomes horribly dark and unpleasant.[157]

Setting a Course for Home

The next morning we traveled by train to Tilbury, where we boarded the steamship *Centennial State*, of the American Mail

Steamship Company, and it felt good to get away from the insuf-
ferable smoke. We had thought to sail with the Cunard or White
Star line, but were convinced to travel with the American line,
which would be cheaper and better. The anchor was weighed at
eleven-thirty, and we proceeded southward until at six we lay to
off Boulogne in France, where a little steamer brought twenty-one
passengers and an amount of mail aboard our ship, and at eight, we
continued onward. The weather was calm and beautiful, and we
got a good rest during the nighttime hours.

The next morning, the sun came up clear and promised a pretty
day. During the day we passed many large and small ships, steamers,
and sail ships, and for part of the day we could see England's southernmost coast until we passed Land's End. Then the course was set
in the direction of Queenstown, where we docked at 2:00 A.M.
After taking on passengers there, the ship sailed onward, and when
it became daylight we could see the southern coast of Ireland. The
sun came up so clear, the sea was almost as still as a mirror, but
further on in the day, the wind picked up and the ship rocked a
little, so that some of the new passengers began to "feed the fishes."
The next day, which was Sunday, it was blustery and rainy, and
several passengers became sick. The Catholic services were held
with many prayers and a short talk by the priest, who maintained
that the differences between Catholics and Protestants were not
particularly great. The main thing was that Catholics have seven
sacraments when Protestants only have one, two, or three. We had
meditation on God's word in the afternoon in our cabin. The next
day was rainy and windy, and it continued to be so for the next
whole week, so that many of the passengers lay sick the whole time.

BACK IN THE LAND
OF THE FREE

At eleven o'clock on Sunday, the coast of New Jersey began to be visible in the west, and soon the coast of Long Island could be seen, too. A pilot came on board and steered the steamer in through Hudson Bay. Soon we saw the tall buildings of New York. The tallest is the Woolworth Building, which is sixty stories high. The Statue of Liberty stands so tall and stately, as if welcoming all those arriving in the land of freedom. Of all the countries we have seen, this one has the greatest benefits to offer humanity. Although our sojourns in other lands have been interesting and educational, it felt good to once again see this great, beautiful, and free country.

Toward evening everything was in order with passports and medical exams, so that we could go ashore. After fussing for a while with the inspection of our travel goods, we took ourselves to the Swedish Lutheran Immigrant House, where we got lodging and meals for a decent price. Otherwise it is very expensive to live in New York. It is a great blessing for traveling Swedes that this home exists. There, they are politely and honorably greeted, and there they receive help and advice in every contingency and many poor travelers get help for free. It is worth remembering that home with a little donation, if one has any regard for their good service.

While we were in New York that time, we wanted to see the Statue of Liberty at closer range. It was given to the United States by France, and was intended to be a symbol of freedom that enlightens the world. It is located on Bedloe Island, at the mouth of the Hudson River. A little steamer carried us to the statue, which is three hundred and five feet tall. Inside the statue there is a spiral staircase that leads to the goddess's head, and there one can look out through her eyes over New York and the sea.

Then we took ourselves to the sixty-floor-high Woolworth Building, the highest in the world. An elevator takes visitors to the top, and from there one has a spectacular overview of the city and environs. Also, we took the underground trolley to the Bronx and visited the zoological garden there.

In Washington, D. C.

The next morning we traveled by train to Washington, D. C., for we wished to see our country's capital. There was much of interest to see, in particular, the White House, the Capitol, and the Library of Congress. There was even a Lutheran Church there, and before it stands a statue of Luther. That was encouraging to see in our capital. It was something we did not see in any other country but Germany. We viewed the Washington Monument, 555 feet high, and the tallest of its kind in the world. It was built of white marble and granite and is topped by a pyramid-shaped roof of aluminum. The monument can be seen from a long distance both night and day. It was begun in 1879 and completed in 1880, at a cost of $1,187,710. That monument is a people's demonstration of love and honor to George Washington's memory. From the top one is afforded a splendid view of the city and surrounding area. To the north one can see the White House, the Treasury Building, and the Department of Defense Building; to the south, the Potomac River, which Washington held so dear; in the east the Capitol and other state buildings; in the west is seen the Arlington Cemetery, the national cemetery, and the Blue Ridge Mountains, seventy miles away.

Westward

After visiting Washington, we traveled westward through the southern states to Corsica, Texas. We stayed there for a couple of days and visited my sister, who lives there. Then we continued travelling on the Santa Fe Railroad homeward over the great

The Larson family of Warren: Albert, standing, and C. J. Larson had adjoining farms and often shared the workload. At right is Signe and far right, Anna. Scappoose Bay is visible beyond Anna.
(Courtesy C. J. Larson Family)

Panhandle plains in northwest Texas, which is mainly rangeland. At the Grand Canyon, we stopped and viewed that famous place, where the Colorado River flows between thousand-foot-high, multicolored cliff walls. When one stands at the top of the precipice, the river below seems like a narrow band of silver.

Our journey continued then through California to calm, peaceful Oregon, to resume there the duties associated with farming, fruit-growing, and dairying. While working we have the opportunity to relive in our memories all that was very beautiful and educational, which we had the benefit of enjoying in our travels.

C. J. and Signe took turns taking pictures of each other with their children. Firstborn Carl, then Naomi, whose full name was Hannah Viola Naomi Larson, came along in 1923 and 1925, respectively. (Courtesy Naomi Larson Brown)

In 1927, Rolf joined the family.
(Courtesy Rolf Larson)

All three children were born on the Warren farm.
(Courtesy Rolf Larson)

AFTERWORD
A Living Tree

By Tricia Brown

My husband's copy of *Genom Sexton Länder*, his grandfather's book, is nearly pristine, because it was rarely opened. Unless you understood old Swedish, it was impossible to read. Perry had told me that it was about a big around-the-world trip his grandparents took for their honeymoon. The newlyweds had even brought along a younger family member, a daughter from his grandfather's first marriage. Beyond what we could see in the grainy pictures, we didn't know what stories the book held. Nobody spoke Swedish anymore.

I had joined the family in 1986, when I married Perry Brown, the son of Naomi (Larson) Brown. We lived in Alaska, so I didn't know the family well. But during holiday visits to Oregon, we trailed after my mother-in-law into the homes of her lifelong friends

C. J. and Signe's family, ca. 1929, photographed outside the farm house. The children, from left, are, Naomi, Rolf, and Carl. (Courtesy Rolf Larson)

and relatives around Warren. We consumed excellent baked goods and many cups of coffee everywhere we visited. The Swedes, I soon learned, are expert bakers and generous hosts.

We moved back to Perry's home county in 2000, and that spring, we connected with the "Swedes to Oregon Society." I mentioned the book, and wondered if anyone might be able to translate C. J.'s Introduction for us. President Bertil Sundvall struck a deal—he'd translate those pages in exchange for a copy of *Genom Sexton Länder* for their library. A few months later, my husband and I, along with his Uncles Rolf and Carl, met Mr. Sundvall in his Mount Tabor home. Lars Nordström, too, joined us for lunch (open-faced sandwiches, of course). Each of us got a printout of the translation. And then it got quiet as we read.

For some of us, it held some surprises.

My husband was unaware that, in truth, the journey *Across Sixteen Countries* was not a honeymoon trip in which the newlywed couple kindly brought along Anna. It was a father-daughter trip, and Signe was the additional traveler. It seems that C. J. and Signe had fallen in love during the trip, and not long after their return to Warren, they married in the little church that he had founded. Shocking? We supposed so, for that time, and perhaps even for now. But theirs was an honorable love and a relationship built on faith, all of which was foundational for their children and grandchildren.

Fifteen years after that lunch with Mr. Sundvall, an out-of-the-blue email from the non-profit Swedish Roots in Oregon once more brought C. J.'s book to light. At the invitation of Rhonda Erlandson, Ingeborg Dean, and Mike Timshel, we met for pizza and learned about SRIO's newest publishing project, born of extraordinary circumstances. Unbelievably, Mike had had found a copy of *Genom Sexton Länder* in a used-book shop, and he'd decided to translate the whole thing just to improve his Swedish language skills. It was written by C. J. Larson of Warren. *Were there any Larsons still around?* They looked, and they found a living family tree. And now the book would be published in English. C. J. would have been so pleased.

As for the travelers, C. J. Larson was writing his life story by hand when he suffered a stroke that took his life in 1951 at age eighty-nine. Anna died in 1963 in Los Angeles, California. Signe passed away from complications of diabetes in May 1972, after twenty-nine years as a wife and twenty-one years as a widow. She was remembered as a warm, loving mother and grandmother, a skilled homemaker, accomplished cook, and a woman who loved Jesus.

The remembrance window. A window honoring Mr. and Mrs. C. J. Larson has a place of prominence at Bethany today. (Courtesy Tricia Brown)

At Bethany Evangelical Lutheran Church, a stained glass window was installed to commemorate the couple and their many years of service to God and to this particular flock. In the cemetery out back, Signe's parents, Gus and Hannah Ekström, are interred near a bend in the drive. C. J. Larson's plot is situated on the highest rise. His grave is flanked by Betty's resting place on one side; Signe's on the other. Other loved ones are buried nearby: the couple's oldest son, Carl Larson, his son, Mike Larson. There are Petersons, Dahlgrens, Hammerbecks, Carlsons, names that are not forgotten, as every Memorial Day the cemetery is filled with flowers and descendants tending graves. Here are the Swedes who built Warren and merged their families' histories, sharing work and celebration, sharing their stories with each new generation.

C. J.'s heaven on earth. The couple's eldest son, Carl, would carry on the C. J. Larson dairy with able help from his three sons. They would later switch to raising beef cattle. In the 1960s, Carl and wife Lorene moved into a tidy white house that C. J. had built for daughter Anna in 1922. Nearby, Rolf and Donna built their family home on the old footprint of the family farmhouse. Albert's former spread, now Howard and Della Larson's, is up the road. Naomi would marry a career firefighter and raise three sons in St. Helens. Many farmers can be counted among the descendants of C. J. and Albert Larson today. (Courtesy Tricia Brown)

ENDNOTES

Editor's Note: Travel memoirs are fun to read for many reasons, not the least of which is the quality of discovering stories within stories, synchronicity and strange coincidences encountered by the traveler (and reader) along the way. Throughout their journey, C. J., Anna, and Signe happened upon people, places, and events that were influencing the news of the day and having some measure of effect on the history of the post-WWI world. What I love most about memoirs such as this—and all non-fiction, for that matter—is the opportunity to explore any number of paths. This kind of reading can be as simple as learning something you didn't know before or as profound as uncovering a whole new realm of absorbing reading to pursue. What I hope you'll find is a sense of what was going on around the travelers: what was the news of the day, who were the movers and shakers, and what challenges would continue to ripple into consequences for us in the twenty-first century. So within these notes, which provide context for our travelers' story, it's my hope that you'll discover something that surprises you, entices you to dig deeper, or carries you off in new directions of your own. The majority of sources for these notes are easily available online. Where URLs are not provided, a key word search will get you to the source.

Notes

1. *Oregon Posten* served as the major Swedish Language newspaper in Oregon from 1908 through 1936. It then merged with two other Swedish language newspapers in Washington State and continued on as the *Svenska Posten*, published in Seattle until it ceased publication in 1976.

2. Scott, Franklin D. *Sweden: the Nation's History*, (Minneapolis: University of Minnesota Press, 1977): 366. [Originally sourced from *Den Svenska Historien*, ed. Sten Carlsson and Jerker Rosen, 9: 35 (Stockholm: Bonnier, 1966–68).]

3. "Immigration . . . Scandinavian," *Library of Congress*, accessed March 26, 2016, www.loc.gov/teachers/classroommaterials/presentationsandactivities/presentations/immigration/scandinavian2.html

4. "Primary Documents in American History: Homestead Act," Library of Congress, last modified March 19, 2015. www.loc.gov/rr/program/bib/ourdocs/Homestead.html

5. Scott, 375. [Originally sourced from *Emigrationsutredningen: betäkande med bilagor*, 20 vols. (Stockholm: Norstedt, 1908–1914)].

6. *Svenska Emigrantinstitutet.*

7. Sadly, family tree records reflect that Emil died at the age of twelve in Lee County, Iowa, in 1875. By that time, C. J. was fourteen years old and settled with his stepfather and the rest of his family on the homestead near Brantford, Kansas.

8. For a wonderful glimpse of nineteenth-century life on the prairie, visit the website of author and speaker Virginia McCone at www.sodhouse.org.

9. The psalmodicon was developed by Scandinavians and commonly used in the nineteenth century for playing sacred music. It was viewed as an alternative to the violin, which was considered a "dance instrument" and therefore not appropriate for church. Later, immigrants brought it with them to America. "Psalmodicon." *Wikipedia, the Free Encyclopedia*. Wikimedia Foundation, Inc.

10. Larson, Katherine R. "History of Bethany Lutheran Church, Warren." *Columbia County History*, VIII (1969): 47. In this article, Katherine Regina Larson (née Peterson) refers to C. J. as her uncle. She was married to Alvin Larson, son of C. J.'s brother, Albert. Alvin was born in 1900 during the time his parents and siblings, as well as C. J. and his family, were farming in Colorado.

11. Smith, William Carlson, "The Swedes of Oregon (1946)," in *Swedish Oregon*, ed. Lars Nordström (Portland: Swedish Roots in Oregon Press, 2008), 236.

12. Renhard, Carl J., and Carl H. Sandgren. *Fifty Years of the Columbia Conference, 1893–1943*, (Augustana Evangelical Lutheran Church): 161. Known today as Legacy Emanuel Medical Center, Carl J. Renhard founded the hospital in "the gingerbread house," a three-story home on Southwest Taylor Street, and served as its first administrator. Nurses lived on site and, having no elevator, Renhard was frequently called upon to help carry patients up and down stairs. Retrieved from *Emanuel 100* on April 15, 2016, www.legacyhealth.org/locations/hospitals/legacy-emanuel-medical-center/emanuel-100.aspx

13. Nordström, Lars. "Introduction (about *Oregon Posten*)," Swedish Roots in Oregon, www.swedishrootsinoregon.org/publications/Booklets/about_oregon_posten.htm

14. C. J. Larson founded the Bethany Lutheran Church in Warren, Oregon, in 1907. At its founding, the little church in Warren joined scores of Swedish Lutheran churches across the United States belonging to the Augustana Evangelical Lutheran Synod. The Augustana Synod was formed by

Scandinavian immigrants and existed from 1860–1962. Today it is known as the Evangelical Lutheran Church in America and is the largest Lutheran church body in the United States. The early Augustana Synod was a vital force and critical touchstone in the lives of Swedish immigrants in the United States. The Swedish Lutherans were great readers and writers, being among the most prolific in literary output. Virginia P. Follstad, Director Emeritus of the Irvin L. Memorial Library in Whitewater, Wisconsin, identifies more than three hundred periodicals published by the Augustana Synod in *The Augustana Evangelical Lutheran Church in Print: A Selective Union List with Annotations . . .*, 1855–1962, ... (Lanham, MD: Scarecrow Press, 2007). Throughout his travel memoir, C. J. Larson references books and articles that are no doubt contained in those works documented by Follstad. Her work is an essential starting place for any researcher of Swedish immigrant history in general and Augustana Synod in particular.

15.   Oregon State University started out as Corvallis College, incorporated by Free Masons in 1858. Ten years later, the college was incorporated by the Methodist Church and designated the State Agricultural College. The recipient of Land Grant funds and once again newly named, Corvallis State Agricultural College issued its first Bachelor of Arts degrees to the Class of 1870. The Olmstead Brothers, founding members of the American Society of Landscape Architects, developed the landscape plan for the college in 1909. By 1920, when our travelers visited, the campus would be mature enough to impress any lover of classic landscape design, showcasing tree-lined streets, open lawns, and architectural harmony. "History of Oregon State University." *Wikipedia, the Free Encyclopedia.* Wikimedia Foundation, Inc.

16.   C. J. was likely speaking to university teacher and national economist John Andrew Bexell. Born in Sweden in 1867, he immigrated to America in 1882 with his parents who first settled in Iowa. He received his Master's degree in 1901 from Augustana College in Rock Island, Illinois. He was an assistant professor in mathematics at Augustana College 1895–1903, director of the School of Commerce and also secretary for the Agriculture College in Utah 1903–1908. In 1908 he became Dean for the School of Commerce (known today as the College of Business) and Secretary of Finance at Oregon Agricultural College in Corvallis, Oregon. He was author of *A Course of Study in the Business*

Endnotes

Side of Farming (Oregon Agricultural Press, 1909–1915) and published several papers on agriculture in various periodicals. Bexell Hall on the Oregon State University campus is named for him. Ernst Skarstedt, "John Andrew Bexell." *Oregon och dess svenska befolkning [Oregon and its Swedish population]*. www.swedishrootsinoregon.org/Publications/Biographies/Bexell_John_Andrew.html

17. Common on steeply graded rail lines, horseshoe curves sometimes reach an angle of nearly 180 degrees. The Southern Pacific Line was still under construction in 1920; its last rail route in Oregon was completed in 1926. Our travelers would have passed through nineteen tunnels, and more than one horseshoe curve, on this rail line between Oakridge and Cascade Summit.

18. Shasta Springs was the site of a popular resort in the late nineteenth and early twentieth centuries located on the Sacramento River in Northern California. The natural springs were the source of bottled mineral water from the Shasta Mineral Springs Company. The company later went on to produce its popular Shasta brand of soft drinks. The resort closed in the 1950s and is now owned by the Saint Germain Foundation, an esoteric religious organization with roots in Theosophy. The station near the incline railway where our travelers stopped to view the falls and drink from the springs is no longer accessible to the public. See beautiful period photos of the view our travelers had at "Historical Photos of Dunsmuir and Other Locations: Shasta Springs," Robert Morris Photography, Dunsmuir, California, Photographic Online Catalog, accessed March 10, 2016, www.snowcrest.net/photobob/shspring1.html

19. Two large rail ferries operated in the San Francisco Bay area, the Solano and the Contra Costa. Built in 1878 and 1914, respectively, these were the largest ferryboats in the world at the time and operated until 1930 when Southern Pacific Railroad opened a newly constructed rail bridge. The bridge itself continues to serve Amtrak and Union Pacific Railroad. "Solano (ferry)." *Wikipedia, the Free Encyclopedia*. Wikimedia Foundation, Inc.

20. Vinland, where our travelers stopped, is known today as the small city of Kerman and is located about fifteen miles west of Fresno. These Swedish-American communities in early twentieth-century California all have

interesting histories of their own. In 1921, a year after our travelers passed through this area, Turlock was the scene of violent racial tensions, gaining nationwide attention when a mob of one hundred fifty white men attacked Japanese cantaloupe pickers over a labor dispute. "Turlock, California." *Wikipedia, the Free Encyclopedia*. Wikimedia Foundation, Inc.

Kingsburg was known as "Little Sweden" with 94 percent of its population identifying as Swedish-American in the early 1920s. "Kingsburg, California." *Wikipedia, the Free Encyclopedia*. Wikimedia Foundation, Inc.

Fresno was more diverse; nevertheless many Scandinavian farmers were attracted to its Central California Colony movement characterized by tracts of twenty- to forty-acre parcels of land richly irrigated by canal systems. Judging from his livelihood and background, C. J. Larson would no doubt have been interested in the Central California Colony system of farming. See John Panter, "Central California Colony: 'Marvel of the Dessert." *Fresno Past and Present: The Journal of the Fresno City and County Historical Society* 36, No. 2 (Summer 1994).

21. Anna Larson would marry John Israelson, a member of this Swedish pioneer family who settled in Warren.

22. Given that our travelers wanted to reach specific destinations by pre-determined dates (for example, they hoped to be in Bethlehem by Christmas and in northern Sweden by midsummer, between June 20–22), the side trip to Catalina Island underscores how leisurely, yet well-planned, was their trip. In the 1920s Catalina Island was a paradise for the people newly developed by William Wrigley, Jr. of Wrigley's Gum fame. Wrigley wanted the island to be protected for all generations to enjoy. "William Wrigley, Jr." World Public Library. *World Heritage Encyclopedia*™, 2016.

The island was also a popular spot for the burgeoning Hollywood film industry. In 1920, the year our travelers visited the island, the silent film *Terror Island*, staring Harry Houdini, was filmed on Catalina. "List of films and TV series set in Santa Catalina Island, California." *Wikipedia, the Free Encyclopedia*. Wikimedia Foundation, Inc.

The glass-bottomed boat on which our travelers viewed undersea marine life was first invented on Catalina Island in the 1890s by Charles Feige (aka Fage, Faggie). A glass-bottomed boat tour was essential for any twentieth-century tourist on Catalina Island. "Glass-bottom Boats." *Islapedia: the Encyclopedia about all things California Channel Islands.* Santa Cruz Island Foundation.

23. Professor Thaddeus Sobieski Constantine Lowe, 1832–1913, was a scientist, inventor, and American Civil War aeronaut. In 1861, he was appointed by President Lincoln to head the Union Army Balloon Corps in which he designed and deployed gas-filled balloons to spy on the Confederate army. He began his ill-fated railway enterprise shortly after relocating to Pasadena, California, in 1887. Lowe's history, along with many photos and a map showing our Swedish-American protagonists' trek up Echo Mountain can be viewed at Lance S. Ferm, "Mount Lowe Railway" *Professor Thaddeus Sobieski Constantine Lowe.*

24. C. J. here refers to Angelica Lutheran Church in Los Angeles where Dr. Julius Lincoln took up his duties as pastor in 1918. *The Lutheran Companion,* 28, no. 25 (July 19, 1920).

   Dr. Lincoln was born in Lindsborg, Kansas, in 1872 following his parents' immigration from Värmland, Sweden. He studied at Bethany College in Lindsborg, Kansas. In 1883, he became the youngest pastor to be ordained in the Augustana Synod and commenced a long and distinguished career in the church. Amandus Johnson, "Dr. Julius Lincoln: In Memoriam." *American Swedish Historical Foundation: the Chronicle* (Autumn 1954).

25. C. J. refers to Balboa Park in San Diego which was the site of the Panama–California Exposition, 1915–16, marking the opening of the Panama Canal in August of 1914. The Exposition drew over 3.7 million visitors, among them such luminaries as Mr. and Mrs. Theodore Roosevelt, Thomas Edison, and Henry Ford, and it rivaled the Panama-California International Exposition held in San Francisco that same year. "Panama-California Exposition." *Wikipedia, the Free Encyclopedia.* Wikimedia Foundation, Inc.

26. Despite President Woodrow Wilson's veto, the Volstead Act was passed by Congress on October 28, 1919, establishing the period of Prohibition in the United States which lasted from 1920–1933. Prohibition was supported by Progressive Democrats and Republicans and by many Pietist Protestant

groups including Scandinavian Lutherans. "Prohibition in the United States." *Wikipedia, the Free Encyclopedia*. Wikimedia Foundation, Inc.

The Volstead Act allowed for alcohol use in religious rituals, and it's likely that the Communion wine was the only alcohol tasted by C. J., Anna, and Signe. Our travelers encountered many opportunities on their journey to indulge in a glass of wine or beer which they cheerfully refused, steadfastly standing by their moral beliefs regarding alcohol.

27. Spanish Dagger is the common name for the *Yucca Gloriosa* evergreen plant native to the southeastern American coast and barrier islands. It is now widely cultivated throughout the U.S. and many parts of the world.

28. Our travelers are probably visiting Zion Evangelical Lutheran Church in Salt Lake City. The church was founded in 1882 by five Swedish immigrants who sought to establish a church in Utah that reflected their Lutheran heritage. Services at Zion were held in Swedish through 1935. O. B. Hanson was the pastor of Zion in 1920. It's possible that Dr. Kowl was a guest speaker at the church when our travelers stopped in; however, this research found no reference to him in online Augustana records. "Our Story: A Timeline of Zion Evangelical Lutheran Church." *Zion Evangelical Lutheran Church* (Salt Lake City, UT, 2011).

29. The graveside visit refers to Selma Larson, nee Sandstedt, the late wife of C. J.'s brother, Albert. Selma is buried at Roselawn Cemetery in Pueblo, Colorado. Albert was five years younger than C. J. and shared his older brother's intrepid pioneer spirit, driving him westward in search of making a better living for his family. When he and Selma settled in Colorado, they brought with them one young son. Three more children joined the family before Selma got sick with pneumonia and died in 1903. Their youngest child, Alvin, was only three years old at the time. Eventually Albert and the children moved to Warren, Oregon, where C. J. had already established a farm, and Alvin began farming his own acreage. Today Alvin's grandson, Howard, with seasonal help from his son and grandsons, continues to run the (Alvin) Larson Farm in Warren, Oregon. Thanks to Della Larson for providing this family history on March 9, 2016.

30. Lindsborg, Kansas, has been called "Little Sweden on the Prairie." It was settled in 1869 by a group of Swedish immigrants from Värmland, Sweden, led by Pastor Olof Olsson, who was twenty-eight years old at the time. In *The Smokey Valley People: A History of Lindsborg, Kansas,* by Emory Kempton Lindquist (Bethany College, 1953), Olsson is described as a "musician, thinker, builder, and dreamer of dreams." This seems an apt description for all of the Swedish immigrants of Olsson's era who settled in the American Midwest. It reflects a spirit that certainly infused C. J. Larson.

31. The Reverend Carl Aaron Swensson, along with Swedish settlers in Kansas, founded Bethany College in 1881. The Bethany Oratorio Society is a large community chorus that has performed Handel's *Messiah* each year since 1882 on Palm Sunday and Easter Sunday. In 1946, a Colorado newspaper called the annual event the Oberammergau of the Plains. "In these United States: Little town in Kansas is 'Oberammergau of the Plains.'" *The Pueblo Indicator* (Pueblo, CO), March 30, 1946.

32. The Kansas Conference fell under the aegis of the Scandinavian Evangelical Lutheran Augustana Synod in North America. In 1959 the Kansas Conference was renamed the West Central Conference incorporating the geographic area of Colorado and Missouri. The full text of a 1907 source, *A History of the Evangelical Lutheran Church of Kansas,* by Reverend Hamilton A. Ott, offers a fascinating account of the Swedish Lutheran settlers in Kansas and describes conditions that C. J. would have encountered as a child newly emigrated from Sweden. Available in full text at Google Books.

33. The United Brethren Church was the first truly American denomination in the United States. It was not an outgrowth of other denominations such as Lutheranism which was transplanted from Europe. Today there are about 200 UB churches, the majority of which are located in Pennsylvania, Ohio, Michigan, and northern Indiana. Theologically, the United Brethren are Arminian based on the teachings of the Dutch Reformed theologian Jacobus Arminius (1560–1609). Arminius's followers were known as the Remonstrants and distinguished themselves by their disagreement with Calvinism as articulated in The Five Articles of Remonstrance. With his faith

shaped by the "readers" who defied the official Lutheran church in Sweden, C. J. probably felt quite comfortable on that Sunday morning as he fellow-shipped with these "remonstrators." A brief history of the United Brethren Church can be read at http://ub.org/about/history/

34. While searching for stray cattle in the canyons of southwest Colorado, the discovery of the Ancestral Puebloans' ruins was made on December 18, 1888, by ranchers Richard Wetherill and Charles Mason. In 1891, the Wetherills invited Swedish scholar Gustaf Nordenskiöld, eldest son of polar explorer Baron Adolf Erik Nordensiöld, to have a look at the ruins. This Swedish-Finnish scientist was the first to study the ruins and his work launched the movement to preserve the ruins. "Mesa Verde National Park." *Wikipedia, the Free Encyclopedia*. Wikimedia Foundation, Inc.

35. The World's Columbian Exposition of 1893 was one of the most significant world fairs in the history of both the United States and the world. For coverage of this historical event that reads like a suspense novel, check out *The Devil in the White City*, by Erik Larson (New York: Crown Publishers, 2003).

36. The Pacific Conference of Swedish Lutheran Churches was organized in 1888 from its original Pacific Mission of 1882. By 1893, the Pacific Conference was large enough to be divided into the California Conference and The Columbia Conference, the latter of which was comprised of Augustana Synod Lutheran churches in Washington, Oregon, and Idaho. Follstad, Virginia P. *The Augustana Evangelical Lutheran Church in Print*, (Lanham, MD: Scarecrow Press, 2007): 238.

37. The Bethphage Mission was founded by Rev. K. G. William Dahl in 1913 as a home for the disabled. Dahl was born in 1883 in Halland, Sweden. At the age of 19, he wrote of an irresistible urge to emigrate to America. By 1903, he had graduated from Augustana College in Rock Island, Illinois, and continued his studies in the Augustana Theological Seminary. He arrived in Axtell in 1912 where he became pastor of the newly organized Bethphage Lutheran Church and immediately set to work on building the Mission to be a home "for them that are in bonds." After Dahl died in 1917, his friend and fellow pastor Dr. C. A. Lönnquist, with whom our travelers spent the afternoon,

was elected to succeed Dahl as Director of the Bethphage Mission. The full story of the Mission is found in *A Miracle of the Prairies*, written by the Rev. Arthur A. Christenson in 1944 and available online.

38. The city of Sisseton, South Dakota, is located on the Lake Traverse Indian Reservation, and is the ancestral homeland of the Sisseton Wahpeton Oyate, a tribe of the Isanti or Santee (Eastern Dakota) Native Americans.

39. By this time, C. A. Tolin was the pastor of Chicago's Swedish Evangelical Elim Lutheran Church, organized in 1885 to minister to the Swedish employees of the Pullman Palace Car Works. In 1887, George M. Pullman made a gift of two lots for the church's construction on 113th and Forest Avenue near Pullman Park. "The Evangelical Lutheran Elim Church of Chicago." *The Pullman State Historic Site* (Chicago, IL, February 2016).

    After Pullman's death in 1897, Abraham Lincoln's son Robert Todd Lincoln became the president of the company. Five years after our travelers visited Pastor Tolin in Pullman's legacy church, The Brotherhood of Sleeping Car Porters was formed and became the first African American labor organization to receive a charter. Its founders, including A. Philip Randolph and C. L. Dellums, would go on to play significant roles in our nation's long struggle toward Civil Rights for African Americans. "Pullman Company." *Wikipedia, the Free Encyclopedia*. Wikimedia Foundation, Inc.

40. Dr. Edwin Sandstedt was born in Iowa where his Swedish family was farming in 1876. In 1892, the family moved to Kansas and continued its livelihood in farming and stock-raising. Sandstedt entered the Teacher's Review School in Chicago, Illinois, in 1900, and then went on to study medicine, completing his course at the National Medical University in 1907. Ernst, W. Olson, ed., "Biographical Sketches with Portraits: Chicago," *History of the Swedes of Illinois, Part II* (Chicago: Engberg-Holmberg, 1908): 349.

41. Carl Linnaeus, 1707–78, renowned Swedish botanist was born in Småland and educated at Uppsala University. He is known as the "father of modern taxonomy" for his development of binomial nomenclature, the formalized system of naming organisms, introduced in his 1753 work, *Species Plantarum*. "Carl Linnaeus." *Wikipedia, the Free Encyclopedia*. Wikimedia Foundation, Inc.

42. The Augustana Synod's Evangelical Lutheran Home for Immigrants of New York City was incorporated in 1898. Originally a ministry to Swedish seafarers dating back to 1873, its purpose shifted to aiding Swedish immigrants who passed through New York City by providing room and board at affordable rates. It gave travelers advice, directed them to local churches, and helped travelers in distress with whatever temporary support needed to get them back on their journey. Photos and a brief summary of its history can be found at www.nycago.org/Organs/NYC/html/SeafarersInt.html

43. Gustavus Adolphus Swedish Lutheran Church was formed in 1865. Beautiful photos and a summary of the church's history can be read at http://daytoninmanhattan.blogspot.com/2012/04/1889-gustavus-adolphus-swedish-lutheran.html

44. The S.S. *Imperator* was built for the German Hamburg America Line, and in 1913 at the time of her launch, she was the largest passenger ship in the world, surpassing the Titanic by twenty-four feet. It's doubtful that our travelers knew of the Imperator's disturbing early history. At the completion of her maiden voyage, the luxury ship revealed a marked list and was soon thereafter dubbed the "Limperator." After extensive repairs, the ship returned to service in the spring of 1914. At the end of World War I, she was turned over to the British Cunard Line as part of war reparations. Our travelers must have gone aboard right about the time she was renamed the RMS Berengaria for her final ten years of service. "SS *Imperator*." *Wikipedia, the Free Encyclopedia.* Wikimedia Foundation, Inc.

Marvelous photos and history of the historic ocean liner can easily be found online with a simple search. A lovely three-minute video can be viewed at www.youtube.com/watch?v=mtokYbX2BUI

45. The years of 1914–22 marked the papacy of Benedict XV. His time as pope was overshadowed by World War I, and although he worked tirelessly to mediate peace, his efforts were ignored by both sides. It's not clear what badly embarrassing situation C. J. refers to, but we know that the world was vastly changed after the Great War. There was disruption and concern as several new nations formed after the war, and the Pope had strong opinions on these developments. Pope Benedict believed the economic conditions

imposed on Germany by the Versailles Peace Conference would ultimately lead to more war. He was right, of course, but his views in the immediate aftermath of WWI were controversial and no doubt led to any number of episodes that could be deemed embarrassing. "Pope Benedict XV." *Wikipedia, the Free Encyclopedia*. Wikimedia Foundation, Inc.

46. French architect Paul Abadie, who designed the Basilica of the Sacred Heart, did not live long beyond laying the foundation stone in 1875. Construction was completed in 1914, but the Basilica was not consecrated until after the war in 1919. As C. J. notes, it is located on the highest point in Paris, at the summit of Butte Montmartre. Photos of this stunning landmark abound online; find a brief history and nice assortment of photos at www.sacred-destinations.com/france/paris-sacre-coeur

47. The windmill could be the Moulin de la Galette or more likely the Moulin Rouge. A delightful online walking tour featuring the sights enjoyed by our travelers as they strolled through the Monmartre district of old Paris is available at www.aparisguide.com/monmartre.

48. The American Church in Paris is the first American church established outside the U.S. It is a nondenominational, international Christian church that today includes more than thirty-five different Christian denominations with a membership representing more than forty nationalities. It was begun in 1814, and its first sanctuary was established in 1857. See www.acparis.org/about

49. Author Nancy L. Green mentions the American Women's Club in her book, *The Other Americans in Paris: Businessmen, Countesses, Wayward Youth, 1880–1941* (University of Chicago Press, 2014, p. 259) and notes that it evolved into the American Women's Group, founded in 1949, an educational, cultural and social organization that is still active today and a member of the Federation of American Women's Clubs Overseas (FAWCO). The AWG's Paris office is located in Columbia University's Reid Hall. It was purchased in 1893 by Elizabeth Mills Reid, whose father Darius O. Mills, had been president of the Bank of California. On her newly purchased property, Reid established The American Girls Club in Paris providing room and board for American women, ages eighteen to forty. Although this club closed at the

beginning of World War I, support for young American women stopping over in Paris continues to this day. "The American Girl's Club in Paris." *Wikipedia, the Free Encyclopedia.* Wikimedia Foundation, Inc.

50. No doubt our travelers knew friends and acquaintances who had fought and died "Over There" during the Great War. Seeing these sites where infamous battles took place must have been profoundly moving for C. J., Anna, and Signe. Verdun itself was one of the largest and most costly battles of the war on the Western front between France and Germany. Over 700,000 lives were lost in this battle that lasted more than three hundred days in 1916.

51. Cook's Tours was a British travel agency established by Thomas Cook in the mid-1800s. In 1872, Cook formed a partnership with his son and renamed the company Thomas Cook & Son. By the time our travelers boarded the company's tour bus to view the WWI battlefields outside of Paris, the company was well-established in foreign travel as well as domestic. The company also sold travel accessories and published a series of travel guides that, according to author Rudy Koshar ("What Ought to be Seen: Tourists' Guidebooks and National Identities in Modern Germany and Europe," *Journal of Contemporary History* 33, pp 323–340, JSTOR 261119), were designed to appeal to middle-class travelers like C. J., Anna, and Signe. These guides continue today as *Thomas Cook Travellers' Guides*, published by Thomas Cook Publishing of Peterborough, England.

A strict Baptist and member of the Temperance Society, Cook viewed his work as a religious and social service, particularly for the less affluent traveler. According to Wikipedia (though no citation is given) Cook also ran a small temperance hotel above his office in London, a place where C. J. no doubt would have felt comfortable staying for a night or two. The company has been sold and merged many times and has parented such well known subsidiaries as Condor Airlines. It is still listed on the London Stock Exchange as a global travel company today. "Thomas Cook & Son." and "Thomas Cook AG." *Wikipedia, the Free Encyclopedia.* Wikimedia Foundation, Inc.

For more on this topic, also see *The Golden Age of Travel: The Romantic Years of Tourism in Images from the Thomas Cook Archive,* by Andrew Williamson, Thomas Cook Publishing, 1998.

Endnotes

52. *Kapellbrücke* [Chapel Bridge] was built in 1333 to enhance Lucerne's fortifications. It is the oldest wooden covered bridge in Europe and the world's oldest surviving truss bridge (a structure of connected elements forming triangular units). Chapel Bridge's paintings were done by Swiss painter and cartographer Hans Heinrich Wägmann (1557–1627) and depicted scenes of local history. On August 18, 1993, most of the bridge along with over two thirds of its paintings was destroyed in a fire that also killed one person.

    The bridge was rebuilt within a year and the paintings were replaced with others that had been in storage since 1834. See photos and more history at http://lucerne.all-about-switzerland.info/lucerne-chapelbridge-water-tower.html

53. Our travelers are now on the *Spreuerbrücke* [Spreuer Bridge] viewing the Dans Macabre by Swiss painter Kaspar Meglinger (1595–1670) depicting the universality of death for all people, regardless of their station in life. Concise background and examples of the *Dance of Death* as an artistic genre are found at www.lamortdanslart.com/danse/dance.htm

54. Discovered by construction workers in 1872, Glacier Garden presents a record of the glacial Ice Age in Switzerland.

55. *Bourbaki's Retreat* is a huge panorama, painted by Geneva born artist Edouard Castres in 1881, depicting military scenes from the Franco–Prussian War of 1870–71. Dioramas and panoramas were popular forms of visual entertainment before movies took over the industry, so we can be sure that our travelers very much enjoyed this stop on their tour. Information on the Bourbaki Panorama, along with an excellent two-minute video overview, can be found at www.bourbakipanorama.ch/en/

56. *The Dying Lion of Lucerne* is an incredibly moving rock relief designed in 1819 by Danish sculptor Bertel Thorvaldsen (1770–1884) and carved out of the sandstone rock in 1820–21 by the German stone mason Lucas Ahorn (1789–1856). Writing about the mortally wounded lion in *A Tramp Abroad*, Mark Twain described the sculpture as "the most mournful and moving piece of stone in the world."

57. Bishop Antonio da Saluzzo initiated the construction of the Milan Cathedral in 1386 with support from Milan's ruler, Gian Galleazzo Visconte. It was consecrated in 1418, but heavy construction continued for another two hundred years.

58. This is probably a reference to San Carlo Borromeo (1538–84), a Catholic Archbishop who is remembered as a great reformer of the Catholic Church in the sixteenth century. He was canonized by Pope Paul V in 1610 and his remains lie in the "Scurolo San Carlo" beneath the altar of the magnificent cathedral of Milan.

59. Coverage of President Wilson's trip to Italy in 1919 can be found in *Current History: A Monthly Magazine of the New York Times*, Vol. IX, Part II, No. 2, February, 1919, pp 209–215. A full text digital copy is available at Google Books.

60. As Cicero (106 B.C.E. – 43 B.C.E.) was an accomplished orator, our travelers' volunteer tour guide from the YMCA must have impressed them with her own skill in expounding on the history and landmarks in Venice.

61. St. Mark's Campanile is the bell tower of St. Mark's Basilica in Venice. Original construction dates back to the ninth century; however its familiar design took shape in 1511, after many repairs from repeated fires and earthquake damage over the centuries. The tower continued to be plagued with damage from lightning strikes, but managed to remain standing until its collapse in 1902. The tower was rebuilt in its original design albeit with modern materials and reinforcement and was ready to greet a new era of tourism in 1912. The tower itself has inspired similar designs around the world, including Sather Tower on the campus of the University of California-Berkeley, the Metropolitan Life Insurance Company Tower in New York City, and closer to our travelers' home, the clock tower at King Street Station in Seattle. The Campanile houses five bells, only one of which survived the 1902 collapse. The original bells each had their own name and were rung to signal specific events: *Maleficio* announced an execution; *La Trottiera* called magistrates to the Palazzo Ducale; *La Nona* rang at the ninth hour; and *Pregadi* announced meetings of the Senate. *Marangoni*, the

surviving bell, traditionally rang for workers at the beginning and ending of the work day. "St. Mark's Campanile." *Wikipedia, the Free Encyclopedia*. Wikimedia Foundation, Inc.

62. Although we can't be certain, it is likely that our travelers made the two-hour walk up to San Miniato al Monto, built in 1018 at the site where its namesake saint was venerated. St. Minias was an Armenian merchant whose Christian beliefs ran afoul of Emperor Decius in the third century C.E. and resulted in his beheading. San Maniato al Monto is described as "one of the most unspoiled of all the Romanesque churches in Tuscany." Christopher Catling, DK *Eyewitness Travel Guide: Florence and Tuscany*, (London: Penguin, 2013): 130.

   Available in PDF format online, you'll find photos of the view from the San Miniato and a map of the route (which incidentally winds past the former home of Galileo) at Google Books.

63. In the years immediately following WWI, Italy was embroiled in political and social unrest that foreshadowed the fascism to come. Our travelers passed through Florence in the months after Giovanni Giolitti was elected Prime Minister in 1920. Excellent coverage of the historical events they were witnessing can be read in Douglas J. Forsyth, *The Crisis of Liberal Italy: Monetary and Financial Policy, 1914–1922*, (Cambridge; New York: Cambridge University Press, 1993). For concise coverage and insight into Giolitti's predicament, the symptoms of which were witnessed by our travelers, see "Giovanni Giolitti." *Wikipedia, the Free Encyclopedia*. Wikimedia Foundation, Inc.

64. It is hard to say which hill town was the destination of our travelers' day trip, but the lovely town of Fiesole is a good guess. That trolleys were available for the five-mile excursion is evident in an early twentieth-century fictionalized travel series written by Helen Leah Reed. In particular, see *Irma in Italy: a Travel Story*. Little Brown, 1908. This irresistible novel is available in PDF format at Google Books.

65. For readers interested in the unique geographical and geologic forces that enabled Rome to become one of the most powerful cities in the world, see Grant

Heiken, Renato Funiciello, and Donatella De Rita, *The Seven Hills of Rome: A Geological Tour of the Eternal City*, (Princeton, NJ: Princeton University Press, 2007).

66. Not to be confused with the Shroud of Turin, it was Veronica's Veil that C. J. was hoping to see. For an overview and history of the relic, see "Veil of Veronica." *Wikipedia, the Free Encyclopedia*. Wikimedia Foundation, Inc.

67. The full title is *Stars in a stormy night: or, Light from the Catacombs. A story of the early Christians in Rome.* The author is listed as E.L.M. and the book was published in London by T. Nelson and Sons in 1874. According to OCLC (Online Computer Library Center Inc.) WorldCat database, there are only two copies extant, both held in the British Library.

68. Anti-Catholicism and disdain for the Pope, prevalent among Protestants around the world, began to dwindle in the United States in the early 1960s when John F. Kennedy was the first (and thus far only) Catholic to be elected President of the United States. The Swedish Evangelical Lutherans were no doubt heavily influenced by Martin Luther who, along with other Protestant leaders, regarded the Pope as the Anti-Christ. A good overview of Anti-Catholic sentiment appears in "Anti-Catholicism." *Wikipedia, the Free Encyclopedia*. Wikimedia Foundation, Inc.

69. Waldensians, Waldenses, or Vaudois are names for a Christian movement of the later Middle Ages, descendants of which still exist in various regions, primarily in northwestern Italy. There is considerable uncertainty about the earlier history of the Waldenses because of a lack of extant source material. They were persecuted as heretical in the twelfth century onwards, and endured near-annihilation in the seventeenth century. There are active congregations in Europe, South America, and North America. The contemporary and historic Waldensian spiritual heritage describes itself as proclaiming the Gospel, serving the marginalized, promoting social justice, fostering inter-religious work, and advocating respect for religious diversity and freedom of conscience. Modern Waldensians are gathered in the Waldensian Evangelical Church. For an excellent overview, see the essay titled, "The Waldensian Movement from Waldo to the Reformation," by Dennis McCallum, available at www.xenos.org/essays/waldensian-movement-waldo-reformation.

70. C. J. is probably referring not only to the equestrian statue but to the entire monument to King Vittorio Emanuele II (1820–1878). See a concise description and several photos at "Victor Emmanuel II Monument." *A View on Cities: Sites and Attractions in some of the World's Greatest Cities* (2016). C. J.'s observation that the monument obstructs the view of Capitol Hill is noteworthy; it's possible that he was aware of the controversy around this particular monument, the construction of which destroyed other antiquities that formerly resided on its site. The Free Library, s.v. "Outrage . . ." Accessed March 28, 2016, http://222.thefreelibrary.com/Outrage.-a018950152

71. Lava cameos from Mt. Vesuvius were popular souvenirs during the Grand Tour years of the late nineteenth century. Today some pieces can be valued upwards of $2,000. A fascination with archaeology and with Edward George Bulwyer-Lytton's *The Last Days of Pompeii*, published in 1834, created demand for such cameos. Renee Kientz, "Cameos from the Grand Tour come of age," *Houston Chronicle* (Houston, TX) April 14, 2001. For photos and a short history of the lava cameos go to the website of Antique Jewelry University, *Dynamic Online Encyclopedia*.

72. As C. J. notes, the volcano had last erupted fourteen years earlier in 1906. It was destined to erupt twice more in the twentieth century—in 1929 and 1944.

73. Monta Nuova is located in what is known as the Phlegraean Fields, a large volcanic area west of Naples. Read about its geological phases at "Phlegraean Fields." *Wikipedia, the Free Encyclopedia*. Wikimedia Foundation, Inc.

74. This would be the medieval fortress, Castel Sant'Elmo. Documents indicate a fortified structure has been on this site since at least 1275, the era of Charles d'Anjou (1227–85). "Castel Sant'Elmo." *Wikipedia, the Free Encyclopedia*. Wikimedia Foundation, Inc.

75. Founded in 1836, the Austrian Lloyd Trieste Company set out to build six steamships. The company prospered and was present with three steamships at the opening of the Suez Canal in 1869. By 1894, four new express steamers had been added to the Alexandria line (where our travelers are headed next), making it and its sister line to Bombay the most profitable passenger line in the company's history. The company began offering pleasure cruises

in 1907. "Österreichischer Lloyd." *Wikipedia, the Free Encyclopedia.* Wikimedia Foundation, Inc.

76. C. J. may not be correct in stating that Pompey's Pillar is the largest of its kind in the world. It is one of the largest and certainly the largest constructed outside of Rome and Constantinople. Made of red Aswan granite in 297 A.D., it was erected in honor of the Roman emperor Diocletian. "Pompey's Pillar (Column)." *Wikipedia, the Free Encyclopedia.* Wikimedia Foundation, Inc.

The Corinthian column became mistakenly associated with the military commander Pompey (106–48 B.C.) when Crusaders in the Middle Ages believed his ashes were in a pot at the top of the column. "Pompey's Pillar." *Ask Aladin, Your Egypt Travel Experts* (1999–2016).

77. The final resting place of Alexander the Great continues to be debated to this day. When C. J. identifies the Nebi David mosque, he may actually be referring to the Nabi Daniel mosque, a location that Heinrich Schleimann suspected as the site of Alexander's burial. Schleimann was denied permission to excavate in 1888. Harry E. Tzalas, "The Nabi Danial Mosque: The search continues." *The Tomb of Alexander the Great: The history and the legend in Greco-Roman and Arab times*, Hellenic Electronic Center, 1998.

In 2014, a large tomb, dated between 325 and 300 B.C.E., was discovered at Amphipolis in northern Greece that experts speculate may have been built for Alexander the Great. Nick Squires, "Mystery of Greece's Alexander the Great-era tomb deepens with body discoveries," *The Telegraph* (January 20, 2015).

78. Jane Walker-Arnott founded several schools in Jaffa under the aegis of the Tabeetha Mission. "Tabeetha Mission School, Jaffa." *The Church of Scotland Home and Foreign Mission Record*, Vol. 18. (Edinburgh: Publication Offices of the Church of Scotland, 1892): 246. Text and a photo of Miss Arnott and her students are available online at Google Books.

A fascinating chapter, also available at Google Books, by Michael Marten, "Independent Women Missionaries in the Scottish School in Jaffa, 1918–1936," relates the history of the mission in Jaffa. Naguib, Nefissa and Inger Marie Okkenaug, eds. *Interpreting Welfare and Relief in the Middle East*, (Boston: Brill, 2008): 107–128.

Endnotes

79. According to the *Encyclopedia Britannica*, the Church Missionary Society was an Anglican organization founded in London in 1799. In 1812, it changed its name to the Church Missionary Society for Africa and the East.

    Miss C. A. Newton (referred to as C. E. Newton in various sources) continued the work of an English woman listed in sources simply as "Miss Morgan" who founded the Jaffa Medical Mission in 1878. The fifty-bed hospital headed by an English doctor was built in 1882 and financed largely by Miss Newton. Julius Richter, *A History of Protestant Missions in the Near East*, (Edinburgh: Oliphant, Anderson & Ferrier, 1910): 257, available at Google Books.

80. Founded by Rev. Albert Benjamin Simpson in 1887, the Christian and Missionary Alliance (C&MA) is an evangelical Protestant denomination within Christianity. For a unique timeline of the C&MA providing the organization's history in conjunction with major U.S. and world events from the 1840s through 2014, see "Historical Timeline." *The Alliance*, The Christian and Missionary Alliance, 2003–2016.

81. C. J. is probably referring to Dr. Daniel Paul Rader (1878–1938) who was an influential evangelist in Chicago and senior pastor of Moody Church, 1915–21. This historic church was founded by Dwight Lyman Moody (who also founded Moody Bible Institute and Moody Bible Publishers) in 1864 and was, at the time of its founding, known as the Illinois Street Church, with a seating capacity of 1,500. The current Moody Church was built in 1924–25. Although research does not confirm Dr. Paul Rader's position among Moody Bible Institutes presidents, he is credited with being one of the earliest American nationwide radio preachers. The Wikipedia entry for Dr. Rader does not cite a source for the claim that he was an early radio preacher in the United States. However, the Moody Bible Institute launched its first Christian radio station in 1926, making it plausible that Dr. Rader was part of this endeavor. "Paul Rader (evangelist)." *Wikipedia, the Free Encyclopedia*. Wikimedia Foundation, Inc.

82. Christmas Eve without lutfisk! Anyone of Swedish heritage will understand the significance of this omission on our travelers' holiday menu.

83. Here C. J. is thinking of *Julotta*, a traditional Swedish Christmas morning service that was held at dawn, usually 4:00 or 5:00 A.M. Today, Julotta is

still common in some Lutheran churches of Swedish descent; however, the service is now most often held a bit later at 7:00 A.M.

84. Johan Ludwig Schneller, born in 1850, was the son of German Pietist farmers. He became a missionary and educator, devoting much of his ministry to work in Jerusalem, and is recognized as an early leader in what is now the Lutheran Evangelical Church in Jordan and the Holy Land. "A Brief History." *The Evangelical Lutheran Church of Jordan and the Holy Land.*

Schneller is perhaps best known for developing the Schneller Orphanage, a nineteenth-century academic and vocational institution open to hundreds of orphaned and Arab children from all over the Middle East. By World War I, the orphanage occupied nearly 150 acres. The German teachers were deported at the beginning of World War II, turning the facility over to military uses until it was vacated in 2008. "Schneller Orphanage." *Wikipedia, the Free Encyclopedia.* Wikimedia Foundation, Inc.

85. Contrary to tradition that identifies the Church of the Holy Sepulcher in Jerusalem as the site of Jesus's crucifixion and resurrection, Gordon's Golgotha is considered by many to be the actual site. Major General Charles Gordon (1833–85) was perhaps the most famous proponent of this theory. "The Garden Tomb." *Wikipedia, the Free Encyclopedia.* Wikimedia Foundation, Inc.

86. The American Colony was a Christian utopian community founded by Anna and Horatio Spafford in 1881. Dubbed "the Overcomers" by the American press, the Colony began in Jerusalem with 13 adults and 3 children. Later joined by Swedish Christians, the society gained the trust of Muslims, Jews, and Christians alike as they carried out their philanthropic work, opening soup kitchens, hospitals, and orphanages while refraining from proselytizing. The Colony ceased to exist as a religious community in the 1940s, and then in the late 1950s, the Colony's former communal residence was converted to the American Colony Hotel. In 1992, representatives from Israel and the Palestinian Liberation Operation met at the Hotel to begin historic talks that led to the Oslo Peace Accord in 1993. "American Colony, Jerusalem." *Wikipedia, the Free Encyclopedia.* Wikimedia Foundation, Inc.

Endnotes

A significant feature of the American Colony was its photographic division formed in 1900 and known as the Matson Photographic Service. A rich source of photographic images from the Middle East, most of its images depict Palestine between 1898 and 1946. Consisting of more than 22,000 glass and film negatives and transparencies, this utterly magnificent collection is held by the Library of Congress and can be viewed at www.loc.gov/pictures/search/?st=grid&co=matpc

87. C. J. here refers to Hansen House, established in 1887 to care for patients with Hansen's Disease (leprosy), still incurable at that time. It was run by the Herrenhut brotherhood of the Moravian Church until 1950, when it was sold to the Jewish National Fund. When a cure for Hansen's Disease was developed, patients were gradually released as they recovered. The last in-patients left the hospital in 2000. "Hansen House (Jerusalem)." *Wikipedia, the Free Encyclopedia*. Wikimedia Foundation, Inc.

88. Going back to the thirteenth century, the dragoman served as interpreter, translator, and official guide to those visiting the Middle East. The dragoman had to have knowledge of Arabic, Persian, Turkish, and European languages. His skills were essential to diplomatic relations and economic and trade negotiations. Later, when tourism was common, dragomans offered their expertise to travelers. No doubt the levels of expertise varied widely when it came down to accosting tourists. "Dragoman." *Wikipedia, the Free Encyclopedia*. Wikimedia Foundation, Inc.

89. Captain W. A. Unander was well known in diplomatic circles. Before his assignment in Cairo, he served as Attaché to the diplomatic representatives from Sweden in Great Britain. Martin, Frederick, et al. *The Statesman's Yearbook*. 55 (London: St. Martin's Press, 1918): 1303. Available at Google Books.

90. Climbing Cheops is yet another example of how fit C. J. was at sixty years of age. The girls, too, were athletic and evidently didn't let their fashionable travel skirts get in the way of a good climb. Climbing the pyramids has been illegal for many years; stiff penalties including jail time come with violating the law designed to protect the ancient monuments, not to mention the safety of climbers. A short distance south of Cairo, Sakkara served as the ancient

burial ground for the old capital, Memphis. The stepped Pyramid of Djoser is located here and is considered the oldest complete stone building complex known in history.

91. C. J. seems unimpressed with what he saw; however these "few petrified tree trunks lying in the sand" date back more than thirty million years to the Oligocene, when the climate was much wetter in northern Africa. Designated an Egyptian Protectorate in 1989, this small area is classified as a National Heritage Site. Jano Charbel, "Protectorates not protected: Petrified trees vs. urban sprawl," *Egypt Independent* (February 12, 2010).

92. The German Colony in Haifa was the first of several such German Templer colonies founded in the Holy Land. A Protestant sect, members were urged to resettle in the Holy Land by the Templer's leader Christoff Hoffman and believed that in so doing, they would hasten the second coming of Christ. The affluent Templers introduced modern farming practices to the area including soil fertilization, new types of crops, and crop rotation as well as new farming machinery. Today, on land where The Colony's vineyards once grew, stands the Bahá'i World Centre in Haifa. During World War II, about one third of Colony members were sympathetic to the Nazi party; most were sent to internment camps by the British. "German Colony, Haifa." *Wikipedia, the Free Encyclopedia*. Wikimedia Foundation, Inc.

93. Also known as the Valley of Jezreel, this twenty-five-mile plain divides the hilly areas of Galilee to the north and Samaria in the south and is an integral part of the Via Maris lowland passage between Egypt and the Fertile Crescent. It is an ancient route of commerce and conflict. *Encyclopædia Britannica Online*, s. v. "Plain of Esdraelon."

94. Dating the ruins is uncertain, ranging from the second to fourth centuries c.e. It is certain, however, that the synagogue was built on the foundation of an earlier first century structure. Read a brief but informative article about the White Synagogue, the ruins of which were identified in 1866 by the British cartographer, Captain Charles W. Wilson, at "Archaeology in Israel: the Synagogue at Capernaum." *Jewish Virtual Library. A project of the American-Israeli Cooperative Enterprise.*

95. C. J. is most likely referring to *Sinai and Palestine: In Connection with their History*, by Arthur Penrhyn Stanley (1815–81) who was a leading liberal theologian in the nineteenth century. Stanley traveled extensively in Egypt and the Holy Land, connecting ancient monuments with sites in the Bible. His discussions of "sacred geography" were very popular, resulting in multiple editions of this title.

96. More than two thousand years ago, the Caves of Arbela were inhabited by the Jewish people. The caves were formed by eroding limestone, hollowed out by rainwater over millions of years. The inhabitants enlarged the caves and made them comfortable, adding ritual baths, water cisterns, and internal staircases. For a brief history, including photos and the story of Herod's soldiers being lowered in baskets to gain access, see the article cited here. Aviva and Shmuel, Bar-Am, "Caves of Arbela: the ultimate hiding place," *The Times of Israel*, (Jerusalem, Israel), March 27, 2013.

97. Dr. David Watt Torrance (1862–1923) was born in Airdrie, Lanarkshire, Scotland. Known as "The Galilee Doctor" and "Torrance of Tiberias," he opened the first modern hospital in Palestine in 1894. For Dr. Torrance's story contributed by his grandson to *RootsWeb, an Ancestry.com community*, see "David Watt Torrance, M.D., O.B.E," by David J. Byrne.

98. American University Founder Daniel L. Bliss served as its first president from 1866–1902. The American College had just been renamed the American University of Beirut in 1920 when our travelers visited its campus.

99. Elisabeth Bowen Thompson was largely responsible for founding the British Syrian schools in the nineteenth century. For fascinating background on Thompson, see Jean Said Makdisi, "Elisabeth Bowen Thompson and the Teacher Training College," *Archaeology & History in the Lebanon*. Issue No. 22 (Autumn 2005): 84–89. PDF with photos available at Google Books.

100. The American Presbyterian missionary William Benton and his wife Loanza first arrived in Syria in 1848 and later lived in Bhamdoun from 1857–68. The unique history and flavor of Bhamdoun is captured by Kamal Salibi in his paper, "Bhamdoun: Historical Portrait of a Lebanese Mountain Village," published in

1997 by the Centre for Lebanese Studies. A PDF is available online at Google Books and provides a sense of what our travelers learned while visiting.

101. The author of the paper noted above, Kamal Salibi, born in 1929, was a historian and professor at the American University in Beirut. He was also the founder of the Royal Institute for Inter-Faith Studies in Amman, Jordan. Born to a Protestant family, he came from Bhamdoun and could very well be a descendant of Mrs. Salibi, the Syran widow who welcomed our travelers into her home while they stayed in this historic location. "Kamal Salibi." *Wikipedia, the Free Encyclopedia.* Wikimedia Foundation, Inc.

102. The Druze are indeed secretive about their form of worship. Although disowned by Muslims, they are a monotheistic Abrahamic religion derived from Shia Islam whose beliefs incorporate teachings from Christianity and Judaism, as well as Greek philosophy and Asiatic precepts. The basis of their belief is that God has been divinely incarnated in a living person, most recently in the form of al-Hakim bi-Amrih Alla in 1009 c.e.. A good overview of the religion can be found in an article simply titled, "Druze," by Pam Rohland appearing in the "Countries and their Cultures" section of the online *World Culture Encyclopedia.*

103. Colonel Charles Henry Churchill (1807–69) was a British officer and diplomat. He wrote widely of his experiences as British consul in Ottoman Syria and was the first to propose the creation of a Jewish State in Palestine. With regard to the massacres of 1860, the work that C. J. may be citing is Churchill's *The Druzes and the Maronites under the Turkish rule, 1840 to 1860,* (London: B. Quaritch, 1862).

Coverage of the 1860 Mount Lebanon Civil War abounds in print and online. See a brief but suspenseful article published in the *New York Times* on August 13, 1860, titled "The Syrian Outbreak; Details of the Damascus Massacre. Foreign Intervention in Syria," at www.nytimes.com/1860/08/13/news/syrian-outbreak-details-damascus-massacre-foreign-intervention-syria.html?pagewanted=all

Henry Harris Jessup, one of the founders of the American University in Beirut, gives his stunning on the ground report of the 1860 massacre in Volume 1 of his memoir, *Fifty-three years in Syria,* (New York: Chicago Fleming H.

Revell Co., 1910). See his chapter, "The Massacre Summer of 1860," pages 157–214. Available in full text on Google Books.

Atrocities such as the Syrian massacres of 1860 ignited passions throughout the western world as new technologies in the media brought these events to the forefront of collective conscience. For readers interested in the history of how concerted human rights activism emerged in the nineteenth century, see Gary J. Bass, *Freedom's Battle: the Origins of Humanitarian Intervention*, (New York: Vintage, 2009, 2008).

104. The Grand Mosque of Damascus, also known as the Umayyad Mosque, is one of the largest and holiest mosques in the world. John the Baptist is honored as a prophet by both Christians and Muslims.

105. After the Babylonian Captivity, a schism developed between the Samaritans and Judaism. Samaritans believed that Mount Gerizim is the holy place chosen by God rather than the Temple Mount in Jerusalem. The Samaritan temple on Mount Gerizim was replaced in 475 C.E. and later fortified by Justinian I in 529 and 533 C.E. Ruins still exist on the mountain. Amazing history, photos, and coverage of modern-day excavations can be found online at www.biblewalks.com/Sites/MountGerizim.html

The Easter celebration that our travelers encountered on Mount Gerizim is actually the Samaritan Passover. The Passa is still celebrated in this location just as it has been for thousands of years. See modern day photos depicting scenes similar to what our travelers witnessed on Mount Gerizim in 1921 and a description of the annual event in an article titled, "The Samaritan Passover," by Todd Bolen, reprinted with permission from Bible and Spade 14.2 (2001), www.egrc.net/articles/other/articles_sam_passover.html

106. Excavations in Accra [Acre] continue today. To sample the finds, see the Associated Press article, "Underground Crusader City Revealed Beneath Streets of Acre, *Haaretz* [newspaper in Israel], (June 22, 2011).

Also see photos by H. Smithline, Israeli Antiquities Authority, and an overview of excavation in E. J. Stern's article, "Acre: Historical, Archeological and Ceramological Background," available in PDF format at www.pomedor.mom.fr/sites/pomedor.mom.fr/files/documents/basic%20pages/Acre%20for%20web%20site_130813.pdf

107. Theodore J. Struve assumed his role as American consul in Haifa in 1906. Kark, Ruth. *American Consuls in the Holy Land, 1832–1914*, (Detroit, MI: Wayne State University Press, 1994): 124.

108. The brother and Norwegian consul in Beirut of whom C. J. speaks may very well be Honorary Norwegian consul Albert Joseph Delbourgo who, several years later, received the King Haakon VII Freedom Cross in 1949. "List of awards by King Haakon VII Freedom Cross," *Wikipedia, the Free Encyclopedia.* Wikimedia Foundation, Inc.

109. Ibid.

110. Whatever source C. J. used here was clearly incorrect, although it is doubtless true that much has been learned about the history and archaeology of Cyprus in the years since 1921. The earliest human communities we know of were hunter-gatherers dating back to 10,000 B.C.E. When C. J. refers to 569 A.D., he may have meant to write 569 B.C. This would have roughly corresponded to a period when Cyprus was ruled briefly by Egypt before it came under Persian rule in 545 B.C. "Cyprus." *Wikipedia, the Free Encyclopedia.* Wikimedia Foundation, Inc.

111. Adalia is the modern Turkish city, Antalya. Founded by King Attalus II of Pergamon in 150 B.C.E, the city was named Attalea or Attalia in his honor. Located on the Mediterranean coast, the city was ruled by several empires including Roman, Byzantine, and Ottoman. After World War I, the Allies awarded occupation of the city to Italy. The Italian martial law that prevented our travelers from going ashore was due to the Turkish War of Independence waged during the years 1919–20.

112. C. J. is here referring to the Greek myth of Hero and Leander and to Byron's swim across the Hellespont on May 3, 1810. Byron was twenty-two years old at the time. Enjoy his poem, "Written After Swimming from Sestos to Abydos," on *The Literature Network* website (Jalic Inc., 2000–2016). Accessed April 7, 2016, www.online-literature.com/byron/706/

113. Today this amount of cash would exceed $8,000! Derks, Scott. The Value of a Dollar, prices and incomes in the United States, 1860-2014, 5th edition (Amenia, NY: Greyhouse Publishing, 2014)

114. In 1921, Ramadan occurred May 9–June 7. The noise that kept C. J. awake could have been associated with celebration during the Muslim holiday period. More likely, the gunfire and revelry was associated with Atatürk's birthday, celebrated around this time in mid-May (a national holiday designating the date as May 19 was officially set in 1938).

115. Robert College, a private, co-educational boarding school, was founded in 1863 by Christopher Robert, a wealthy American philanthropist, and Cyrus Hamlin, an American Congregational missionary who would later serve a five-year term as president of Middlebury College in Vermont. Situated on 65 wooded acres in Istanbul, Robert College is the oldest American school still in existence on its original location. "Robert College." *Wikipedia, the Free Encyclopedia*. Wikimedia Foundation, Inc.

116. The medieval citadel of Galata belonged to the Republic of Genoa between 1273 and 1453. Rising nine stories, the tower was built by the Genoese in 1348 on the highest level of the citadel. The panoramic view that our travelers enjoyed was captured on canvass by French panorama painter, Pierre Prévost, in 1818. Some twenty years later, the photographic company, Sébah & Joaillier, compiled ten photos to create the entire panorama. See it at "Galata Tower," *Wikipedia, the Free Encyclopedia*. Wikimedia Foundation, Inc.

117. The Greek Evangelical Church is a Presbyterian Reformed denomination and the first Protestant church established in Greece.

118. For nearly six months, America was riveted by the "Miss Stone Affair," in which American Protestant missionary Ellen Maria Stone and her fellow missionary and friend Katerina Stefanova-Tsilka, were kidnapped in August 1901, by the Internal Macedonian–Adrianople Revolutionary Organization (OMARA). Taken near the town of Bansko in Bulgaria, Tsilka was pregnant at the time and gave birth during her captivity. Extensive negotiations and a sizable ransom resulted in the captives' release in February 1902. Considered the first modern American hostage situation, it posed a considerable dilemma for Theodore Roosevelt at the beginning of his presidency. Carpenter, Teresa. *The Miss Stone Affair*, (New York: Simon and Schuster, 2003).

For a brief recap of the story along with great photos, see Ivan Dikov, "Bulgaria and USA in the Miss Stone Affair: Terrorism as it once was," *Novinite.com Sofia News Agency*, November 29, 2010, 19:46.

For a contemporary news article on the release of the captives, see "Stone Party Freed," *The Herald Democrat* (Leadville, Colorado), February 24, 1902.

119. Empress of Austria, Elisabeth of Bavaria (born on Christmas Eve, 1837, and assassinated on September 10, 1898) loved to spend her holidays on Corfu. In 1890 she designed the large, splendid house to resemble an ancient Phaeacian palace inspired by Greek mythology and the last destination in Homer's Odyssey. The Empress called the palace Achilleion for the mythical hero Achilles, and after her death, it was purchased by Kaiser Wilhelm II. "Achilleion (Corfu)." *Wikipedia, the Free Encyclopedia*. Wikimedia Foundation, Inc.

120. Before World War I, Italy and Austria-Hungary had helped create an independent Albanian State. At the outbreak of war in 1915, Italy moved to occupy the southern half of Albania, hoping to thwart any chance of capture by the Austro-Hungarians. In 1920, the Italians gave up the occupation in response to a number of factors including Albanian resistance and pressure from the United States. "Italian Colonists in Albania." *Wikipedia, the Free Encyclopedia*. Wikimedia Foundation, Inc.

121. This grand boulevard began as a bridle path developed by Elector John George of Brandenburg (1525–98) to reach his hunting grounds in Tiergarten. The linden trees that lined the boulevard were planted in 1647. By the nineteenth century, Unter den Linden was the grandest street in Berlin. In 1934, long after our travelers admired the scene, many of the trees were cut down to build the Nord-Süd Tunnel for the Berlin S-Bahn. What was left of the trees were cut down and used as firewood during the final desperate days of World War II. Today the street is once again lined with linden trees, replanted after the war in the 1950s. "Unter den Linden." *Wikipedia, the Free Encyclopedia*. Wikimedia Foundation, Inc.

122. Known as "The Golden King" and the "Lion of the North," King Gustavus Adolphus (1594–1632) is regarded as one of the greatest military commanders

of all time, leading Sweden to military supremacy during the Thirty Years
War. His intervention in the war turned the tide in favor of the Lutheran side.

123. This is the story of *Jätten Finn*. The giant is linked to a number of medieval
churches in Scandinavia and Finland and particularly to the Lund Cathedral
where it relates specifically to pillars in the church.

124. Lake Vänern is the largest lake in Sweden and the third largest lake in Europe
after Ladoga and Onega in Russia. It is also the country's largest hydro power
reservoir. About 10 percent of the Swedish population takes its drinking
water from Lake Vänern. See how big and beautiful it is at www.lakev-
anern.se/en/. No reference to a "path of love" could be found in this research;
however, it's safe to say that this would not be the last time C. J. and Signe
found themselves on such a metaphorical path.

125. Constructing a canal and series of locks across southern Sweden began in
1811. To date, it was the greatest civil engineering and modernization project ever undertaken in the country and took twenty-two years to complete,
employing more than fifty-eight thousand workers before it was completed.
Today the canal, known as "Sweden's blue ribbon," is used primarily to serve
the tourist industry. "Göta Canal." *Wikepedia, the Free Encyclopedia.* Wikimedia
Foundation, Inc.

126. Signe's father was Gustaf Henning Ekström, so we can be quite sure our
travelers were visiting Signe's grandmother in Mortala, which is situated on
the eastern shore of Lake Vättern. With the construction of the Göta Canal
in the nineteenth century, Mortala became an important center of commerce
along the canal route.

127. Fredrik W. Lönegren, born in Kronoberg County, Sweden, was founder,
editor, and publisher of the *Oregon Posten*, which published its first issue
on December 2, 1908. Lönegren was active in politics. Before moving
to the Pacific Northwest, he was a delegate to several Democratic state
conventions in Minnesota and actively supported John Lind's guberna-
torial campaigns in 1894, 1896, 1898, and 1900. He worked on several
Swedish language newspapers before launching the *Oregon Posten*, including

Svensk-Amerikanska Posten in Minneapolis, *Nordvesterns Handelstidning* in Duluth, and *The Pacific Tribune* in Seattle. Owenius, Victoria. *Oregon Posten: the Story of an Immigrant Newspaper* (Portland, OR: Swedish Roots in Oregon, 2005).

128. Pastor P. A. Ahlberg was a leading figure in the Lutheran Pietist movement in Sweden. In 1860, he set up the Ahlberg School in Vetlanda, Sweden, providing instruction in Christian doctrine and preaching. He encouraged his students to emigrate to America where they would go on to set up missions, schools, and Lutheran churches. Many of the Lutheran immigrant pastors became leaders in the Evangelical Lutheran Augustana Synod of North America. Ahlberg's book of devotions and missionary journal were widely read in Augustana circles. Bergendoff, Conrad, "The Augustana Pastor: Saga of a Thousand Immigrants from Sweden," *Swedish-American Historical Quarterly* 31, no. 1 (1980): 34–50.

129. David Östlund coordinated the Swedish Temperance movement and founded the Anti-Saloon League of Sweden. In 1922, he was among ten pastors associated with the Swedish Temperance movement who were sent by the World League Against Alcoholism (WLAA) to fight for prohibition in Sweden. Tyrell, Ian. *Reforming the World: the Creation of America's Moral Empire* (Princeton University Press, 2010): 214–215.

130. Laestadianism is a conservative Lutheran revival movement founded in Lapland by Lars Levi Laestadius in the mid-nineteenth century. A leader in the temperance movement, his teachings were strongly Pietistic.

131. Gustaf V was king of Sweden from 1907–50. He married Princess Victoria of Baden in 1881.

132. Ytterlänne's old church is truly a national treasure. Its front door bears a bronze lion's head dating to the 800s. The interior has well-preserved frescoes from the late fifteenth century. The Madonna painting that C. J. mentions is thought to be a gift from Archbishop Jacob Ulfsson Örnfot when he visited the parish in 1507. The baptismal font dates to the fourteenth century and is made of marble from the island of Gotland. "*Ytterlännäs gamla kyrka*." *Wikipedia, the Free Encyclopedia*. Wikimedia Foundation, Inc.

133. The EFS is an independent organization within the Church of Sweden. It was founded in 1856 and continues today, working with independent churches in Africa and India.

134. Ulrik Frederik Gyldenløve (1638–1704) was commander in chief of the Norwegian army during the Scanian War, fought in 1675–79. The acknowledged illegitimate son of Frederick III of Denmark and Norway, he advocated for reforms in Norway, including a simplified tax system, and he constructed numerous fortifications along the Swedish border. Known as the Count of Laurvig, Gyldenløve founded what is today the city of Larvik located in the southeastern portion of Norway.

135. Norwegian writer Bjørnstjerne Martinius Bjørnson (1832–1910) was the recipient of the 1903 Nobel Prize in Literature and is considered one of Norway's four greatest authors along with Henrik Ibsen, Jonas Lie, and Alexander Kielland. In 1870 he published *Poems and Songs* and the epic cycle *Arnljot Gelline*. "Bjørnstjerne Bjørnson." *Wikipedia, the Free Encyclopedia.* Wikimedia Foundation, Inc.

136. The opera's character Arnljot Gelline is mentioned in Snorri Sturlusson's saga about Olaf II of Norway who reigned as king from 1015–28. The former king was canonized as St. Olaf one year after he died in the Battle of Sticklastad, regarded as one of the most famous battles in Norwegian history. The original performance of the opera took place in the Royal Theater in Stockholm in 1910. "Arnljot." *Wikipedia, the Free Encyclopedia.* Wikimedia Foundation, Inc.

137. Storsjön is popular for its Loch Ness-like monster, Storsjöodjuret. The first description of Sweden's only lake monster appeared in a tale by vicar Morgens Pedersen in 1635. The Frösö Runestone from the eleventh century is said to bear the image of Storsjöodjuret. Read Pedersen's tale and see a photo of the Runestone at "Storsjöodjuret." *Wikipedia, the Free Encyclopedia.* Wikimedia Foundation, Inc.

138. Åreskutan is a 4,660-foot mountain in Jämtland, central Sweden.

139. *Rikets Ständer* translates literally as "Estates of the Realm." The Swedish word for Parliament is *Riksdag*. King Gustav III reined from 1771 until his

assassination in 1792. He was an admirer of Voltaire and endeavored to enact many reforms, particularly those he regarded as abuses of the nobility. A great lover of the arts, he founded several academies including the Swedish Academy known for its annual selection for the Nobel Prize in Literature. Gustav III also created the Royal Swedish Opera and even established a national costume to help his fellow upper and middle class citizens save money on clothing. In 1782, Gustav III was the first neutral head of state to recognize the fledgling United States as it fought for its independence from Great Britain. "Gustav III of Sweden." *Wikipedia, the Free Encyclopedia.* The Wikimedia Foundation, Inc.

140. Gustav I Vasa (1496–1560) was king of Sweden from 1523 until his death. C. J. references his speech to a group of people in Dalarna, Sweden, who spoke dialects unintelligible to mainstream Swedish speakers. The most famous Dalecarlian dialect is Elfdalian, a North Germanic language that was spoken through the thirteenth century. Elfdalian is now taught in some schools, and an attempt to establish it as a regional minority language through the Council of Europe is underway. To read about the history of this language and listen to an audio recording of its rhythmic cadence, go to the *Ancient Origins* website and access the article by Liz Leafloor, "Elfdalian, the Ancient Viking Forest Language of Sweden Set to be Revived," posted on May 20, 2015.

141. Gustav I Vasa had more than one adventure escaping the Danes. Margit's scheme to hide him in his basement is depicted in a painting by Johan Fredrik Höckert. Later in his travels, C. J. recounts more of Gustav's exploits that captured the popular imagination.

142. Bohuslän is a Swedish province in Götaland, situated in southern Sweden.

143. See a fascinating expansion on the story of the American Colony and its founders Anna and Horatio Spafford in a piece published in 1996 titled, "Faith and Fate in Jerusalem," by Birgitte Rahbek and Mogens Bäckne, available in PDF format at www.birgitterahbek.dk/faith_fate.pdf

For an update on the American Colony wherein "The landmark hotel . . . unveils its archives, illustrating a tumultuous, passionate, and sometimes eccentric history," see Jessica Steinberg, "From Commune to Oasis: Postcards from the American Colony," *The Times of Israel*, April 23, 2014.

144. C. J. may have transposed his digits here. The steeples rise 389 feet.

145. In this passage, C. J. refers to a number of well-known figures in Swedish history. King Johan III, the son of Gustav I, assumed his crown in 1568. The "murdered Stures" refers to five members of the nobility who were incarcerated in Uppsala by the seriously mentally ill King Erik XIV (1533–77). Ebba Magnusdotter Brahe (1596–1674) was a Swedish countess and the great love of Gustavus Adolphus. St. Birgitta, aka Bridget of Sweden, was a mystic who founded the Bridgettines nuns and monks. Information about Eric IX (1120–60), who was also known as Eric the Lawgiver, comes largely from legend as no official records for this king survived.

146. *The Codex Argenteus* is a sixth-century manuscript. Known as the "Silver Bible," this primary surviving example of the Gothic language can be viewed online at http://app.ub.uu.se/arv/codex/faksimiledition/contents.html

147. Gunnar Wennerberg (1817–1901) was a Swedish poet, composer, and politician.

148. Also known as Birgir Magnussson, Birgir Jarl (1200–66) was a Swedish statesman who played an important role in the consolidation of Sweden. He also led the Second Swedish Crusade, which established Swedish rule in Finland. He is considered the founder of Stockholm.

149. Despite his promise of amnesty, Danish forces under the command of King Christian II (1481–1559), executed eighty to ninety members of the Swedish nobility and clergy. The Stockholm Bloodbath took place over a period of three days, November 7–9, 1520.

150. Carl Michael Bellman (1740–95) was a Swedish poet, songwriter, and composer. He has been compared to Beethoven, Mozart, and Hogarth, and he remains a powerful influence in Swedish music and literature to this day.

151. Reverend Fredrik Hammersten (1846–1922) became pastor of Stockholm's Jacob Church in 1908. Among his writings were "Daily Meditations upon the Church Year Gospels" and "Epistles and Evening Lyrics," which were reprinted in *The Lutheran Companion*, a widely read Augustana Synod periodical.

Against Fredrik's wishes, his daughter Signe Hammersten became an artist and married Finnish sculptor Viktor Jansson. The couple went on to become the parents of photographer Per Olov Jansson; author and comic-strip artist, Lars Jansson; and author, painter, graphic artist, and caricaturist, Tove Jansson creator of the "Moomin" characters. Tove described her mother as the "wild pastor's daughter" of her generation. See excerpts and photos of Tove Jansson's childhood memoir, *Sculptor's Daughter* (London: Benn, 1968) at www.tovejansson.com/eng/perhe.html

152. Olaf Kyrre (1050–93) ascended to the Norwegian throne as Olaf III in 1067 and remained King of Norway until his death.

153. Born in Bergen, Ole Bull (1810–80) was a Norwegian violinist and composer. While the Bergen city park is named in his honor, another Ole Bull Park exists in the United States. In 1852, Ole Bull purchased more than eleven thousand acres in Pennsylvania and formed a colony he called Ole Bull Colony. The land consisted of four communities: New Bergen, Oleana, New Norway, and Valhalla. Today the site is the location of 132-acre Ole Bull State Park. "Ole Bull." *Wikipedia, the Free Encyclopedia.* Wikimedia Foundation, Inc.

154. "Feed the fishes" was a euphemism C. J. enjoyed using whenever his fellow passengers suffered from seasickness. Occasionally he, too, succumbed, but for the most part, he seems to have had a strong pair of sea legs.

155. King Macbeth, on whom Shakespeare's famous play is based, was an eleventh-century ruler in Scotland. The location of the castle to which C. J. alludes was east of the present-day castle at Inverness and was built around 1057. A well-sourced post on the subject can be found at "Do the locations and settings Shakespeare used in Macbeth exist in real life?," *Fresh Meaty Words: the Final Works* (blog), January 13, 2011, https://freshmeatywords. wordpress.com/2011/01/13/do-the-locations-and-settings-shakespeare-used-in-Macbeth-exist-in-real-life/

156. Burns was born in Alloway. Brig o' Doon is a bridge nearby.

157. The noxious smoke-filled air that C. J. describes in London climaxed with the Great Smog that settled on the city for five continuous days in 1952.

The smog paralyzed the city and shut down most transportation. Sporting events were canceled and livestock brought to the famous Smithfield Show choked to death. Pedestrians gasped for air and could barely see their own feet as they walked in the greasy thickness. Initial reports estimated four thousand deaths attributed to the Great Smog. Later reports put the death rate as high as twelve thousand lives lost. The event precipitated Parliament's passage of the Clean Air Act of 1956. Christopher Klein, "The Killer Fog that Blanketed London 60 Years Ago," *History in the Headlines,* December 6, 2012.

ALSO FROM SWEDISH ROOTS IN OREGON PRESS

compiled and edited by Lars Nordström

Swedish Oregon
Ten New Lives
Swedish Roots, Oregon Lives

———— • ————

BIOS

Originally from southern California, Michael Timshel has now lived in the Willamette Valley in Oregon for more than thirty years. His father was a Swedish immigrant, and he has had a life-long interest in the Swedish language and culture. His employment at the University of Oregon afforded him the opportunity to study and improve his Swedish language skills. In retirement, he now has more time to devote to translation.

The daughter of a Swedish immigrant, Rhonda Erlandson grew up surrounded by the beauty of Swedish culture and the musical cadence of its language. Like C. J. Larson, she too has roots in Warren, Oregon. A professional librarian for the past 23 years, Rhonda lives in Portland, Oregon, and currently serves as the President of Swedish Roots in Oregon.

Tricia Brown joined the C. J. Larson family in 1986 when she wed C. J.'s grandson and Naomi Larson Brown's son, Perry Brown. She is an author, editor, and book developer specializing in Alaska titles, and was thrilled to join the publishing team for *Across Sixteen Countries.*

Made in the USA
Charleston, SC
19 November 2016